Wilson Barrett

The Sign of the Cross

Wilson Barrett

The Sign of the Cross

ISBN/EAN: 9783337300210

Printed in Europe, USA, Canada, Australia, Japan

Cover: Foto ©Lupo / pixelio.de

More available books at **www.hansebooks.com**

Mercia, by look and caress, urged him to be calm.

Page 292.

The Sign of the Cross

By
Wilson Barrett

Philadelphia
J. B. Lippincott Company
Mdcccxcvii

Copyright, 1896,
BY
J. B. Lippincott Company

PREFACE

BY THE BISHOP OF TRURO.

To purify the stage, that the stage might raise men, to go straight to the source of high emotion, to bring together the old and the new natures till each told the truth of the other, to bring the nineteenth century face to face with the first,—this seemed to me heroic.

And the more so, because great actors and good men said it was impossible, for the English playgoer was best caught with broad pieces and the things which he would condemn in the real life of his own home.

Many a tragedian preferred the things that make for good, but their audience seemed of another mind.

We only seemed so; at the bottom of our hearts all the time there was a scorn of base thoughts, and a kindling to whatever is pure and true and honourable and lovely, although we did not always know it. And

PREFACE

when the *Sign of the Cross* reached us, we knew its kindred touch, and the story found itself at home.

So we thank Mr. Wilson Barrett for his work, his success seems to be ours, his success is the mother of Plays that live, and ideas of life that make men live.

JOHN TRURON.

TRENYTHON, CORNWALL.

Contents

CHAPTER	PAGE
I.—MERCIA	9
II.—MARCUS	14
III.—NERO	21
IV.—MELOS	28
V.—MERCIA'S SORROW	35
VI.—THE PERSECUTIONS	41
VII.—SOME PATRICIANS	50
VIII.—BERENICE	71
IX.—THE ARREST OF STEPHANUS	85
X.—THE TORTURING OF STEPHANUS	101
XI.—THE DEATH OF FAVIUS	116
XII.—THE WOOING OF BERENICE	130
XIII.—SOME PERPLEXITIES	164
XIV.—POPPÆA WINS	191
XV.—ANCARIA	206
XVI.—MERCIA'S PERIL	224
XVII.—MERCIA'S CONDEMNATION	255
XVIII.—THE REMORSE OF MARCUS	262
XIX.—A ROMAN FESTIVAL	280
XX.—THE GATES AJAR	286
XXI.—MERCIA SAVES MARCUS	294

PROEM

In Jerusalem, in a low workshop, under the shadow of the Temple Mount, two labouring men—one stalwart and ponderous of movement, with dark, surly face, thick, pendent lower lip, and beady, twinkling, black eyes; the other short, bloated, and wheezy of breath—were engaged constructing a rude gibbet of unplaned wood, in the form of a cross. The upright bar was about twelve feet high, the transverse about six in length; upon this was to be crucified the following day one Jesus, a Nazarene, by many called Christ. This gibbet was the last of three that they had been making that day.

No sculptured stone of Phidias or Michael Angelo, no painting of Apelles or Raphael, no masterpiece of art, however valued, no manuscript or precious record of the history or thought of man, could so stir the imagination, touch the heart, move the soul, or bring so large a price as one authenticated foot of that roughhewn gallows would realise this day. Offered for sale, a world would bid for it. Little dreamed those two men plying their trade, eager to be done and get to the wine-shop, that for thousands of years untold

PROEM

millions would make of this handiwork of theirs a Sign, as the outward acknowledgment of their faith; and that for countless ages the most potent factor in civilising and humanising the world would be—

The Sign of the

The Sign of the Cross

CHAPTER I

MERCIA

In the atrium of the house of a merchant, in a secluded street in Rome, two children were playing—a boy and a girl. The boy was between nine and ten years of age—a sturdy, well-made lad, with earnest, blue-grey eyes, and a round, honest, comely face. The girl was some five years younger—a lithe, lissome little maiden, with large, brown, lustrous, wondering eyes, and a mass of dark-brown curls, glinted with threads of gold in the sunshine; curls which the child had a pretty little trick of tossing from her eyes and forehead. Her lips were thin and sensitive—almost too sensitive—but they were full of life and colour. Her hands and feet were small; her complexion of a marble clearness and smoothness, rose-tinted with health and good temper.

At the east end of the room the embrasure of the window had been built in the form of a long, narrow cross; through this the sun poured on to the shaded floor and formed there a cross of golden sunshine, in the rays of which the children gambolled.

"Yes, dear Mercia," said the boy, "and I shall—

THE SIGN OF THE CROSS

being older than thou—have to wait for thee; but I *will* wait, and, when thou art old enough, I will wed thee."

"Wed?" asked the tiny little woman innocently. "Wed? What is wed?"

"<u>Make</u> thee my wife," the boy replied, blushing slightly at his own temerity.

"<u>Make</u> me thy wife?" lisped the little maid demurely. "Nay, that thou shalt *never* do. I am very, very grieved, dear Melos, to deny thee *aught*, but *that* I *cannot* promise. Do not let it vex thee, for, though I cannot let thee make me thy wife, I will be thy dearest friend, dear, dearest Melos."

"But, Mercia," began the lad.

"No, Melos, no; I cannot," firmly replied the child. "<u>Pray</u> thee, do not ask such things."

Years afterwards, when the little Melos was grown to manhood, and the child had become a lovely woman, he pleaded thus to Mercia once again, for the boy was faithful to his child-love all the days of his life.

Melos was an orphan, the son of a dead friend of the owner of the house, in which he lived as one of the family. The owner was one Lucius, a merchant, descended from an ancient family of honourable traditions, whose distinctions had passed away in poverty.

Lucius was a man of high integrity, excellent capacity, and untiring industry. To dispose of his merchandise he travelled into many lands and met many men. He went to Palestine, abiding for a time in the Port of Cæsarea. Here he met a centurion named Signinus, who saw Jesus die. <u>Many</u> were the conversations these two had together in the house of Signinus, where men of all nations gathered together to talk of their Redeemer. Eagerly Lucius drank in the new gospel, and, in the end, he embraced the new faith.

Returning to Rome he married a pure and lovely woman, named Galata. Younger than himself by several years, of a bright and beautiful nature, she was a perpetual delight to him. His graver spirit basked in the beams of her sunny temperament, and happiness came to him that he had never dreamed of. On her side, his knowledge, probity, and gentleness of spirit instilled a depth of love and devotion which filled the whole of her being.

Galata, too, had heard of Jesus from an acquaintance of both—one Favius, a man deeply respected, well past the prime of life, who led a quiet existence, gaining a livelihood by copying for the booksellers. This Favius, fervent of disposition, impatient of wrong, had embraced with ardour the doctrines of Christ, and with no less energy and fervency did he strive to disseminate them amongst all with whom he came in contact.

That this mutual belief in the new creed should bring husband and wife still closer together was but natural; equally natural was it that it should tend to draw them farther apart from the pagans around them. In this quiet seclusion and self-sought isolation their daughter, Mercia, was born and reared.

Inheriting the cheerfulness of the mother and the calm dignity of the father, little Mercia was a happy child, quiet and lonely though her surroundings were. Favius grew to love the tiny maiden almost as dearly as

THE SIGN OF THE CROSS

her own father, and, at his earnest request, Lucius and Galata confided to him her education.

Thus, in the protection of these three noble and devoutly affectionate souls, Mercia's nature was moulded. Her first lispings were the prayer that He gave to His disciples; and with the first beginning of knowledge came the knowledge of Him who died on the Cross for her and for the world. Unconsciously there grew up in the child a habit of restraint towards strangers and those towards whom her parents exercised reserve, but there was an inner circle in which she felt herself free of utterance—friends who visited the house of her father and Favius as more than friends, with whom she felt a pure and binding fellowship, even as a child.

When Nero came to the throne, Mercia was eight years old. She knew little of the world around her, yet even childhood must be conscious of atmosphere, and, from whispered talk, she gathered a crude but just idea that her parents and friends were objects of suspicion and dislike to the government and the general populace.

Claudius and his court had been objects of dread to the Christians, as they were called. Claudius was dead, and Nero reigned in his place. Much was hoped for from Nero. Men spoke of his youth, his beauty of face, and his aptitude for learning. His master, Seneca, was proud of his pupil, and almost afraid of him.

Seneca her father spoke of as a man of much worth and a teacher of many good things, and it was believed that he and honest Burrhus together would guide the young Emperor to just rule and sovereignty.

MERCIA

When Mercia was twelve years old there was much excitement and expectation among the little band of Christians in Rome. A lady from Greece was coming to visit them, and this lady brought a letter from Paulus himself, that one-time persecutor, now teacher, guide, and leader of the faithful. Joyfully was the epistle received, and quickly was it passed from mouth to mouth among the brethren. Many were the secret meetings called to hear and discuss it—in caves, in granaries, in the deep recesses of the woods it was read and re-read. Every man and woman of the Christian community had each precious word thereof stored up in their memories to transmit to their children and their children's children after them.

The years went on, and Mercia had reached the age of sixteen. Tall beyond the common for her years; of beautiful but exquisitely fragile figure; with the face of a Madonna, clear cut as a cameo; eyes of a deep, rich, velvety dark-brown, eyes that glassed a soul of absolute purity; a carriage of perfect grace, and a step so light and elastic that she seemed more to tread the air than the earth: it was no marvel that she should compel earthly love in the hearts of the men who were privileged to meet her. Of this Mercia knew little, and heeded less. Happy in the devotion of her father, mother, and her teacher, Favius, she sought no other ties; and those who were inspired with love for her felt the hopelessness of their passion, and kept the knowledge of it to themselves.

CHAPTER II

MARCUS

At this period of Mercia's life, Nero appointed as Prefect of Rome one Marcus, a young Patrician of some eight and twenty years of age. The Prefectship was given to Marcus as it was usually given—more as an act of favour than one of right and justice. Theoretically the post of Prefect was an onerous one, practically it was a sinecure. Generally it was held by young men of the best families who had, or whose friends had, great influence at court. In this case it was bestowed by Nero partly for immense favours received from the father of Marcus, whose wealth was boundless, and partly out of liking for the manly, free-spirited, lighthearted young noble himself.

The home of Marcus was one of the most magnificent in Rome. A palace in a city of palaces. Luxury, grandeur, beauty, taste, and wealth were stamped on every corner of it, from its white marble coping to its tessellated basement. Its courts were daily thronged with the fashion, wit, wisdom, manhood, and loveliness of Rome. Lavish hospitality and reckless extravagance were common enough among the patricians of the time, but nowhere was hospitality more markedly lavish and extravagance more reckless than in the house of Marcus. His father was a man of ancient lineage, possessed of talents not unworthy of those ancestors who had, in the Senate and the battlefield, contributed to the building up of Roman power and grandeur. But it was a time when to exercise talent in Rome was a dangerous thing, nor had he any great inclination for exertion. He filled offices in the usual course, because his family was accustomed to take office, and it would have seemed derogatory to his position as head of the house if he had not; but he was naturally too indolent and too content to be at ease to possess either zeal or ambition. In his office he was ready to execute the laws with tolerable intelligence and impartiality; not inclined to rigour, he yet could be—as Rome could ever be—merciless if roused. In his private life he was somewhat better than his compeers. He had his vices—they were a natural adjunct to his place and position—but he kept them within bounds, and, to his credit, it may be added that he never obtruded them upon his wife. She, like himself, was the descendant of a great family, and brought with her a dower which formed a sensible addition to even his vast wealth. Handsome, stately, with all the habits and bearing of high place, she was a dignified mistress of a household peculiarly dignified. Her innate pride, and perhaps some vague feeling of the traditional virtues of the women of her ancestry in purer Roman days, made her disdain the looseness of the average woman of the day. Her husband's lapses were never thrust upon her, and she moved on her own way without curiosity or inquiry—content with his ever graceful and sufficiently considerate regard, of which she always felt pleasantly and perfectly secure.

Between this somewhat cold couple one great bond existed—their intense and absorbing affection for their only child, their son, Marcus. In him was centred all the ambition they knew, and, as his mind and person developed, their pride and hopes became more and more concentrated upon him. Romans had been, and might still be, great; in Marcus they saw—or thought they saw—every element of greatness; and no care was lacking to make his training and education complete.

He was not left, as were most children of the better classes of the time, to the charge of a Greek chambermaid and a casual slave or two, but to the care of a woman of some education, considerable character, and good reputation; and with this nurse were associated some specially selected slaves to minister to his wants, and teach him as little evil as was possible in such a time at Rome. The claims of society were often ignored by the mother, that her beloved boy might nestle in her arms or play by her side, while the father would never hesitate to give up even a pet dissipation in order to spend the time with his son.

To their son both parents showed the best side of their character, and he, in return, loved and honoured them. Their judgment in the choice of tutors was sound and good. Men capable and honest of purpose were at that time hard to find, but they were found, and they unfolded to the quick and eager youth the history of Rome. Her literature, the meagre but virile works of her older authors, and the splendid writings of the golden age of Augustus were constantly in his hands. Greek became by easy habit a second language to him, and he knew fairly well the literature of Greece, her poetry, drama, history, and philosophy. If the inclinations of his parents were towards over-indulgence, it was to a great extent counteracted by his teachers, who found a moral support in the boy himself, who gave but little occasion for discipline. He showed every indication of talent, and was by no means devoid of application when he was interested, though he was difficult to pin down to any set rules or regular course of industry. Quick to apprehend and learn where his desire was excited, drudgery of any kind repelled and disgusted him. Great deeds and great thoughts would inflame his mind and soul,—but great deeds and thoughts were rare among those with whom he mingled. The days of his youth had not been cloistered, and those of his young manhood were spent with the youthful bloods of his time.

As has been shown, his father and mother alike were no stern moralists, nor did it alarm or distress them that their son should indulge in the fashionable follies and vices of the period. Ample means were at his disposal, which he was encouraged to spend, and, while he had intellect enough to be attracted by the thoughts of philosophers and dreams of poets, there was in him enough of the animal to impel him to the gratification of desires by no means philosophical or ideal. From the utter degradation of many of the fashionable young men around him, and from their effeminacy, his innate manliness preserved him. Their more brutal indulgences disgusted him, and from many well-born amongst them he held absolutely aloof, and, when questioned, did not hesitate to give the reason why. Trained in martial and athletic exercises, he rejoiced in the practice of them. When of fit age he was sent for a season to the army on the borders of Germany. He revelled in the soldier's life, and, although the time was one of peace, took part in a few skirmishes in the course of necessary expeditions for the preservation of order on those dangerous frontiers. In these he showed utter fearlessness and a natural aptitude for war and the command of men. The Germans interested him—barbarians though they were—and his own bold, free spirit sympathised naturally and easily with their vigour and independence. When a German chief said, "A land to live in we may want, but a place to die in we cannot," he recognised the same noble spirit which distinguished many a hero of old Rome.

The strict severity of the matrimonial bond among these savages half amazed and half amused him. The wife, he saw, came to her husband as a partner in toil and danger, to suffer and to dare equally with him in peace and war. Thus she was to live and thus to die. The punishment of adultery was as instant and inevitable as under the old Mosaic law; none looked on vice with a smile. The woman took one husband as one body and one life; no thought, no desire was to range beyond him. Many a camp joke was passed as to the fate of some of the loveliest ladies of Rome, were morals so enforced with them; but none the less the nobler nature of Marcus, corrupted as it was by indulgence, could, and did, appreciate the loftier ideal. But his soldiering was cut short by the sudden death of his mother, and his recall to Rome by his surviving parent.

The loss of his mother was a great grief to Marcus. Her entire wealth she bequeathed, by the father's consent, to her son. This gave him still further power and importance in Rome, and Nero sought him out and attached him to his court.

His father outlived his mother but a short time. To his own astonishment, possibly, he found that he missed her as a better part of himself, and, having lost her, persuaded himself that he had deeply and truly loved her, and, refusing to be comforted, set about pining for her with a plenitude of sentimental sorrow that was at once the wonder and admiration of Rome. His own devotion and constancy to her sweet memory was a thing so pathetic to himself that in absolute self-pity he gave up the ghost and followed her.

Thus Marcus became the richest man in Rome and in the Emperor's favour. It was difficult to keep aloof from the most abominable of Nero's orgies, but he did avoid them, and, in so doing, excited the hatred of Cæsar's most trusted councillor, Tigellinus, a man of great cunning and ferocity, who ministered to and encouraged Nero in the vilest excesses. No intrigue was too low, no tyranny too cruel for this creature. Mercy was unknown to him, and he was never so happy as when instigating his royal master to some hellish deed, or helping him to accomplish it.

THE SIGN OF THE CROSS

The knowledge of Nero's liking for Marcus was as wormwood to Tigellinus, and his dearest wish and dream was to find some means of discrediting him with Cæsar. In the fulness of time his opportunity came, but it was not yet.

CHAPTER III

NERO

TIGELLINUS had announced a public reception to Nero. Rumour averred that it would exceed in prodigality and licence anything that even Rome had witnessed. Public holiday was proclaimed, all business suspended; the schools and Senate were closed. So degraded were the people as a mass that, although it was freely stated that the spectacles were to be of the most licentious character, parents did not hesitate to scramble for seats and positions where their children could witness the orgies side by side with themselves.

But few, save the Christians, expressed any abhorrence of the coming saturnalia; they determined to remain within doors until all was over.

So colossal was Nero's vanity that no homage was sufficient, no flattery too gross to satisfy him. He was, in his own estimation, a god above the gods, and was madly jealous of any devotion to the deities of which he did not receive the lion's share. Any defection from his feasts brought instant and condign punishment upon the absentee. To avoid this, men had recourse to all manner of artifices. Sickness was feigned—even serious wounds were self-inflicted in order to explain or excuse non-appearance. A seeming slight to his own "sacred person" Nero resented and punished. A message would be sent to the defaulter to quit not Rome only, but the world, where his presence was a constant insult to Nero's godhead.

Tigellinus was as vile as his august master—a being without shame, humanity, or decency; with almost unlimited authority from Nero for debauchery and cruelty, he spurred his filthy imagination to absolute riot in the planning and execution of this particular feast.

He caused to be built on the lake of Agrippa, which was in the public gardens adjoining his house, a huge raft, luxuriously appointed, on which he arranged a magnificent banquet. This raft was drawn up and down the lake by boats striped with gold and ivory, and the rowers were ranged according to their ages and their proficiency in the practice of debauchery. The raft was fitted with exquisite divans and couches of the softest silks; the awnings were of the same materials; braziers, burning the sweetest incense, were placed at intervals along the raft; a band of the most famous musicians of the city discoursed voluptuous music; tents, lavishly furnished and decorated, margined the whole of the lake, wherein ladies of distinction indulged in the grossest profligacy.

In the centre of the raft, reclining upon soft couches, were Nero and his favourites of both sexes, who paid him the most fulsome compliments; but even their slavish obsequiousness and gross flattery, that should have wearied and sickened him, could not keep pace with his inordinate appetite for adulation.

At his side was Poppæa, his Empress; at his feet

Acte, the beautiful woman whom he had bought as a slave and emancipated. At some little distance stood Marcus, the young Prefect of Rome, a frown of disgust upon his handsome face. Richly and tastefully dressed, he formed a conspicuous figure, even amongst all the glitter and show by which he was surrounded. Poppæa flashed under her long lashes a glance in his direction, and turning to Nero, said—

"How rapt our Marcus seems! How silent!"

Nero turned and looked at Marcus, and beckoned him to approach. Marcus did so, with a slow and stately step that contrasted strangely with the fawning servility of the rest of the court.

"Well, well, my Marcus! What dost thou think of this?" said Nero, indicating with a broad sweep of the hand the spectacle on either side of the lake.

"I think, Cæsar," replied Marcus, "that it is worthy of a Tigellinus."

"But not of a Marcus, eh?" muttered Tigellinus.

"A Marcus could assuredly never have designed such a feast," said Marcus. "He lacks the taste—and skill."

"Come, come, Marcus, taste thou hast—of a kind. Indeed, that last banquet of thine was a marvel—but cold, my Marcus, cold! The women were beautiful—that is, what one could see of them, but somewhat frigid, eh? Reserved, eh? Not like these, eh? Look at that. There's life, eh? And fire, eh?" and the bloated sensualist pointed to a group in one of the open tents.

Marcus turned away his head with a look of such

abhorrence and disgust that Poppæa, ever alert and watchful in his interests, called to him to pick up her fan, which she had dropped, in order that Nero should not see the look of loathing on the face of Marcus.

Poppæa was an extraordinary woman, her power over Nero would alone prove this. Undoubtedly she, with Acte, held longer sway over his erratic nature than any other of his wives or women; but Poppæa's influence was seldom used for good. She was unscrupulous and ambitious, and, for power, as hungry as Nero himself. Her beauty was of the ethereal type. Fair in the extreme, with an abundance of flossy hair, soft as spun silk, which she delighted in letting loose about her shoulders; eyes of an intense blue, that looked up at men with an expression so childlike and artless that it made them doubt the evidence of their own senses and knowledge, and set them wondering whether, after all, she was not maligned and libelled, whether she was not as innocent as report implied she was base. That she loved Nero was impossible. A certain refinement in vice was hers, and Nero's degrading practices were hateful to her; but she had to pander to them, or lose her hold upon him. This she did so cunningly, and with such consummate realisation of shocked and terrified modesty, that Nero was deceived again and again.

The contrast of Nero's baseness and the inner nobility of the nature of Marcus was so strong that Poppæa's fancy was inflamed by it, and such love or passion as she was capable of went out to the handsome young Prefect. Often had she endeavoured to draw Marcus into an intrigue and failed. Her failures served but to make her desire to subjugate him the more ardent, and, had not the suspicion with which all around Nero's court were regarded prevented her, she would have gone to any extreme to attach him to her side. She knew Marcus was fearless, indeed reckless, and, not wishing that he should publicly show his detestation of the scenes being enacted around him,—an act which might lead to some equally public rebuke from Cæsar, —she tried, by engaging him in conversation, to direct his attention from his surroundings. Mentally she contrasted the fine, athletic figure of Marcus with the prematurely aged and bloated satyr at her side. But just turned thirty, Nero was more feeble than many men of twice his years. The result of his horrible dissipations could be seen in the shaking hands, loaded with rings, the twitching mouth, and in the restless eyes, to which habitual fear had given a hunted and tormented look that came and went alternately with glares of insane ferocity and unbridled lust. His ability could not be questioned. His rebuilding of Rome, for example, was a magnificently devised and executed work. His vanity was a mania that undermined his whole being, and made of him the unnatural monster that he was. Yet he could at times show the greatest kindness, while his remorse and terrors were, at times, horrible.

A revolting creature he looked as he sat there in state. His face was puffed and swollen, the lower jaw underhung, and the chin doubled; his auburn hair was carefully curled over his forehead in stiff, unnatural ringlets. He was splendidly but effeminately dressed, and when he moved, he did so with all the airs of a peacock. This was the being who terrified the whole of Rome into a state of moral degradation unparalleled in the history of the civilised world.

"What an exquisite piece of music," said Poppæa, anxious to divert Marcus's attention. "Is it not?"

"Enchanting, lady; too enchanting to accompany a scene so vile."

"Hush, hush, impetuous one!" whispered Poppæa under her breath. "Be more guarded. Had Nero heard that speech, or seen the look that went with it, it might accompany a scene as solemn as thy death. Thou knowest Cæsar brooks no frown when he is pleased to smile."

"I am no comedian, as Cæsar is," answered Marcus. "What my heart feels my face must show."

"What's that, eh?" queried Nero, partly overhearing Marcus. "No comedian? Ah, no! I *can* act. All Naples fought for places to see me, and so overloaded the theatre that the foundations were shaken, and, when the vast audience had left, it fell—a heap of crumbled ruins. Didst hear of that, eh, my Marcus?"

"Yes, Cæsar, often," said Marcus drily. And indeed he had heard of it many a time, for Nero never wearied of boasting of his theatrical achievements and triumphs, which he bought or terrified the people into ascribing to him.

"Ah, thou shalt see me play soon. I must let all Rome know what an artist I am. Ah! See there, my Poppæa," said Nero, pointing to one of the tents from which a group of ladies waved rose-garlanded wine-cups, "they beckon me. I will go to them. Order the rowers to take me thither, my Tigellinus."

This was done, and Nero landed and strutted to the tent, where the women fell upon their knees before him, as they proffered him the richest wines in exquisitely-wrought cups of bejewelled gold.

Marcus took the opportunity of Nero's momentary absence to beg Poppæa to excuse his departure and explain to Cæsar, should his defection be noticed, that some important duty had escaped his memory and he had departed to perform it. Poppæa, thinking that of the two evils his absence would be the less, consented, and Marcus eagerly and swiftly strode from a scene that wearied and disgusted him.

If the profligacy was great in the open day, when night fell it became hideous. Cæsar revelled in licentious scenes; nothing was too degrading for him, and on this night nothing was left undone to pander to his distorted appetite. Women vied with men and with each other in degrading themselves for his amusement. It was as though hell had emptied itself of all its pollution to help to make this filthy Roman holiday.

Within a stone's-throw of these awful scenes a little band of Christians, led by Favius, were locked within a disused granary, praying for their enemies and glorifying their Master. Verily, a new force for good was wanted in such a world, and it had come in the teaching of the lowly Nazarene and His faithful disciples and followers.

CHAPTER IV

MELOS

THE home of Mercia presented a great contrast to that of Marcus. Simplicity took the place of luxury, and quiet comfort that of magnificence and display. Instead of crowds of idle, chattering, worldly patricians, there were a few sedate, dignified friends, and the multitudes of slaves were represented by a few freed men and women,—themselves Christians,—orderly, methodical, and devoted heart and soul to the household they served. Lucius and Galata, their master and mistress, they loved and reverenced, but Mercia they idolised. Her every word was treasured, her every action lovingly discussed, her wishes anticipated. It was happiness to serve her, a joy to be commended by her. Her sweet cheerfulness, her quick sympathy, her constant care for their smallest wants, her knowledge by intuition of their feelings and wishes, made them feel that she was, as it were, the guardian angel of their welfare. To her all their troubles and pleasures were confided, and into them all did Mercia enter with a wisdom and appreciation wonderful in one so young. Her circle of friends and acquaintances being small, and her soul and sympathies being large, with much to bestow and but few to receive, those who did need sympathy and consolation received it in bounteous plenty. Little wonder that she was beloved.

MELOS

Her special attendant was a girl named Decima, who cherished for Mercia a dog-like devotion that carried with it a dog-like jealousy, although she seldom showed it. One more kind word or caress to another than she received herself was as the slash of a knife to her, but her devotion to her young mistress was absolute.

Mercia was at work at her loom in the atrium, which was at once the reception and work room of the family. It was plainly, though not poorly, furnished, and was brightened by flowers, palms, and evergreens. Mercia's lute and tambour-frame were on the stone bench, resting on a cushion covered with embroidery wrought by her own fair hands.

Mercia was busily spinning, humming the while softly to herself the refrain of a Christian hymn that she was committing to memory (the metre and time of which would not harmonize with the tap-tap of a sculptor's hammer chiselling out the base of yet another statue to Nero across the road), when Decima entered, announcing Melos.

Melos was now a handsome, well-proportioned young man. Mercia esteemed him highly—indeed felt for him the tender affection of a devoted sister. Melos was a youth of many excellent qualities. From Favius, who had been his teacher as well as Mercia's, he had imbibed a simplicity and strength of faith in the doctrines of Christ that nothing could ever take away. His days were spent in the service of one of Rome's most distinguished architects, who was at once his employer and professional tutor, and with whom he lived. His evenings he devoted to the study of his profession and the meetings, discussions, and prayers of the Christians.

On his entrance, Mercia rose to meet him with a warmth and tenderness that sent a swift rush of blood to his forehead and a pleasurable thrill to his heart.

"Welcome, Melos," said Mercia, in her sweet, low tones. "This is unexpected. What hath brought thee hither so early in the day?"

Melos paused a moment before answering.

"I have obtained special leave for an hour to confer with thee, Mercia," he said, looking at her with such deep earnestness that Mercia wondered what could be the purport of this most unusual visit. Now she remembered that her mother had desired her not to venture out at this hour. Why was this? Mercia knew not—but Melos did. He had, the evening before, confessed his love for Mercia to her parents, and they had joyfully consented to his speaking to her, for they held him in most affectionate esteem; and this visit was arranged to give him the opportunity of avowing his love to Mercia.

"To confer with me? On what matter, Melos?" Mercia asked.

Melos was silent. The happiness of his life hung upon the next few moments, and the words carefully thought over and prepared had left him. A tame linnet twittered from bar to bar in an open cage, and the tap-tap of the mason's hammer and chisel in the street sounded in his ears with a distinctness that he never forgot to the day of his death.

His silence lasted so long that a premonition of some

coming evil smote Mercia's mind, and, with a swift movement of inquiring fear, she placed her hand on his shoulder and, looking intently at him, said—

"Melos, no evil hath befallen thee?"

"Ah, no," he answered, throbbing under her touch. "Indeed, I should be passing happy to-day."

"Should be, Melos? And are you not?"

"I scarce know, Mercia; I am happy to be here with thee, but"—and again Melos hesitated.

"But what, my friend? Come, sit with me here and tell me what stands between thee and happiness." And Mercia moved with him to the stone seat, and sat beside him.

"One word, Mercia, no more—one word from thee."

Had Mercia been less innocent, had any real love touched her heart, she could not have failed to understand what Melos meant; but no thought of the love of man for woman had ever crossed her mind. Her face looked troubled at his reply, but her eyes met his with the gaze of an affectionate child, and a dull sense of coming disappointment crept over him. What use to question further? Was he not already answered? There was, he knew, no vestige of guile in Mercia's nature. And yet, might he not be mistaken? It might be possible that her calm, clear spirit had long understood his feeling for her, and only waited his word to yield herself up to him. In any case he could not bear the suspense. He must know.

"What word of mine that will give happiness to my friend can remain unspoken a single moment?" asked Mercia.

THE SIGN OF THE CROSS

And then love spoke. The words came readily enough now.

"Mercia, that little word which will bind thee to me for ever—that thou lovest me as I love thee, with a love that knows no limits but the grave and His commandments,—the love of a wife for a husband who worships her next to his faith."

Mercia stood silent, and her beautiful face, the mirror of her pure soul, quivered with the emotions that swept over it. Surprise, regret, pity—all were in her looks, but, alas for Melos, not one trace of love. She had risen from the seat and was looking away from him. With a half-sigh, half sob, she murmured—

"How pitiful! How grieved I am!"

"Grieved for what, Mercia?"

"For the friendship that is fled," she replied; "I never thought or dreamed of this."

"But thou wilt think of it," he pleaded. "I have startled thee in my haste—forgive me—I had thought and conned so many things to prepare thee for what I have said so blunderingly and roughly; but one sight of thy sweet face, one touch of thy dear hand, and all was forgotten. Forgive me, Mercia," he pleaded.

Two glistening crystal drops hung on Mercia's eyelashes, and her voice trembled as she answered—

"Melos, there is naught to forgive in thee, but, I fear, much to pardon in me. I must have been to blame."

"Blame? How, sweet Mercia?"

"Something in my conduct, my manner towards thee, must have given thee cause and warrant for this avowal; but indeed and indeed it was all unconscious. Thou didst ever seem to me so close a friend, so dear a brother, that, having no brother in blood, I looked upon thee as such. And now—now——" and Mercia sank back upon the seat and covered her face with her hands to hide the hot, welling stream of tears that flooded her eyes.

Poor Melos. He knew now. Friendship and pity—but a pity that was hopeless and far removed from love—were all that could ever be his share of the beautiful nature he thought he had known so well.

"I understand, Mercia. Let it not grieve thee. The heart is not as the wheel of thy distaff, to be moved at a touch, as the will dictates. I was presumptuous—love is ever so. Thou art so far above me—so much nearer His throne than I, that——"

"Hush, hush, dear Melos! Make not my regret—my abasement—more deep, more hard to bear. I did not know. Thou art so worthy, and, next to my loved father and my dear Favius, thou art the most esteemed; but this other feeling—this love, as thou dost call it—it terrifies me. I know it not, seek it not—can never know it, never seek it. It—not thou, dear Melos—is abhorrent to me. Ah, forget it, forget it!"

Thus Mercia, at the first shock of contact with an earthly love, spoke in her innocence of that passion which was to come to her all too soon—to her wonderment and pain; but he who was to create and bring it into life was not the honest, God-fearing man who listened with sinking heart to her words.

"Forget it?" said Melos sadly. "No, Mercia, that I

THE SIGN OF THE CROSS

cannot do while memory lives. This love of mine is no mere thing of yesterday; it is a part of all my life. If I had a mean or despicable thought, thy sweet memory shamed it into oblivion; if a worldly ambition, thy bright image shaped it worthily. I—I have known no thought that was not chastened and made pure and sweet by thee. All toil was for thee, all—all. And now——" And Melos turned away, his grief and bitter disappointment choking him.

Neither could find words for a few moments. Mercia's heart was aching with pity and regret, but she felt that no more could be said by her. Melos knew nothing he could say would help his helpless cause, and yet he dreaded to tear himself away to face the busy world once more, that world that a few hours—a few moments—ago seemed all so fair, now clouded and dulled to him forever.

With a great effort he drew himself towards Mercia, and taking her hand gently, he bowed over it with a reverence that honoured both his nature and hers; and, with a low-murmured "Farewell, Mercia!" he was gone.

Mercia, with her face buried in the soft cushion, sobbed softly to herself. The pet linnet had flown across to the corner of the couch, and, with head aslant, was gravely watching her.

CHAPTER V

MERCIA'S SORROW

For some few days Mercia saw nothing of Melos. He wisely refrained from obtruding himself upon her in her father's house, and at the meetings, her parents, who had learned of her rejection of his suit, out of pity for Melos, kept the two young people apart. Mercia's sweet disposition could not but suffer under the thought of so much grief occasioning to Melos, for his altered manner, his pale face, and the hopeless look of pain in his eyes told her, what his manliness prevented him from saying in words, that his grief was deep and sincere. This was a sorrow to Mercia; but a still more poignant one was to come—a sorrow that abided with her, a grief destined to change the whole course of her life. A terrible disaster was to occur to Rome, in the great fire which took place in the tenth year of Nero's reign. That this fire was the work of Nero there can be little doubt; the historians agree in imputing the blame to him. What inspired him to commit this crime will never be known. It might have been done in revenge for some real or fancied slight on the part of the nobles towards himself; from a desire still further to terrify and subjugate the hapless populace; to gratify his insatiable lust for cruelty; or from the cynical desire to enjoy some new experience. Someone repeated in his hearing his own saying, "When I am dead let the whole world burn"; and he had replied, "No, let it burn while I am living."

Mercia was sitting at home one evening with her parents and Favius, when suddenly there was heard a great rush of chariots passing the house and a loud confused roar in the distance. Running to the portals to learn the cause of the disturbance, Lucius beheld a great glare of flame in the direction of the circus. Realising that a conflagration of more than ordinary importance was raging, Lucius called to Favius to come to him.

"What is it, friend?" asked Favius, in calm, dignified tones.

"Surely a terrible fire is there. Look! Is not that by the Mount Palatine?"

"Ay, it is in the circus."

Just then there was a dull roaring heard, and the flames shot up into the air, while myriads of sparks were showered in every direction.

"Some large building has fallen in," said Mercia, who, with her mother, had joined the group at the door. At this moment a troop of mounted soldiers dashed past at full gallop, hotly followed by a dense crowd of running men, horsemen and charioteers, all crying aloud—

"Fire! fire! Rome is on fire!"

Even as they watched, the flames not only increased in volume, but fresh fire seemed to start up in several places at once.

"This is no accident, brother Lucius," said Favius

hurriedly, but with great decision; "this is design. There are new horrors abroad. Give me my toga—this is no time for quiet converse, but for action. Yonder is danger, terror, bloodshed, death, and my place is there. I must go."

"Yea, good Favius, but not alone," gravely replied Lucius; "I will go with thee."

"Good! Let us waste no time; each moment may mean a life sped, a soul lost."

"Husband, I must go with thee," said Galata. "Quick, Mercia! all the linen that will serve for bandages! Decima, a skin of wine! Haste, haste!"

"And I too, mother; may not I also help?" asked Mercia.

"No, no, child; no!" firmly answered her father. "That cannot be. The house must not be left empty; neither are the streets at such a time a fitting place for thee. It may be that we may send some poor wounded and distressed ones back here—be thine the work to tend and succour them. May He protect and guard thee!"

With a tender embrace, her parents and Favius left her, and, bearing the wine and bandages, hurried off in the direction of the flames. Fast as they travelled, the fire outstripped their speed in its seeming haste to meet them. The narrow streets and the inflammable materials of which the buildings were composed seemed to be hungrily licked up by the raging flames; they tore down the passages and, fanned by the wind, seemed to drive straight through the houses as the flame from the alchemist's blow-pipe pierces the precious metals.

THE SIGN OF THE CROSS

The heat was intense, the smoke blinding. Into the dense throng of men, women, and children, the three brave souls fought their way. There was no lack of work for their willing hands. Those of the mob who were not frantically fleeing for their lives stood helpless and dazed. Here stood a poor mother, with one wailing child in her arms, staring and screaming that her other little ones were still in the tottering home. Without one thought of self, Favius and Lucius rushed into the house, and emerged, scorched and blackened, with two children, senseless with the smoke, and, placing them in their mother's charge, they pursued their noble task. Favius, especially, worked like a giant; his tall, majestic figure, his flowing white hair and beard, stood out against the background of fire and smoke like that of some rescuing deity. Never for a moment flurried, nor for an instant dismayed, no matter what the peril, he seemed to see everything and be upon the instant just where he could render the greatest service.

The noise and heat were deafening and suffocating. Men, women, and children, burnt, scorched, battered with falling masonry and timber, were lying helpless and groaning in every direction. Galata's meagre store of wine was soon exhausted, and water could not be found. All the linen she had brought for bandages was used up; she tore her own and her husband's draperies to shreds for more to bind up the wounds of the sufferers.

For hours these brave ones battled with flame, smoke, pain, despair, madness, and death in their efforts to help those who were either too severely injured or too stupefied with terror to help themselves. Even as they toiled, Death overshadowed them, and often they could almost hear the beat of his wings. The wall of a house quivered, shook, and fell crashing outwards, covering them with its dust, and leaving barely three feet between it and their devoted lives.

The confusion caused by the rapidity with which the flames spread was terrible. But little effort was made to check the progress of the fire, and that little was frustrated by bands of men who threatened and attacked those who attempted it. In their grief and madness at seeing their homes destroyed and their loved ones perish, many threw themselves voluntarily into the blazing buildings, preferring death to life without the dear ones who had been taken from them.

Mercia, at home, was racked with anxiety and fear for her parents' safety, and, finding the suspense at last unbearable, she seized her mantle and rushed into the streets. The hurrying crowds, in their wild rushes for safety, beat and hustled her hither and thither. Bruised and bleeding, the poor girl dragged herself from place to place; the streets were no longer recognisable—where once a palace stood there was naught but a heap of smoking ruins. The selfishness of despair seemed upon all the people; no answers were made to her questions, no heed paid to her entreaties. Her agony of mind was pitiable; she had lost all knowledge of her whereabouts, and now, anxious to go back to her home, with a faint hope that her parents might have returned in her absence, she was unable to do so.

She was burning with fever and parched with thirst;

her limbs failed her, but even in the last moment of consciousness and failing strength she saw a woman falling senseless just where a tottering wall must surely crash down upon her. With a last effort she rushed forward and dragged the helpless woman out of the danger, only to be struck by a falling beam herself, and to be flung to the earth stunned, bleeding, and unconscious. Some soldier, more pitiful than his fellows dragged her into the shelter of a ruined doorway, and there left her; and there, when the dawn of day came, Favius and Melos found her, still insensible.

Using a shattered door as a litter, these two faithful souls bore her to the house of Favius, and tended her back to life and to the knowledge that, save for themselves, she was alone and friendless in the world; for, in saving the lives of others, her father and mother had laid down their own.

CHAPTER VI

THE PERSECUTIONS

For six days and nights the fire raged with undiminished violence and fury. The helpless citizens were driven to the fields to escape its ravages, where, homeless and starving, they bemoaned the losses of friends and property. During this time of horror it was said that Nero, on the roof of his palace, calmly watched the progress of the flames, and, dressed in fantastical stage costume, sang an ode of his own, commemorating the destruction of Troy, to the twanging of his lute,—thus assimilating the two catastrophes.

Learning that suspicion was pointing to him as the author of the disaster, Nero at once set to work to conciliate the people. He caused the field of Mars, the monumental buildings erected by Agrippa, and his own gardens to be opened to shelter the homeless people. Eventually he stopped the conflagration, after it had destroyed ten of the fourteen sections of Rome. Then he started rebuilding the city, erecting for himself a palace the magnificence of which was beyond description. Gold, silver, and costly gems were lavishly used in the decorations, and the most exquisite statuary that Greece could furnish adorned its courts and passages. The gardens were of vast size and beauty, and contained many large and picturesque lakes. This "Golden Palace" had long been a dream of Nero's, and it was now realised by the blood and property of those unfortunates who were killed by the fire and whose estates he confiscated.

Public suspicion began to grow to popular fury, and Nero, to divert the rage of the sufferers, fixed the crime of the burning of the city upon the Christians. These were accused wholesale, and, under the flimsiest pretexts, were put to the most horrible tortures to induce them to confess their guilt, in order that Nero might free himself. Practically he ordered a war of extermination. He spared no one—the whole accursed race of the Christians was to die. Some were given to the wild beasts in the arena; some crucified in horrible mockery of the death of the Redeemer; of others Nero made torches; wrapping round their bodies tow soaked in oil and turpentine, he caused them to be chained to stakes, and quietly watched their dying agonies.

No defence was accepted; the mere accusation of an informer or a spy was enough; the hapless accused was haled off to the cells, and, with or without the formality of a mock trial, was tortured or put to death. The Christians not only remained faithful to their Lord and Master under such trials, but went to their horrible deaths with a calmness and firmness that at once astounded and exasperated Cæsar.

Mercia had been quietly living in a small house in a retired portion of the city with her faithful servant, stirring abroad but seldom, and then only to visit the sick or her guardian Favius. Still true to her faith, she was at all times exposed to the most deadly peril. Her youth, her strange charm, her unusual beauty—all

THE PERSECUTIONS

were so many dangers that opened traps and pitfalls for her at every footstep. As yet no direct charge had been made against either her or Favius, but an accident was to start the suspicion all too soon.

One afternoon, shortly before sunset, two men were seated on the steps of a house in Rome. The house was handsome; the portico and steps were garlanded with roses; the street was a short one leading from the main thoroughfare to the quay bordering the Tiber. Above the solid stone embankment of the bridge lay a striking view of the river and the palaces beyond. The two men were of the poorest class, dirty, ragged, and unkempt. One, who was called Servilius, was almost wolf-like in appearance—a resemblance he heightened by a badly-cured skin of one of those animals, which he wore as a half shoulder cloak. The other man was taller than his companion, with a more stupidly brutal expression of face, though cunning and vindictiveness were the common features of both. They were apparently intent upon a game of dice, but, as they rattled them in their hands and threw them, with loud comments, upon the marble steps, it was obvious to an observer that their interest in the game was not so great but that, from time to time, each was casting furtive glances on all that passed around him. There was much to interest them, for the street, though not thronged, was busy. Porters bore their burdens from the landings a little distance off; women of the middle class were on their road to purchase their provisions for the morrow; flower-sellers and, of course, a swarm of beggars; men hurrying from business, and the variety of loiterers usually to be met in any part of a great city. From the turning opposite the men, a small party of soldiers and a minor officer crossed the road, guarding a man somewhat advanced in years. The prisoner's hands were tightly bound to a heavy triangle of wood passed over his head and fastened there by an iron lock. The man looked ill, worn, and feeble. Impatient at the slow progress he was making, one of the guards struck the poor wretch so violent a blow that he staggered and fell. Rudely and brutally dragging him to his feet again, with an oath and another cruel blow, the soldier pushed the prisoner onward. A woman following the party and holding by the hand a little girl of five or six years of age, who was loudly sobbing, seeing the brutality of the soldier, made a piteous gesture of entreaty to spare the man; but her only answer was a rude and violent push and a curse. The poor soul staggered back, terrified; the guards passed out of sight with their prisoner, the helpless wife and child, with streaming eyes, disappearing in their wake.

"That was a hard knock, my Servilius," said the taller of the two spies (for such was the occupation of these ruffians).

"Well, what matters?" replied the other; "it was only a dog of a Christian."

"Oh!" grunted his mate; and with that grunt what little sympathy he had felt departed.

"Yes," continued Servilius, "I have been watching him for weeks, but Caius got hold of him, and I lost Nero's reward of two hundred sesterces."

THE PERSECUTIONS

"Christian-hunting pays well, then, eh?"

"Yes, my Strabo, it pays well, and is good sport withal. It is as exciting as wolf-hunting, and has none of its dangers," he added with a grim chuckle, "for, with all their child-killing and secret murders, they are a poor-spirited lot; they never strike back. Ugh! they are a cowardly crew."

At this moment a file of handsomely-dressed and equipped guards, headed by a still more richly-clad officer, crossed the street. The two men looked after them with great admiration.

"That is Viturius, captain of the guard to Marcus Superbus," said Servilius.

"Ah, I should like to be that fellow," said Strabo enviously.

"Or Jupiter, or Apollo," sneered Servilius. "As well wish to be a god as Marcus Superbus. Next to the Emperor, he is the richest man in Rome."

"Ay, and the luckiest," scowled Strabo, moved by the thought of his own impecuniosity. "It's an accursed shame that one man should have so much and another nothing."

"Ay, Strabo, we're goodly men enough, but we haven't a copper coin between us, while Marcus has his horses shod with gold. Why, on the last banquet he gave to Nero, he spent six million sesterces."

"Whew!" whistled the envious Strabo; "is there so much money in all this hungry world?"

"Yea, is there, Strabo," said Servilius, drawing closer to his companion and lowering his voice, "and some of it may be ours, if we can but trap a Christian or two.

THE SIGN OF THE CROSS

Hush! here are strangers. Keep your eyes and ears open, my Strabo."

The men to whom he was alluding were approaching from opposite directions. Though dressed in the ordinary costume of respectable citizens of the time, there was about them, their faces and bearing, that which would have attracted the attention of a much less alert observer than the spy. The elder man was Favius, who looked as the prophet Moses might, so dignified and majestic was his carriage and bearing. His mantle partly covered his long, snowy locks; he held a staff in his hand, but scarcely used it as a support; his clear, eagle-like eyes swept the whole street in once glance. He saw and noticed with a look of keen interest the stranger who was approaching him. This man was evidently a traveller; his garments were soiled with the dust of the country roads. He was a man of some fifty-five years of age; he was sturdily built; his frame was formed for exertion, and capable of enduring much fatigue. He, too, bore a staff, but it was more to accelerate than to support his footsteps. He walked steadily and swiftly, as though intent upon some weighty and important mission. On the faces of both these men there was an expression of calm and peaceful dignity that contrasted strangely with their humble attire.

As they neared each other, some mutual attraction induced both to make a moment's pause, as if each intended to speak. Neither did so, however, but moved on a few paces, then instinctively turned, and, with a meaning look in their eyes, they once again drew near.

THE PERSECUTIONS

——The traveller had traced with his staff two simple marks in the dust of the road.

"The Sign of the Cross! Who art thou?" asked Favius of the stranger.

"A fisherman from Galilee."

"How know you me?"

"By the Master's badge."

"What is that?"

The Galilean quietly lifted the sleeve of Favius' tunic and then his own. On the forearm of both was marked a cross. The men's hands met in a warm and fervent clasp.

"Thy name?" Favius asked of the stranger.

"Titus," he answered.

"Who sent thee hither?"

"Paulus of Tarsus, Apostle of Him they crucified," replied the man.

"Speak lower," said Favius, warningly. "Even the stones of Rome have ears. Dost thou tarry here long?"

"Only long enough to give Paulus' message to the brethren. Where meet they to-night?"

"At the Grove near the Cestian Bridge," whispered Favius.

"At what hour?" The messenger's powerful voice was also lowered.

"The tenth."

"How many?"

"Hush! Even the stones have ears," said Favius, who had perceived that the spies had silently crept up close on either side of them.

"In the name of Cæsar, hail!" said Strabo, whose greeting seemed more threat than welcome.

"Hail, friend," courteously responded Favius, and, taking his friend's arm, he was about to go, but was stopped by Servilius, who came swiftly down to intercept him.

"Whither so fast?" queried Servilius, half as in good-fellowship, half as in threat, as his comrade's tone had been.

"About mine own business, friend," was the composed reply.

"Where dwellest thou?"

"What is that to thee?"

The quiet question was baffling. The spy tried another tack. In a more sympathetic tone, he said—

"Thy friend seems wayworn and weary; hath he come from afar?"

"I have travelled some days," said the fisherman.

"Thou art athirst, I'll wager," and the spy's tone became insinuating. "Come with me; a cup of good wine from yonder wine-shop will wash the dust of the road from thy throat."

"So will a cup of good water from yonder fountain," was the grave reply. "I thank thee for thy courtesy, good friend, but I have no time to tarry with thee."

"Strangers tarry in Rome longer than they plan to do at times, especially strangers who come from Galilee; Nero looks not with favour on Galileans or Nazarenes. He finds rest for them, however," sneered Servilius.

"I have heard as much," quietly said Paul's messenger.

THE PERSECUTIONS

"Nero may find rest for thee," grinned the spy.

"When my day's work is done, I shall welcome rest and peace, whoever sends them," serenely answered the Christian.

"What is thy work?"

"My Master's."

"Whom dost thou serve?"

"The Son of Man."

And, with a slight, but courteous, inclination of the head, the Christian laid his hand upon the arm of Favius and walked away.

For a moment the spies remained still, staring after the two dignified men who had so quietly baffled them; but, recovering himself, Strabo cried, with greed and cruelty in his voice,—

"'The Son of Man'? What means he?"

"My Strabo, I smell money here. Sport and money both." Swiftly running to the spot where the Christians had traced the marks in the dust, he hoarsely cried, in fiendish triumph,—

"The Sign of the Cross! Christians these, Christians! Come, good Strabo, follow, follow!" And stealthily and swiftly they crept down the street after the two Christians.

CHAPTER VII

SOME PATRICIANS

THE house upon the steps of which the spies had been gambling belonged to a nobleman named Barcinus, with whom our story will have little to do; in truth, he was but a nonentity even in his own household, where his wife, a beautiful blonde of some two-and-twenty summers, held absolute sway. People who knew them both troubled themselves but little about him,—especially the men of their acquaintance,—but most—and again the male sex may be particularly implied—were much interested in the doings of his wife. And, indeed, that lady gave her friends and enemies plenty to talk about, even if she did at times cause the conversation concerning her doings to savour more of censorious gossip than respectful admiration. If her friends took interest in her actions, she certainly did not fail to reciprocate their concern for her. What Dacia, for that was the lady's name, did not know of the doings of the rank and fashion of Rome was certainly not worth the knowing—at least, to her. She was a witty, clever, careless, thoughtless butterfly of a creature, utterly incapable of any deep feeling even for herself, but not ill-natured at heart (if such a thing was included in her composition), but with a tongue that would do more mischief in a day than it could undo in a year.

SOME PATRICIANS

In spite of this little weakness, the "fair Dacia," as she was called, was much admired and sought after, and no fashionable gathering was considered complete without her. Exceedingly pretty and good tempered, ready of speech and not too squeamish in her choice of topics, or mode of dealing with them, she was a continual source of amusement to the golden youth with whom she, for choice, passed most of her time. Her husband, good, easy man, troubled himself but little about his wife's affairs, save when he was called upon to pay her bills, and, to do him justice, not even then, save when they were more than exceptionally heavy, or he was more than usually pressed for money. On these occasions he would, for a moment, lose his temper, which moved the fair Dacia not a tittle; she would laugh at her lord and master until he either paid the bill or left the house. Then the lady would scurry off to one of her many gossips, or send for one of her equally numerous admirers, and extract either sympathy from the one or gold from the other. Among her crowd of adorers none was more pliable or pecuniarily squeezable than Philodemus, an effeminate young nobleman possessed of an exceedingly empty head and a very plethoric purse. This elegantly-garbed and sweetly-perfumed fledgling had neither the wit, heart, nor manliness to feel a real passion (even a distorted one) for Dacia or any other woman, but it seemed to him it was necessary to his dignity to have the reputation of being irresistible and invincible among women, and, as he could pay handsomely for such notoriety, many of the fair creatures indulged him in his weakness. Never exacting, and quite content to go when he was likely to stand in the way of a more exigent lover, he was as useful an appanage to her suite as any fine lady could hope for or desire.

On this particular afternoon, at an hour bordering on sunset, Philodemus brought to Dacia's house a band of singers. They were richly dressed, and garlanded with roses. Halting in front of Dacia's door, they sang the following verses, accompanied by musicians with lutes, citharas, and pipes:—

> "What is life where love is not?
> A sunless world.
> Life is love itself begot.
> Then love and live.

> "Life is love—and love is fire,
> Those who love not live in vain.
> Life is but one long desire;
> Either love or die in pain.
> Then love and live.

While this song was being sung a young and exquisitely graceful girl, lightly clad in rich sky-blue silk, danced airily in front of the steps of the house, scattering roses over them. The sound of music brought Dacia out of the portico. With her came two richly-robed slave-girls, who spread cushions upon the seats, and embroidered draperies upon the balcony. Dacia was beautifully dressed in soft, close-clinging silk, which accentuated rather than concealed the lines of her handsome figure. The richest jewels sparkled in her hair, and over the bosom of her dress. She was laughing merrily at some jest with her attendants, and her eyes sparkled with pleasure at the ceremony arranged in her honour.

"Looking at the singers, she said—

"Well sung! Who are your masters? Oh, I see! Philodemus and Glabrio!" she added, as these two individuals came forward.

Philodemus was robed in a pale-yellow silk tunic and toga, heavily trimmed with gold and jewels. His face was worn, his frame slight, his manner effeminate in the extreme; he had a slight lisp, rolling, vacant eyes, and a languid, listless air that betokened weakness— physical as well as mental. His companion, Glabrio, was a great contrast to him. A man of fifty years of age, rotund of body, rubicund of face, beaming with humour and good-temper; a rich, unctuous voice, and a continual chuckle, as though life to him was one huge joke,—which indeed it was. The old reprobate avowed that he had lived all the days of his life, and all the nights as well, and intended so to live until he died. Not for him was mere existence, but *life*. The vine-leaves and roses were never out of his hair, or, to speak more correctly, were never off his head, for of hair his store was small; his bald pate shone with the lustre of ruby wine, his nose blossomed gaily under the same fierce warmth, while a heavy droop of the left eyelid suggested a perpetual wink at all and sundry. It was a boast of his that he had not been drunk since boyhood. There was some truth in this: so soaked was he, so inoculated with the virus of the grape, that drunkenness was now impossible. Still, to say that he was never drunk, was but half a truth; he should have added that he was never sober. His dress was symbolical, being of the colour of his favourite red wine, trimmed with vine-leaves worked in gold. On his head was a fillet, which, in sympathy with the drooping eyelid, had slid down over his brow. His gait was not too steady, and he seemed cautiously to feel his way with his gouty toes, as though those members had learned by long and bitter experience that marble was harder and more enduring than flesh, and that it was well to tread gently, and treat the stones with due respect.

Both men carried fans of feathers, after the effeminate custom of the time.

"Welcome, gentlemen; welcome!" continued Dacia. "What would you?"

"Leave to worship," answered Philodemus.

"Leave to worship Nero grants to all, save the Nazarenes. At whose shrine wouldst thou bend the knee?"

"Venus, I," replied Philodemus, with a languishing look at his charmer.

"And Bacchus, I," greasily chuckled Glabrio.

"Hast thou not worshipped the ruby wine-god enough already, good Glabrio?" asked Dacia.

Glabrio's mouth moved as though tasting wine of some particularly good vintage; the flavour must have been pleasant, for the old toper's face broadened with a smile, and his double chin waggled with satisfaction as he answered—

"Never can I worship him enough! The sacred fire of Bacchus is in my veins . . . my heart . . . my blood——" and, reeling slightly, he chuckled, "and, to a certain extent, in my legs, as—er—you may per-per-perceive," looking down at them with intense amusement. "Look at them! they are a trifle at variance with—each—other—other," he repeated, as he smiled at his own thoughts. "While my right leg would fain go east, my left doth struggle to convey me west."

"At variance thus early in the day?" asked Dacia smilingly, not in the least shocked or surprised by so very common an occurrence.

"In truth they've never been otherwise since—since —oh, since that last banquet Marcus gave. Oh, the good Marcus! he spares nothing. What wine!" He smacked his lips, and seemed to roll the fine old Falernian unctuously round his capacious and well-seasoned mouth. "Yes, and what women!" and now he gave a roguish leer as he looked round at his companion, whilst making a pretence of hiding his blushes with his fan. "He hath a pretty taste in both."

"And remains unmoved by either," laughed Dacia, dropping her fan.

"True," drawled and lisped Philodemus, slightly envious; "he hath a head of iron for wine, and a heart of stone for women."

"Iron melts, and stone breaks. He will get caught some day," said Glabrio, with tipsy philosophy.

"Marcus? Never!" Thus Philodemus.

Glabrio had waddled to the steps, and was vainly trying to reconcile the recalcitrant legs and make the perilous ascent to Dacia's side; his cautious toes acting as advanced guards or feelers. Not sorry to pause in his upward progress, he turned upon Philodemus with an assumption of sober gravity that his watery eyes and stumbling feet denied, and said—

"My son, let an older and a wiser, and, of a surety, a more sober man advise thee. I have lived" (here a vain endeavour to mount the next step) "in this somewhat unsteady world for two-score years and ten; have seen many sights, and vis-vis-vis-ited" (overcoming the obdurate word at last) "many lands, but never yet saw I a young and high-mettled man who did not, sooner or later,—usually sooner,"—with an unctious laugh—"succumb to some fair woman."

"Never Marcus!" lisped Philodemus, with languid assurance.

"Wait, my Philodemus, wait!" retorted Glabrio, with smiling confidence.

A sudden howl of execration, and a rush of idlers to the corner of the street, attracted the attention, and stopped the conversation of the patricians, who rose and peered over the balcony to discover the cause of the uproar. A dense crowd, composed chiefly of the rabble and the lower orders (but several were of the better class) had surrounded some person, and were evidently hustling and otherwise illtreating him. All seemed absolutely furious with the man, and, headed by the spies, Servilius and Strabo, they were dragging him bare-headed and dishevelled along the roadway. The object of their hostility was the old man, Favius, at whom those nearest to him aimed blows with their fists and sticks. His garments were torn, and a deep cut on his forehead testified to the savagery of the attacks upon him.

As the surging, howling mob reached the centre of the street, opposite Dacia's house, the old man was hurled violently to the ground by the rabble, who, led by the two spies, were yelling—

"Death to the Christians! Death! death!"

But death there and then would have robbed the informers of their blood-money, so they cried, "Take him to the Ædile!"

Glabrio, from the steps, moved with some pity for Favius, asked—

"What hath the old man done?"

"Bowed down to the god Anakoites. He is worth two hundred sesterces, and Nero will make a torch of him!" shouted Servilius.

"Ay!" roared the mob. "To the lions with him!"

And again they rushed at the good old man, as though he were some wild and dangerous beast.

Now down the street sped a girl so lightly and swiftly that she appeared to skim rather than tread the ground. Clad in pure white, she seemed to the brutal mob a daughter of the gods rather than of earth, and, for the moment, they slunk back, awed and ashamed. It was Mercia. On her way to the house of her friend, Favius, she had seen a crowd of people attacking an apparently helpless man, and, not pausing to count the probable cost of her action, had run boldly forward to assist, and, if possible, save the victim of their fury. With a force and energy amazing in one so seemingly slight and frail, she pushed the men away, and stood

THE SIGN OF THE CROSS

protecting the fallen Favius and braving the mob. How divinely beautiful she looked! Her arms were outstretched as if to shield the old man from further peril, her eyes shining with the fire of righteous wrath, and her lovely face alight with inspiration.

The tribute that manhood ever pays, involuntarily or willingly, to innocence and womanly purity, was hers. This weak girl, whom any man there could have brushed aside with ease, cowed them all. As they gazed upon her with mingled fear, wonder, and admiration, her sweet voice rang out clear and strong, and her words cut some of them as might the lash of a whip.

"Are ye men or wolves? Are ye blind? Are white hairs no longer reverenced in Rome?" Stooping to Favius, she tenderly helped the bleeding and stunned man to his feet; then, seeing the wound upon his forehead, she added with gentle solicitude—

"Are you hurt, my father?"

"I feel no pain, daughter," said Favius, who, in sooth, was dazed with the blows showered upon him.

"But there is blood upon thee! Look, men of Rome! Are you not ashamed?" Mercia indignantly asked, turning to the rabble.

"By Bacchus, what a beauty!" said Glabrio, from the balcony.

Mercia wiped the blood from the face of Favius, and, taking his hand, said, "Let me lead thee home, my father."

But by this time Servilius had recovered his wits, and he stopped her, saying—

"Not so fast! What say ye, citizens, shall a pair of

pretty eyes and a baby face rule Rome and Romans?"

"No, no!" yelled Strabo, inciting the others to join him.

Mercia turned, and, with a touching gesture of entreaty, said—

"I beg of you to let this old man go! There is no harm in him; I know him well. He hath wronged no one—unless it be a wrong to nurse the sick, comfort the weary, help the helpless. All these things hath he done. Would you slay him for that?"

Servilius and Strabo redoubled their energies, and yelling, "He is a Christian! To the lions with him!" induced the crowd to close once more round the hapless Favius, to whom Mercia was clinging, vainly endeavouring to shield him from the ruffians who were trying to drag him away. But her efforts were futile against the blind hostility of the rabble. A dozen strong, pitiless hands were upon her, tearing her from Favius; their wild and savage execrations were ringing in her ears as she continued to struggle in defence of her aged teacher. Death to both seemed inevitable; but there was a quick tramp of armed men, a swift rush of shining armour, a few heavy thuds, as the handles of spears fell upon heads and bodies, and, like a flock of frightened sheep, the cowardly crowd fell back on either side of the street, gazing with terrified eyes at the guard of soldiers, led by Viturius and commanded by Marcus, the Prefect of Rome.

And thus, for the first time, these twain met and looked upon each other. What is the subtle, mysterious thing men call affinity? What the magnetism that, with a look, a touch, draws, in the twinkling of an eye, two souls together, never to be parted through all eternity? For one instant only had their eyes met, and yet, in that moment, all the currents of their lives were changed. For a moment neither moved. Some strange spell seemed upon both. It was as though soul was speaking to soul, and both wondered. But this was no time for self analysis; Marcus had to act, and, recovering himself he asked, with the manner and voice of a man used to command and to be obeyed,—

"What hath this old man done?"

"He is a Christian!" shouted the too busy Servilius.

"Silence that fellow, Viturius!" quickly interposed Marcus, and Viturius, nothing loth, smote the spy over the mouth with the back of his hand, and he fell back among the crowd holding his face in both hands, whimpering, "Nay, nay, good Marcus, I have done nothing wrong." And the wretched turncoats among the mob waved arms and sticks in the air and shouted, "Marcus! Marcus! Hail! Hail!"

With a shrug of contempt Marcus turned from them and looked once more on Mercia. With open, wondering eyes she was gazing at the shining figure which still stood between her and death. It had seemed to her that the mob had recoiled as dark spirits of evil would fall back before the might of some strong angel of light. Marcus looked, indeed, a goodly picture of manliness. Firm set in the full vigour of his virile beauty, his bearing full of command, his face slightly flushed with excitement, and yet his whole being steady as a rock, he dominated the men about him as resistlessly as the waves of the incoming tide sweep over the beach. He was dressed in military costume; a short white linen tunic, barely reaching to the knee, was covered by a coat of mail, heavily studded with bosses and plates of brass, and jewelled with emeralds and rubies; from under this fell lambrikins of white leather, heavily trimmed with gold and jewels and edged with gold fringe. A helmet of polished brass glistened on his head, and a short mantle of old-gold-coloured silk hung from his shoulders. His sandals were topped with flat rings of gold, and over the centre of each was the head of a lion wrought in the same precious metal. His armour and jewels glittered in the sunlight, and half dazzled the eyes that looked upon them. But Mercia's eyes were upon his face. His gaze seemed bent upon seeking her very soul. In a deep, rich, yet gentle tone, he addressed Mercia—

"What is thy name, girl?" and this, the first spoken word to her, sent a strange shiver through Mercia's body. Her voice, sweet and low, trembled a little as she answered—

"Mercia."

Marcus thought he had never heard music so tenderly exquisite as that sound. Turning his eyes for a moment upon Favius, he asked—

"Thy name, friend?"

"Favius Fontellus," was the answer. Then again the eyes of Marcus flashed upon Mercia.

"Is this maid thy daughter?"

"Nay, sir," and Favius seemed to interpose to shield Mercia from the young Prefect.

"Nor any kin of thine?" asked Marcus.

"No."

"I have no kin," softly and sadly murmured Mercia.

"Why is she with thee, then?" said Marcus to Favius, his eyes still upon Mercia.

"She came between me and the rabble when they set upon me, to protect me," replied Favius.

A slight smile flickered on the face of Marcus as he exclaimed—

"Protect thee! The lily protect the tottering oak." "What a lovely face!" he thought. "What is this old man to thee?" he asked of Mercia.

"He is my teacher."

"So. Teach you in the public schools?"

"No."

"Of what sect art thou?"

"I am a philosopher."

"He is a Christian!—death to him!" here yelled the mob.

"Clear the streets, Viturius," commanded Marcus, and Viturius and the soldiers drove off the crowd, who reluctantly departed, shouting and murmuring, "Death to the Christians."

Glabrio, who had been an amused observer of the scene, turned to Philodemus, and said, "Dost see, my Philodemus, beauty hath defeated the brute."

"If ever thou shouldst be in need of a friend, girl, come to me," said Marcus impressively, still regarding Mercia with earnestness.

SOME PATRICIANS

But Mercia shrank a little from him, and Favius came between them and said, "Shall the dove seek the hawk for friendship?"

"Not if the hawk be hungry. But am I the hawk?" queried Marcus laughingly.

"Thou art Marcus Superbus," said Favius.

"Well?"

"One woman more or less is naught to thee. This child is purity—innocence itself."

"Canst thou vouch for that, old man?"

"With my life."

"Innocence is a rare jewel in Rome, and, for its rarity, much desired," said Marcus, with a slight sneer.

With much dignity Favius answered, "Thou hast done a noble action in saving her from the rabble; it will be recorded in thy favour. Do not stain that record with evil—let this maiden go her way unharmed."

There was something in the nature of Marcus which responded to this dignified appeal of the aged Christian, but he was loth to let the fair vision depart, and again he paused and looked upon Mercia. His bold, searching eyes had in them—even against his will—some deeper sentiment than mere passion;—was it respect? A sense of something nobler in her than anything he had known before? A craving in his own heart that she alone could satisfy? He knew not what it was, but he knew that some subtle, indefinable change was stealing over him. Mercia, in her turn, was lost to her surroundings, and was a passive instrument in the hands of Favius. In her eyes there was that which showed that her heart gave full response to all the nobler feelings which found expression in his eyes, while all that was suggestive and base was lost to her sight. There was no excuse for longer detaining them, and Marcus said—

"I do not hinder her or thee; prithee go thy ways."

"Oh, promise, Excellence," pleaded Favius.

"Enough," said Marcus haughtily, "I have saved her life and thine—let that suffice. Go!"

Quietly and with dignity Favius turned to Mercia and led her slowly away, but to the last her eyes were fixed upon Marcus, who, calling Viturius to his side, said quickly—

"Viturius, follow them—find out where they dwell— of what family the girl is. Quick, learn all you can about her. Go."

"Yes, Excellence," and hastily saluting his master, Viturius followed after Mercia and Favius.

"What a lovely being!" thought Marcus. "Young, too. Young, lovely, innocent, and alone—quite alone in cruel, heartless Rome. The sweetest, most enticing piece of womanhood I've seen for many a day." His thoughts were interrupted by Dacia, who called to him from the balcony—

"Most noble Marcus!"

Marcus turned, at first with something like a gesture of impatience, but curbing his feelings, he saluted Dacia, and said—

"What would you with me, fair Dacia? Ah, Philodemus and Glabrio."

SOME PATRICIANS

"Hail, Marcus! That was a pretty piece of flesh—eh?" leered Glabrio.

This remark of Glabrio's, uttered a few minutes before in relation to some other woman, would have passed unheeded by the ears of Marcus, but applied to Mercia, it sounded like a profanation, it jarred harshly upon him, and he turned with a reply to Dacia.

"What would you with me, fair Dacia?"

"Thy company, most noble Marcus. Join these gentlemen; come, honour my poor dwelling with thy presence."

"Alas! fair Dacia, duty—stern, inexorable duty—calls me elsewhere," lightly answered Marcus, looking in the direction in which Mercia had gone.

"Art afraid?" smiled Dacia.

"Afraid of what?"

"Of the sharp tongue of Berenice?"

"Neither of her sharp tongue nor of thy sweet lips. Why should I fear Berenice?" asked Marcus.

"Rome doth link thy name with hers," answered Dacia.

"How?"

"'Tis said thou art betrothed to Berenice."

"Indeed!" said Marcus coldly; "Rome is all too kind. It honours me beyond my deserts."

"Marcus and Berenice—it would be a glorious match," Dacia rattled on. "Tigellinus is thy rival, not only for Nero's favour, but for the hand of Berenice; Marcus and Berenice united need fear no Tigellinus. What say you, Marcus?"

"That Marcus alone has yet to learn to fear a Tigellinus."

Not heeding the quiet but cutting scorn of the reply, Dacia continued, "Ah, well! all Rome doth know it is a race between thee, and Tigellinus is not the man to throw a chance away. You are both ambitious. Berenice is not only rich and beautiful, but clever withal, and a clever woman——"

"That is true, Marcus," broke in Glabrio; "you should take to yourself a wife."

"Why?" asked Marcus.

"Eh? why—yes—ah, yes—why?—well, why do men marry?"

"Why—ah, why indeed?" drily echoed Marcus.

"'Tis every man's duty to take a wife," argued Dacia.

"To take a wife, or to marry—which?" lightly asked Marcus.

"Both," laughed the gay beauty. "Marry, Marcus; thou art rich enough to support a wife royally."

"True; but nowadays, in Rome, as friend Seneca writes: 'It is thought so much more honourable to support the wife of your friend'—eh, Philodemus? And to be married is scarce a pleasure, while women reckon their lives not by their years, but by the number of their husbands?"

"Come, Marcus, come," still smiled Dacia; "some noble ladies keep their husbands."

"Yes, most of them," murmured Marcus.

"Rumour saith——" began Dacia afresh, but Marcus was weary of the discussion, and he curtly stopped her with—

SOME PATRICIANS

"Rumour hath many tongues, and most of them lying ones. No, lady, no; I may commit many acts of folly, but marriage will not be one of them."

"Berenice will make thee change thy resolve," insisted Dacia. Then, turning to go, she beckoned to her friends. "Farewell, Marcus."

"Farewell, Dacia!" answered Marcus, bowing. "Remember, Philodemus and Glabrio, you sup with me to-morrow."

"I will not fail thee, Marcus," simpered the effeminate youth, escorting Dacia into the house.

"Nor I," said Glabrio, but he staggered as he moved, and laughingly added as he went, "that is, if my legs do not fail me."

"Marriage! no, by the gods!" mused Marcus. "But this girl,—how her face haunts me! What innocence! —what grace! Is it possible that such purity can dwell in the heart of one of these despised Christians?"

Viturius swiftly crossed the street, and saluted Marcus.

"Ah, Viturius, where left you the girl?" questioned the Prefect.

"In a small house: the fourth on the right from the statue of Hercules, Excellence," quickly replied the officer.

"Know you aught of the inhabitants of that house?" Marcus asked anxiously.

"The house is suspected, Excellence."

"Of what?"

"Of being a meeting-place of these Christians."

This reply sent a thrill of dread to the heart of

THE SIGN OF THE CROSS

Marcus, that he did not quite understand, and still more anxiously he asked—

"Ah! is this mere rumour?"

"No, Excellence. I know that the ædile of the district hath set a special watch upon the house."

"A secret watch?"

"Yes, Excellence."

"Who is the ædile of the district?"

"Licinius."

"Licinius! the most cruel, merciless, and bloodthirsty officer in Rome! The gods protect these poor people if he do suspect them, for if there is no evidence against them, he will invent it. Viturius, return at once to the spies; learn all you can from them. If any arrest is ordered or contemplated, let me be advised instantly. You understand?"

"Perfectly, Excellence."

"Then go."

Viturius wondered a little at the unwonted interest his young master was showing, but he only asked, "Will you go unattended, Excellence?"

"Yes; go."

"I obey, Excellence," and, saluting once more, he swiftly re-crossed the street in the direction of the house of Favius.

"Licinius!" thought Marcus,—"a wolf, from whose ravenous fangs this sweet white lamb must be protected. I have another fate in store for her. What grace! what tenderness! I have never been so moved by womanhood before: I thought all women were alike to me. I was wrong. And a Christian, too!"

SOME PATRICIANS

Marcus wondered at himself. Resting against the base of a gilt statue of Nero, he gave himself up to thought. The plebeians who passed him looked at him with curiosity, and some wonderment, but did not dare to pause, or give him more than a quick glance as they went on their way. So still was he that the pigeons from the Quay fluttered round him, and strutted fearlessly almost to his sandalled feet. "Mercia," he murmured softly to himself; "Mercia!" trying unconsciously to reproduce the music of the sound of Mercia's voice repeating her own name. His heart beat faster at the recollection. He had grown weary of the wiles of the women he had constantly to meet. He knew their weaknesses, their vices, and their allurements by heart. The flesh alone had been moved,—never his soul. The brightest, wittiest, and most clever among them he had found some pleasure in, but there was always a something wanting in them that usually drove him with impatience away. They were not all vicious actually, but vice was not abhorrent to them. All who dared hope for the honour (and there were few who did not) schemed and plotted to become his wife. "Marriage! faugh! a mere licence for profligacy, immunity from shame; the husband a shield that protected, but did not hide the wife's laxity. No; he would have none of it." And yet his home was lonely; his life, in spite of its gaieties and pleasures, its constant change of faces and companions,—male and female,—was dull and profitless. Women appealed to the brute part of him—always—either impelled by the brute in themselves, or from cunning and greed of gain! He

THE SIGN OF THE CROSS

had scarcely to ask to obtain, and if any for a moment refused through coquetry, he yawned, left and forgot them. "Virtue!" bah! another word for fear! In the feminine spiritual constitution there was no such thing as virtue for virtue's sake, and yet this girl, this Christian, this Mercia,—and again he murmured the name of "Mercia" softly under his breath,—what a lovely face! Mercia! Mercia!

CHAPTER VIII

BERENICE

THE reverie of Marcus was broken by a musical, cultivated voice breathing his name. He turned and beheld a beautiful woman, seated in a *lectica* chair, carried on the shoulders of two gigantic negroes; by her side walked a bluff and heavy-moving man of middle age, in the dress of a Roman general. At a little distance behind her were two elegantly attired and handsome female slaves. The lady, who looked every inch the well-born patrician that she was, smiled graciously upon him as she gave him her hand to kiss, saying, "Hail! noble Marcus!"

"Hail! lady!" replied Marcus, bowing gracefully over the outstretched fingers.

This lady was one of Rome's most beautiful and proud patricians. She was an orphan, of twenty years of age. Her father had been a general in the time of Claudius, and, like many of his class, had amassed great wealth. This he had invested with such skill and foresight that, when he died, he left his daughter a fortune exceeded by that of no other woman in Rome. His wife had preceded him to the grave while his daughter was still a child, and he lavished on the young Berenice all the affection of a not unloving nature.

His wife was not a Roman. He had fought a battle with a German prince, whom he captured and made prisoner. The daughter of this prince—or king—was a lovely blonde of chaste and dignified character, and a mutual love resulted in a happy marriage that was ended only by her death. He brought her to Rome, and Berenice was born. The child inherited the almost black hair of the father and the large blue eyes of the mother; the blue was the light azure of the morning sky. She was above the average height of woman; splendidly proportioned, she moved with all the grace of a thoroughly well-bred woman. She was as clever as she was beautiful. Young, enormously wealthy, intellectual, with an unstained reputation, she was looked upon as the greatest prize in the Roman matrimonial market.

Such was the woman with whom her friend Dacia said the name of Marcus was coupled by all Rome. Any man might well be proud of such a distinction; but, truth to tell, the somewhat over-blessed Marcus did not feel a single heart-beat or one pulsation of his veins quickened either by the compliment or the lady's presence. Not that he held her in no regard; on the contrary, he esteemed her as one of the most virtuous women of his acquaintance. She had always evinced a liking for him, which showed itself in a thousand pleasant ways. He, in turn, did not hesitate to show his friendship for her by attentions and gifts that would have turned the heads, if not have moved the hearts, of most women. Berenice's heart was moved to its utmost depths, and she loved the young Prefect with all the warmth of her Roman, and all the constancy of her German, nature.

BERENICE

Berenice was not of a placid or listless temperament; her young blood was full of life, vivacity, and passion. Her tongue could be sharp at times, but the wounds it gave were inflicted with a polished weapon, not as with a bludgeon.

As she sat in her *lectica* she looked a very queen in stateliness and distinction. She needed no rich dress to make her noticeable, but she was both richly and tastefully attired, and she leaned back in her gold and ivory-bedecked carriage with the comforting conviction that among all the fair sights of Rome none could be found more fair than the picture she presented to the man she idolised. She had been listening wearily and listlessly to the heavy, blundering compliments of the lovelorn soldier by her side, but her eyes had lit up with a sudden gleam of fire as she caught sight of Marcus. Her colour rose as Marcus lightly touched her fingers with his lips, and she bent down upon him a glance that was direct and warm enough to have pierced the armour and heart of any save the one and only man she cared to waste a thought upon.

Lifting his hand, Marcus saluted the officer with, "Hail, Metullus!"

"Hail, Marcus!" gruffly responded that gentleman.

"What is the latest gossip, Marcus?" asked Berenice.

"That Berenice is still Berenice," he answered gallantly.

"Is that a compliment?"

"If I say the sun is still the sun, can I pay a higher tribute to its light? If I say the rose is still the rose, can I extol its sweetness more? And if I say Berenice

THE SIGN OF THE CROSS

is still Berenice, can I pay Berenice a greater compliment? What say you, Metullus?" said Marcus.

The glib tongue of Marcus annoyed the more stolid Metullus, and he growled out—

"Nay, Marcus, I am but a rough soldier, and tricks of tongue are not for me. I can give an order, or obey one; I can fight for a woman with my sword—but not with my wit."

"Ah," replied Marcus, "the man who would carve his way into a woman's heart is like to find love butchered there."

"So! Well, being butchered, it could not be another's."

"Metullus, terrible Metullus!" said Berenice, shrinking in mock fear, and then to Marcus, with a sweet glance of the blue eyes, "Good Marcus, shall I be honoured?"

"How, gracious lady?"

"With thy escort home?"

"Nay, thou hast thine escort, lady," said Marcus evasively, with a glance down the street in the direction Mercia had taken.

"Wilt visit me to-day?"

"To-day? I am busy upon State affairs. Alas! I must deny myself that joy."

Berenice let her little white teeth close for a moment on her under-lip before she said—

"To-morrow, then?"

"To-morrow I feast some friends."

"And you invite not me! That is scarcely kind or flattering."

"It is a man's feast, fair Berenice."

"Will there be no ladies present?"

"I think I may truly say there will be no ladies present."

"No women either?"

"Well, some players or singers, perchance."

Here Glabrio, freshly charged with Dacia's hospitality, staggered on to the balcony and sank rather suddenly on the seat at the top of the steps.

"Marcus at least is frank; he does not hide his vices."

"Is it a vice to love?" questioned Marcus.

"Love! Does the word apply in such cases?" questioned Berenice, with angry contempt in her tones.

"It serves," lightly retorted Marcus.

"Have you no heart, Marcus?" asked Berenice softly.

Glabrio broke in with tipsy jocularity—

"Heart? I thought not, until a moment ago; but beauty vanquished the brute, and I know now——"

"I hardly understand," said Berenice, with a coldly questioning glance.

"No? Why . . . pretty Christian . . . black eyes . . . Marcus rescue . . . lovely girl," spluttered Glabrio.

"Christian? Lovely girl? What is this, Marcus?" Berenice was now thoroughly alert and anxious.

"A slight hallucination of Glabrio's, the result of an all too early devotion to the god of wine."

"Eh? What? What? Early luce-e-luci-lucination! Not at all," hiccoughed the tipsy jester, and, rising with no little difficulty, he groped his way to his friend Philodemus.

THE SIGN OF THE CROSS

"Philodemus, come here," and Philodemus, looking flushed and more vacant of mind than ever, came, asking—

"Why have you left the table, Glabrio?"

"Only to taste the air," answered Glabrio. "Did not beauty vanquish the brute?"

"Certainly."

"Who was this beauty, Philodemus—this Christian?" asked Berenice, a jealous fire already in her eyes.

Glabrio was about to answer, but Marcus imperiously interposed.

"Enough, Glabrio; this jest has gone too far. Wine is a good servant, but a tyrannical master. Go and rest, good Glabrio. Philodemus, give thy friend thine arm, and conduct him within."

The manner of Marcus was too stern for the weak Philodemus to resist, and he took his friend by the arm and endeavoured to carry out the dictates of Marcus.

"Thou hadst better follow me, Glabrio."

"But beauty . . . black eyes . . . Christian girl."

"Yes, yes, of course; within," protested Philodemus.

"Within? Why within?" said Glabrio. "I desire to tell the lady Berenice that the pretty Christian——"

There followed from Marcus a look of such swift menace that Philodemus hastened Glabrio with a sudden jerk that sent the graceless old toper reeling into the house, and Philodemus shut the door upon himself and his friend.

Not a look or a movement on the part of Marcus had been lost to Berenice. He had betrayed impatience and anger, unusual weaknesses for the Prefect to indulge in. Why? Who was this Christian girl? And what was she to Marcus? Berenice shivered slightly as she looked at Marcus and asked—

"Were you afraid that he would speak too freely?"

"He hath spoken too freely already."

"And this strange girl—this Christian?"

"There is no evidence that she is a Christian. A young girl and an old man were attacked by a rabble. My guard protected them. That is all. Glabrio saw too much, or heard too little. Not an uncommon failing with men in his condition."

"Men in wine speak the truth, Marcus."

"Another, and still older proverb for thee, sweet lady, 'When the wine is in the wit goes wandering.'"

Fain would Berenice have concluded that Glabrio's remarks must be but the babble of a tipsy gossip, but Marcus' manner gave the lie to any such thought. He was restless, uneasy, even nervous. Indeed he had cause to be so. Glabrio had started a stone rolling down a steep hill. Who could say where it would stop? The whisper, the hint that a person was a Christian carried with it such terrible dangers, that the mere thought of them in connection with this innocent girl, Mercia, made Marcus shudder. He knew, too, that his office and position would compel him to use his power to bring any so accused to punishment, and the thought of being compelled to use his authority against Mercia was horrible to him. And yet, why should he fear? He would protect Mercia—in his own way; Nero would understand, and be the last to interpose between him and his desires. There need be nothing to trouble him or her; he had but to beckon, and Mercia would follow. Yes, there lay a clear way out of the difficulty. He would make further inquiries about the girl, and shield her with his affection and his rank. She, of course, would be only too glad to accept immunity with his advances. There would be resistance, a little more prolonged than usual perhaps, but that mattered not; the end would be the same. No, the law should not touch her; he would take good care of that!

"What are thy thoughts now, most silent and preoccupied Marcus?" quietly asked Berenice.

He was spared the trouble of inventing an answer by the approach of Tigellinus and a file of soldiers. The Councillor frowned slightly as he saw Marcus standing so close in converse with Berenice, but he saluted him with elaborate courtesy, and said—

"Well met, Prefect."

"Hail, Tigellinus!" answered Marcus, with a slight inclination of the head.

Approaching Berenice, Tigellinus said to her—

"Hail, gentle lady! Hail, Metullus! Prefect, I was on my way to seek thee. The Emperor greets thee, and sends thee this," and upon the word he handed a scroll to Marcus.

"Is it so very urgent?" asked Marcus haughtily.

"Most urgent."

Marcus, accepting the scroll, smiled coldly upon Tigellinus, and, bowing low to Berenice, said, "Will you pardon me, lady?"

The scroll contained the following message:—

BERENICE

"To MY WELL-BELOVED SERVANT, MARCUS,—GREETING: The accursed sect of the Christians is increasing. They plot together to destroy my throne and life. They will not bow down to me nor call me Cæsar, nor pay tribute unto me. They are murderers and fanatics, venomous and bloodthirsty. Spare none of them—men, women, nor children. Slay those who are dangerous; the rest I will give to the beasts in the arena. Thou hast full power. Show mercy to none. On thy life I charge thee to be faithful.

"CÆSAR."

Marcus had read, and was gazing abstractedly at the mandate, when Berenice said to Tigellinus—

"Your news seems to trouble the noble Marcus."

"It should not do so," he answered, looking at Marcus with suspicion. "'Tis but a fresh edict from Nero to exterminate, at any cost, these accursed Christians. To Marcus is allotted this special duty."

"To exterminate, at any cost, the Christians?"

"Ay, gentle lady. The Emperor has been informed by traitors in their sect that they plot against his life. His edict condemns to torture and to death all who are proved to worship with them or help them in any way."

"Torture and death!" mused Berenice, gazing at Marcus, who turned towards Tigellinus and said—

"I kiss the mandate of the Emperor, Tigellinus."

"And will obey it?"

"Can you doubt it?" icily responded Marcus.

Tigellinus turned on his heel and addressed Berenice.

THE SIGN OF THE CROSS

"Go you homeward, lady? Let me add to your escort?"

"Gladly," she said. "Farewell, Marcus. The Emperor hath chosen wisely. Torture and death to all Christians, without distinction of sex! A wise decree, and a timely one. Farewell, Marcus," and casting on him a meaning look, which he did not fail to understand, she was borne away by the negroes, followed by Tigellinus, Metullus, and the slaves.

As they left him, Marcus again unrolled the scroll he held in his hand, and re-read the command of Cæsar. "Spare none of these Christians—men, women, nor children. . . . Thou hast full power. . . . On thy life I charge thee to be faithful." Faithful to such a mandate! And this girl, this fair and innocent creature, Mercia, was she too a Christian?

Slowly pacing the street, he encountered Viturius, who saluted him hurriedly, and said—

"Excellence—the young girl——"

"Mercia?" eagerly inquired Marcus.

"Yes, Excellence. I was watching the house, as thou didst command me, when I saw the door cautiously opened; a boy came out and looked carefully up and down the street; not observing me, he beckoned, and the girl, Mercia, with a mantle over her head, came softly forth. I doubled upon them to tell thee. See! here they come." Viturius pointed down the street, where Marcus beheld the maiden who had caused him so much anxious thought, accompanied by a boy some twelve years old, dressed in a short brown tunic, girded in by a buff leather belt. Across his shoulders hung a strap of similar make, from which was suspended a pouch. His face was handsome and ingenuous; his long light brown hair fell in clusters over his forehead, which was broad and well-shaped. The eyes were frank and affectionate; his mouth and lips were curved; his chin rather too sensitive and pointed for the rest of his face and head. He held Mercia by the hand and chatted gaily as he strolled along by her side. As the two approached, Marcus and Viturius moved away until they were hidden by the base of Nero's statue.

The sun was setting and warming the streets and palaces with its ruddy glow. Mercia wore a mantle over her white robes, of a delicate puce colour, one end of which formed a kind of hood and partly concealed her face. As they neared the statue she paused, and looking at that spot where, a short time ago, she had met Marcus—that meeting so fraught with fate to both—she sighed softly to herself, then said to the boy—

"Indeed, I am safe now, Stephanus; return to Favius."

"Nay," said the lad, with manly assumption, "I will not leave thee, Mercia, until I see thee within thine own doors. The streets are not safe for thee."

Marcus moved from the shelter in which he had stood unobserved, and broke quietly in upon their words—

"No indeed, they are not; nor for thee, either, boy."

"I care not for myself, but for her," replied Stephanus, with a smile of surprise at the stranger.

THE SIGN OF THE CROSS

"Come, Stephanus, come," said Mercia, nervously, trying to pass Marcus.

"Let me attend thee, lady. In the streets of Rome this boy is no protection," Marcus urged, with winning courtesy.

"I thank thee, sir, but do not need thy help,' said Mercia, and, as he moved towards her, a slight shrinking movement betrayed her alarm.

"Dost thou fear me, lady?" asked he, with a note of resentment in his voice.

"I have been told to avoid thee," she replied innocently.

"By the old man, Favius?"

"By him—and others," and her beautiful eyes gazed sadly upon him.

Marcus pondered a moment, and then with an inquiring smile asked—

"Ah! I have a bad reputation?"

"Yes," she replied quietly; and Marcus bowed with satirical humility.

"Perchance I deserve it—and, perchance, do not. Perchance I have been a trifle spoiled. Never knew I cause or inclination to deny myself aught that I desired. It is long since I have desired anything ardently. To-day I have had quite a revelation;" the rich low tones grew deep and earnest. "There is, I find, in all this worn-out Rome, one thing I really want—and really mean to have. Canst guess what that thing is?"

"I do not wish to try. Please let me pass."

"Pray, let me attend thee. I cannot bear to see so

rare a jewel go unguarded," Marcus said, still gently barring her way.

Even as he spoke Tigellinus and Servilius entered the street and rapidly approached the Prefect, unperceived by him.

"Indeed, I wish to go alone," said Mercia urgently.

Servilius slunk, with his wolflike motion, round the base of Nero's statue, behind Marcus, as Tigellinus strode to the Prefect's side, and, pointing at Mercia, exclaimed—

"That is the very girl, Excellence!"

"Who is this woman, Prefect?" Tigellinus asked with studied insolence.

Marcus met him with a look that amply repaid him for his contemptuous tone, and, with quiet dignity, answered—

"This lady's name is Mercia."

Tigellinus stared contemptuously at Mercia for a moment, and then said—

"This man accuses her of being a Christian. If that be so, it is your duty to arrest her."

Marcus' hand moved quickly to the handle of his sword, a movement which startled the spy, and made even the scornful Tigellinus blench. But Marcus looked at Mercia, and, with some effort, controlled himself, and quietly he said—

"Be sure I know my duty, Tigellinus,—not only to the Emperor, but also to myself."

Then, turning to his captain, he said—

"Viturius, accompany this lady home."

THE SIGN OF THE CROSS

His quiet assurance enraged Tigellinus, who angrily exclaimed—

"Have a care, Marcus! If thou dost neglect Cæsar's commands——"

"Enough, sir," said Marcus sternly, and turning from him, he added, in ringing tones, "Viturius, I hold you responsible for this lady's safety. Go!"

Then, with a bow in which reverence and admiration were curiously blent, he said to Mercia—

"Farewell, lady."

Almost reluctantly Mercia moved away, Stephanus still holding tightly to her hand, and Viturius following and keeping faithful guard.

CHAPTER IX

THE ARREST OF STEPHANUS

MARCUS returned slowly and thoughtfully to his palace. He had, in sooth, food in plenty for reflection. The events of the past few hours were burnt into his brain; he could never erase them so long as he lived. Moreover, his sensations were new and strange to him. In his many adventures with women, he had never been so much as scratched by Cupid's arrows. He had begun to doubt, if not the actual existence of love, at least his own capacity to feel it. Was he feeling it now? He could not, try as he might, analyse his own sensations. Mercia had produced in his mind a novel sense of tenderness towards mankind in general that might have embraced even Tigellinus himself, had not the Councillor attacked Mercia. That he could not endure. Mercia! how he longed to follow her. Why had he not done so? What folly on his part was this to send Viturius with her. Why had he not gone himself? True, she had firmly refused his proffered escort, but that was before he had saved her from Tigellinus. She would surely not have rejected his offer again. Whither had she gone? Even that he did not know, and must await the return of Viturius ere he could learn.

He summoned a slave and inquired if Viturius had

yet arrived. No, of course not; there was not yet time. Impatiently he paced the marble floor of his room. It was now night, and Rome was flooded with the soft light of the early moon. He went to the casement and gazed over the city towards the quarter whither he supposed Mercia was gone. How was he to see her again? She had given him no encouragement to attempt to find her. She had repulsed his every advance, and yet, he was sure, not because he had made no impression upon her, or that the impression, if made, was a disagreeable one. That he knew from her eyes, however her words and actions could be construed. Again he upbraided himself for his folly in not accompanying her. And Tigellinus? What cared he for Tigellinus? He might inform Cæsar—let him do so. Ah, but stay, what if Tigellinus used his authority to persecute Mercia and her friends? That thought struck him with a chill of apprehension. He must warn her—how? He did not know where she was. She did not live at the suspected house by the statue of Hercules, that was certain. Where, then, did she live? Why did not Viturius return? Surely he might have traversed the city twice by this time. How was he to warn her? Not by a message. He, the guardian of the law, to warn the transgressors of the law, and so assist their escape! That could not be. Yet that pure, sweet girl must not fall into the hands of a brutal Tigellinus. Ah, her purity!—what of that? How was she to fare with him? He had no scruple; she was to be his. Of course, she would come to him. Was he quite sure of that? Something in those clear

THE ARREST OF STEPHANUS

innocent eyes gave birth to a momentary doubt. How lonely the palace seemed—how lonely he was! Why had he not arranged some feast for to-night? There was not a sound anywhere except the distant hum of the city. He would fare forth to some of his friends. Whom? Who was there to interest him? Berenice? No. Ancaria, his last mistress? No. How flaunting and brazen her image seemed to him now. What, in the name of all the gods, was Viturius doing that he came not? Striking the gong, again he interrogated the negro slave, who swiftly glided to his master's feet, with body bent and eager, watchful eyes, ready to die for him whom he worshipped, content that he should put his foot upon his neck and crush his life's breath out of him if it so pleased him.

"Has Viturius returned?"

"No, Excellence!"

"Send him to me the moment he arrives."

"Yes, Excellence," and with swiftness the lithe slave left him again alone. Alone? Ye gods! *how much alone.* And yet, why? Was it because he had found, and for the time lost his other self—his soul's affinity? What! in this *Christian* girl? Ah, no! how could it be?

The black slave noiselessly re-entered, and, with his low, salaam, announced—

"Viturius, Excellence." And vanished from the room as Viturius entered.

"At last!" breathed Marcus. "Well, my Viturius, what news?"

THE SIGN OF THE CROSS

"I accompanied Mercia and the boy to her home, but it was some distance, Excellence; near to the Palatine."

"She is safe?"

"At present, Excellence, but she is closely watched. The spy, Servilius, must have followed us, for I saw him near her house as I returned."

"Servilius? Is that the man who was with Tigellinus?"

"Yes, Excellence."

"Then Tigellinus means mischief, that is sure. Who lives with her? Didst thou learn?"

"Yes, Excellence; no one but a freedwoman, who is her servant and only companion."

"I must warn her of her danger. If Tigellinus can, he will at once arrest her. I will go to her."

"Excellence, forgive thy servant—but is that wise or safe? Thou knowest the jealousy of Tigellinus; if he dared, he would disgrace thee in the eyes of Cæsar, for his own advancement."

"That I know full well, my Viturius, but I match my wits against his. Meantime, keep your guard ever at hand. By some means I will reach this girl—at once. Follow me at a safe distance, but be within call. Choose your best men; at any moment they may be required, and swords must be ready and arms strong. Go! lose no time."

"I go, Excellence." And the fine soldier, who knew no will but his officer's, was gone.

Marcus persuaded himself that the safety of Mercia and her friends was his first thought, but above that

THE ARREST OF STEPHANUS

was the longing and yearning to look upon her sweet face again.

The house of Favius was simple and plain even to barrenness. It was but a rude hut of wood and rubble, with a slight foundation of brick, and consisted only of two small rooms. The living room had in it but one rough deal table, two stools, and a small trunk, which held some books and writings. The other room contained a small pallet bed couch and his few household necessaries.

After the attack upon the aged Christian he had returned home, where the Galilean fisherman awaited him. It was now the ninth hour, and Stephanus, having accompanied Mercia to her home, had returned to Favius, to whom he acted in the capacity of messenger.

The room was dimly lit by an oil lamp, placed upon the table by which Favius was seated. Titus stood behind it. Both were deeply interested in the answers which the boy, Stephanus, who was on his knees by the side of Favius, was making to their questions.

"And Marcus ordered his soldiers to accompany thee?" said Favius.

"Yes," answered Stephanus.

"He had speech with Mercia?"

"But a few words."

"What thou hast already told us?"

"Yes."

"You did not again see either Tigellinus or the spy?"

"No."

"Stephanus, thou art but a child, but thou knowest

evil from good," said Favius, gently stroking the boy's curls.

"Yes, my father," answered Stephanus, looking up at his teacher with loving reverence and trust.

"And thou lovest Mercia."

"I do love Mercia," answered Stephanus earnestly.

"She is in deadly peril, Stephanus!" At these words the boy started. "This Marcus seeks her"—Favius hesitated—the boy would not understand Mercia's peril, and he said, "destruction. He is bold, unscrupulous, and powerful. As yet he knows not that Mercia is a Christian, but she is suspected. Thou hast been seen in her company; it may be that thou wilt be arrested. They will think that thou, being young, mayst be induced to betray us and Mercia."

"I betray thee and Mercia? Never, father!" said Stephanus, with glowing earnestness.

"Thou dost know what the Saviour did for thee?" gravely asked the reverend man.

"He died for me." And the boy's face shone with a spiritual fire.

Here Titus said, with tender impressiveness—

"And if thou betrayest the smallest of His children, thou betrayest Him." Titus was bending over the table watching the boy's face intently.

"I know it," said the child.

"So that thou wilt be faithful?" asked Titus.

"Unto death!" firmly replied Stephanus, his hands crossed over his breast and his eyes uplifted.

Patting the boy's head affectionately, Favius rose and, leading Stephanus to the door, said—

THE ARREST OF STEPHANUS

"Now speed thee to our brother, Melos. Tell him the brethren are gathering at the Grove next the Cestian Bridge, at the tenth hour, and we require his presence. Be faithful and vigilant, my son. Keep to the byways; see that thou art not followed or watched. Go; and may the Spirit of Him we serve be with thee now and for ever!"

"Amen, my father," solemnly answered the boy.

Stealing to the door and looking warily out, he swiftly and cautiously ran up the street, while Favius watched him for a moment, and then closed and carefully bolted the door, saying as he did so, with a tender smile upon his face,—

"A brave child, and faithful."

"But still a child," said Titus, with a warning accent in his tone. "Why choose a child for such an errand?"

"Because he is less likely to be suspected and followed. Until he was seen with Mercia, none have met him with the brethren."

"Now that he has been seen, take my counsel, brother, and choose another messenger," said Titus.

"After to-night I will," replied Favius.

At this moment three peculiar knocks were heard upon the door, and Mercia's voice was heard calling—

"Father! Open, open quickly!"

Hurriedly opening the door, Favius admitted Mercia. She was excited and trembling. Her drapery partly concealed her face. This she removed as she spoke, letting it fall upon the table.

"What is it, daughter?" asked Favius.

THE SIGN OF THE CROSS

"I have been followed, father," said Mercia, sinking into a seat beside the table.

"Followed? By whom?"

"I know not. As I left my house I saw a man with his mantle over his face start up from behind a pillar. I tried to elude him by turning back, but could not. I hid in a doorway and he passed me. When he was out of sight I ran on here." Mercia was pale and breathless.

"He did not see thee enter here?" anxiously asked Favius.

"I think not."

Favius turned to Titus, who had been eagerly listening to Mercia's story, and said, in his rich, deep, mournful tones,—

"Thou seest, Titus, how the brethren fare in Rome. Hunted like beasts—neither age nor sex is regarded. At his last Carnival in the Amphitheatre, Nero threw young maidens into the arena, where hungry tigers leapt out upon them and lapped up their blood; and they died glorifying the Shepherd. The aged brethren he ordered to fight with his trained gladiators, and when they threw down their weapons and refused to defend themselves, Nero commanded the gladiators to slay them; and they died praying for their persecutors. Others who would not abjure the Saviour he coated with pitch and set up on high poles and burned as torches to light up his infamous orgies; and, as they burned, they sang the song of the Redeemer. Were they not faithful unto Him?" And the face of Favius was all aglow with religious ecstasy.

THE ARREST OF STEPHANUS

Titus replied with kindred fervency, "Yea, brother, even as thou art, and thou wilt be, my daughter, when thy time comes. So, in the blood of the saints, the message shall be written to the whole of the earth, and to the millions yet unborn the glad tidings shall be given that He died that they might live."

His words were barely uttered when a loud knocking was heard at the door. The impatient summons bore no resemblance to the signal in use among the brethren. This must be a stranger. While Favius went to the door and asked, "Who knocks?" Mercia arose and stood by Titus in breathless suspense.

"Open and see," said a voice outside. It was the weak and quavering tone of an aged man.

"What want ye?" asked Favius.

"Speech with Favius," was the reply.

"Do I know thee?"

"Open and see."

"Dost know the voice?" Titus asked.

"It reminds me of——" Mercia was about to continue, but the loud knocking began again.

"Better open the door," said Titus.

"Yes, but go thou within, Mercia," urged Favius.

"Yes, father;" and going to the inner door, which Titus held open for her, she left them. Cautiously Favius opened the outer door, and an old man, in a cloak and hood drawn well over his face, entered, saying as he did so—

"Hail, Favius!"

"Who art thou?" said Favius, closing the door, but leaving it unfastened.

THE SIGN OF THE CROSS

The stranger did not answer, but, looking hard at Titus, asked—

"Who is that with thee?"

"A friend," said Favius.

"Is he of Rome?" asked the man, still carefully watching Titus.

Titus answered for himself and said, "No."

"May I speak before him?" asked the stranger of Favius.

"Why not?"

"May I?" persisted the man.

"You may. But who art thou?"

"My name is Tyros," said the man with barely perceptible hesitation. "I am a boatman of the Tiber, but I wax old apace and my arms grow too feeble for my work."

Favius, pointing to the stool, courteously requested the man to be seated, and asked—

"What is thy errand, Tyros?"

Sitting down, the man gave a slight start, as he touched the drapery Mercia had left upon the table; but he continued—

"Thou wert accused to-day of being a Christian."

"I was," quietly answered Favius.

"Art thou?"

Favius paused before replying, and regarded the stranger earnestly. Then he said, "What gives thee the right to question?"

"The wish to serve thee," said his visitor.

"How canst thou serve me?" noting the apparent poverty of the man.

THE ARREST OF STEPHANUS

"It may seem strange to thee, but I know men who have influence with those who sit in high places; those who have the power over life and death. Some there be who hate these Christians as men do hate the plague."

"That all men know," sadly acquiesced Favius.

And the man went on—

"Others there be who care little one way or the other, but who must obey, and will obey, blindly those who do command them."

"Well?"

"And still others who would fain spare, even if guilty, those who are misguided, or, in their innocence, misled."

At this the stranger looked towards the door of the inner room, as though his words applied to someone there.

"Of what speak you now?"

"Of this strange worship, this foreign superstition."

"Know you of what you speak?" Favius asked, with a grave smile.

"I know that these Christians worship strange, new gods, and work in secret to overthrow the Government and effect the downfall of Cæsar."

"I have heard no such tales, sir," sternly answered Favius. "It has been told me that they worship but one God, and Him the Everlasting. That they seek the downfall of no man, even be he such a thing of evil as Nero, the monster whom you call your king; whose mouth is full of bitterness and curses, whose feet are swift to shed blood, under whose reign Rome hath

THE SIGN OF THE CROSS

become as a wanton, filled with lust and drunkenness. Woe unto him and unto Rome, for the kingdom of heaven is at hand." And the old Christian towered above the stranger, prophetic alike in soaring look and warning words. But Titus arrested his further speech.

"Brother!" he exclaimed.

"Thou art bold, old man. That speech, heard by other ears than mine, would cost thee thy life, and the lives of all who consort with thee. Have a care!" said the stranger sternly.

"Thy errand, Tyros?" curtly asked Favius, ignoring the caution.

"I come as a friend, to warn thee. Thou art watched. Beware of Tigellinus and Licinius, for they seek thy life and the life of the maiden whom thou dost call Mercia. If thou beest what men do call thee, followers of this Christus, for the sake of the maiden, cast her from thee. Thou art old, as I am, and thy time draws near; she is young, with all youth's young blood in her veins. Let her live her little life in happiness."

"Happiness?" said Favius. "Dost thou know what that word means?"

Crossing to the door of the inner room, he called, "Mercia!"

"Yes, father!" Mercia called, and the stranger started, and looked eagerly in the direction from which the sound of Mercia's voice came.

"Come hither!"

"Yes, my father," said Mercia, entering the room.

THE ARREST OF STEPHANUS

The stranger surveyed her with undisguised interest, and greeted her with—

"Hail, gentle lady!"

Mercia gazed curiously at the man, but made no reply.

"This stranger desires me to cast thee from me," Favius said.

"Why, my father?" cried Mercia, startled and alarmed.

"That thou mayst live in the world, for the world, as others live who know not the truth. Wouldst thou so live?" asked Favius.

"No, my father," was the calm and firm reply.

"He saith that there is happiness."

"He knoweth not of what he speaks," said Mercia radiantly, advancing towards the stranger. "The kingdom of heaven is not meat and drink, but righteousness and peace and joy." Then, with an arresting gesture, she turned to Favius and cried, "Father, this is the man who followed me."

"Why didst thou dog this maiden's footsteps, Tyros of Tiber?" asked Favius.

"He is not Tyros of Tiber, but Marcus Superbus, Prefect of Rome," exclaimed Mercia.

"Marcus the Prefect?" Favius was startled. "Marcus?" looking anxiously at the cloaked and hooded figure.

"Dost thou deny it?" quietly asked Mercia.

The full, deep tones of Marcus answered—

"Maiden, those eyes are as keen as they are beautiful," and with a sweep of his hand the disguise was

THE SIGN OF THE CROSS

brushed aside, and Marcus stood revealed in the humble garments of the stranger.

Mercia instinctively moved towards her teacher, Favius.

"I should have thought Marcus would have paid others to spy for him," said Favius, with indignation.

"By the gods, old man, and so he might," answered Marcus. "But there was someone here he wished to see for himself, and would go far and through much to behold. Well, Tyros hath no existence, but Marcus lives, and would fain befriend thee, but he holds Cæsar's command to exterminate all Christians,—men, women, and children. At present there is no evidence against thee; let there be none, for, as Cæsar liveth, I will obey him. For thy sweet sake, maiden, I would do much, but my duty I must do. So, again, be warned in time!"

Before answer could be made, the three signal knocks were heard at the outer door, and Favius asked, "Who's there?"

"Melos, thy friend," was the reply. "Haste; I bring bad tidings."

"Enter, Melos," said Favius, and Melos burst into the room, excitedly crying as he did so—

"Licinius hath arrested Stephanus."

"Arrested Stephanus?" cried Mercia in great distress.

"Yes," said Melos, "and——" here he caught sight of Marcus, who still wore the cloak in which he had disguised himself. "But who is this?"

"Marcus Superbus, Prefect of Rome," answered Marcus.

THE ARREST OF STEPHANUS

"What doth he here?" asked Melos in some amazement.

"Let that rest. Who is this Stephanus? The boy I saw with thee?" questioned Marcus of Mercia.

"Alas, yes!" answered Mercia, her sweet voice broken with tears.

"When was he arrested?" Marcus asked of Melos.

"But now," replied Melos.

"By Licinius himself?"

"I—I——" And Melos hesitated, knowing not whether Marcus was a friend or an enemy.

"Speak, and speak quickly," haughtily commanded Marcus.

"Yes."

"Whither have they taken him?"

"To the prison of the district—and——"

"Tell me no more," Marcus interrupted; and hurriedly turning to Mercia and her friends, he said, "if that boy knows aught against thee, fly the city, for he will be made to speak by torture. I go to Licinius. I cannot prevent him doing his duty—I may stay him from doing more. Heed my words, and farewell. Lady, I am thy servant." And, with a low bow to Mercia, he was gone.

Mercia had watched his every look eagerly, but her heart was torn for the boy, and she said—

"Oh, my father, poor Stephanus! Can we not comfort and succour him?"

"We cannot, but there is One who will," reverently replied Favius.

THE SIGN OF THE CROSS

"Would that I could be near him to share his pain," said Mercia, with tears in her beautiful eyes.

"There is other work for thee, my daughter," Favius answered kindly. "We cannot stay our march because one falleth by the way. Art thou afraid, daughter?"

There was a look of divine inspiration on the face of Mercia, as she replied—

"Nay, my father. That which He calleth upon me to do, I will do, let the task be what it may; I have set my hand to the plough, and I will not look back."

"Even though death and the grave lie before thee?"

"Even though death and the grave lie before me."

"Let us go hence," said Favius, after an instant's solemn silence. "We cannot stay the brethren; they are by this time on their several ways to the trysting-place by the waters of Tiber. Let us go to them, to pray or to suffer with them as He willeth. Though the wicked encompass us around, He will be with us, and though we go down into the depths, He will uplift us."

And together they started on what was to prove, to two at least of this devoted little band, their last earthly journey.

CHAPTER X

THE TORTURING OF STEPHANUS

AFTER leaving Favius, Stephanus ran swiftly in the direction of the house in which Melos lived. Fast as he travelled he did not outstrip the spy, Servilius, who had been watching the dwelling-place of Favius, and was now pursuing him. Darting into the shadows, hiding when Stephanus turned his head, Servilius kept the boy well in sight the whole way. As Stephanus neared the residence of the employer of Melos, Servilius saw Melos leave it and meet the boy; they stopped by a colonnade of arches, behind which the spy crept until he was separated from them by the width of a marble column only, and low as was the hurried conversation, he overheard it. Stephanus was about to tell Melos the place of meeting of the Christians for the night, when he caught sight of the evil face of the spy peering at him from behind the pillar. Clutching the arm of Melos, he stopped speaking and drew him away. Together they crossed the street, and Servilius sped on to tell Licinius, the ædile of the district, what he had seen and heard. Licinius immediately despatched guards in every direction to trace and arrest Stephanus.

Melos had gone to pass the name of the trysting-place round among the brethren, while Stephanus started to walk to the Cestian Bridge alone. He had not gone far before he was seized by two of the guards sent out by Licinius, and by them dragged to the prison. No answer was made to his questions, no explanation given as to the cause of his arrest. It was evidently the intention of Licinius to terrify him into betraying his associates. To this end he ordered the soldiers to chain the boy's wrists together, and thrust him into a filthy cell below the level of the river. One small torch gave a fitful light to this noisome hole; the floor was dank and green with ooze, and the boy's bare feet slipped over it whenever he attempted to move. The place was empty; he could not lie down upon the slimy stones, and it was too small to walk about in. Fungi of fantastic shapes formed blotches on the walls, and the place smelt like the foul and gruesome vault that it was.

Licinius had despatched an urgent message to Tigellinus, telling him how he had arrested Stephanus, who could give valuable information concerning the Christians Marcus had protected that day, and begging him to be present at the examination of the prisoner. While he waited for the answer, the poor boy was left shivering in his cell, a prey to anxiety and fear. Although he had not been told, he readily guessed the nature of the charge that would be made against him. His associations with the Christians had been discovered, and he felt that no mercy would be shown him on the score of his youth. What his fate would be he divined and shuddered at. How many of his friends had disappeared suddenly, never to be seen again save in the arena, or at one of Nero's revolting feasts! All

THE TORTURING OF STEPHANUS

the stories he had heard of the horrible deaths by burning, by the wild beasts, and by gladiators, came back to him with a vividness that made him tremble. He could have screamed aloud, but he remembered the words of the revered Favius, "Thou wilt be faithful, my son?" and his own promise, "Unto death, my father!"

"Unto death!" Yea, death was a terrible thing; and this foul dungeon; if he were not slain, would they keep him there always? Would not death be preferable? "Unto death!" Had he not been taught that death was but a stepping-stone to life? Had not He died that all might live? Yes! He would be brave and endure for His sake. Still, he was but a child, and his heart sank with terror, and his body trembled at the thought of what he was about to suffer.

Eager to find some excuse for undermining the friendship, if such it could be called, of Nero for Marcus, Tigellinus had at once yielded to the request of Licinius that he should be present at the examination of Stephanus, and, accompanied by his guards, he hastened to the prison where the frightened little captive lay.

This Licinius was a plebeian ædile. His office carried with it curiously varied duties. The ædiles had the care of the public buildings,—the temples, theatres, baths, aqueducts, roads, and sewers. They inspected the markets and the provisions exposed for sale there. They broke unjust weights and measures, limited the expense of funerals, fixed rates of interest with the money-lenders, banished men and women of bad character, after trial, and were empowered to take precautions against any new gods or religious ceremonies being introduced. To them, therefore, fell the task of watching and detecting the Christians. According to the statutes, the ædiles had no power to arrest save by the order of the Prefects or Consuls; but in the case of the Christians, so hated and loathed were they, the laws were often contravened and defied, to enable wholesale arrests to be made.

This particular ædile, Licinius, was a remorseless, bloodthirsty, and ambitious man, who sought to gain promotion by an excess of vigilance in persecuting the unhappy Christians, hoping, by so doing, to curry favour with those who had the power to advance him. He was but a tool in the hands of Tigellinus, from whose influence he expected much.

It was into the power of this man that poor little Stephanus had fallen; he had, indeed, cause to tremble and be afraid. In a room above him were Tigellinus and the ædile, questioning the spy, Servilius. The two officers, richly dressed, grim, grizzled, fierce, and relentless, were seated at a table; the spy cringing and fawning at their feet; the guards, heavily armed, at the doors, silent and immovable as statues. The room was ill-lit by a lamp which threw distorted and monstrous shadows crawling up the walls and on to the ceiling and back again, as the lamp flared up or flickered down. The voices of the officers were subdued, but firm and authoritative, as they put question after question to the spy, who paused for a moment, to be sharply ordered by Tigellinus to "Go on!"

"I followed him until he met one Melos. I heard

THE TORTURING OF STEPHANUS

him say, 'The brethren meet at——' then he saw me and ceased at once. I came on here to inform the ædile," said Servilius.

"Hast thou yet seen him?" asked Tigellinus of Licinius.

"No," was the reply.

"Bring him before us," ordered Tigellinus, and the guards left the room.

"We must terrify the boy into confession. This girl, Mercia, may be useful to us, can we but get her into our hands," said Tigellinus.

The guards returned, dragging with them Stephanus, who was pale, but who still had a look of determination on his young face. At his heels followed a jailer, a big, burly brute of a man, with a bushy, black beard, who held a whip of several knotted cords in his hand. The guards roughly thrust Stephanus into the room. Tigellinus furtively peered at him for a moment before he asked—

"Thy name, boy?"

"Stephanus," he answered.

"Art thou a Christian?"

Stephanus hesitated a moment; to confess this was death. He replied, "I serve my Master."

"Where dwelleth he?" asked Tigellinus.

"By the right hand of the Father," replied the trembling boy.

"Answer directly, you cub of darkness!" said Licinius. "Cease this jargon, or the jailer's whip shall let it out with thy blood. Art thou a Christian? Answer!"

THE SIGN OF THE CROSS

"I have answered," murmured Stephanus.

"Answer again," fiercely said Tigellinus. "Art thou a worshipper of the strange god, Anakoites?"

The boys lips quivered. These two strange, merciless men were watching his every movement! they, the guards, the jailer, were all so big and strong, and he so small and weak! He looked round, as though searching for some means of escape. His utter helplessness was so evident that he felt nothing that he could either do or say could save him, and a great lump arose in his throat and prevented him answering Tigellinus, who repeated his question with redoubled sternness.

"Dost thou hear me, boy? Art thou a follower of this strange god, Anakoites?"

Then his teaching came to his aid, and he replied, almost joyfully,—

"No! I worship the living God; no brazen image of any kind!"

Half rising, with a hideous scowl upon his forbidding face, Licinius demanded—

"Are you a follower of this Nazarene—this Christian? Answer, you spawn of evil!"

Stephanus trembled, but was silent. Licinius gave the jailer a sign, and he raised his whip, and the cruel thongs decended upon the boy's thinly-clad shoulders and twined themselves around his arms and breast like snakes of fire, eating their way into his flesh. The boy gave a muffled cry like that of some wounded animal, but no other sound passed his bloodless lips.

"Answer!" again roared Licinius. "Follow you this Christus?"

THE TORTURING OF STEPHANUS

The pain was horrible, but the child set his teeth to bear it unflinchingly, and answered—

"I will not deny my Master; I do."

"Ah!" grunted Licinius, with a grin of satisfaction.

Now Tigellinus took up the examination. "This man heard thee tell Melos that the brethren meet to-night. Who are the brethren?"

"That I will not tell."

"Where is the place of meeting?"

"I will not say."

"Thou dost know it?"

"I do know it."

"Then tell it," interposed Licinius.

"I will not tell it."

"Let him taste that whip once more," cried Licinius.

Again the jailor lashed the poor boy, who fell to the ground with a stifled cry of pain.

"Thou shalt answer, or I will slay thee."

Faintly the boy replied—

"Thou canst slay my body; thou canst not kill my soul."

"Answer, and save thyself further pain," said Tigellinus.

"He who suffered for me will help me," moaned the boy.

"The calmness of these fanatics passes my understanding," muttered Tigellinus. "Put him to the rack —that will shake his calmness," said Licinius. "Stay —once more, boy—give us the names of the brethren and their place of meeting, and we may pardon thee," urged Tigellinus.

THE SIGN OF THE CROSS

"Thou mayst pardon me, but not my conscience."

"Thou dost refuse, then?' asked Licinius.

"I do," firmly answered the trembling child.

"Enough. Put him to the rack," commanded Licinius.

"The rack!" What was that? Stephanus had heard vaguely of this torture, but nothing distinct or clear. Poor little fellow! he was to learn all too soon. He was dragged into an adjoining apartment, followed by Tigellinus, Licinius, and Servilius. The floor and walls were of stone. Hung round it were strange instruments of unusual shapes. There was an iron vice in the shape of a boot, worked with a screw, which, when the victim's foot had been placed within it, was contracted, crushing it to a pulp, if he refused to confess. There, a huge wheel on an axle, which could be turned swiftly when the person to be tortured had been bound to the wheel, and he would be whirled round and round until unconsciousness or death came to relieve his agony. There was a brazier for heating pincers white hot to tear the flesh in pieces from the body; and, in the centre of the room, was a structure like a rough hobby-horse, made of two stout beams of wood; this was called by the Romans, Equuleus. Stephanus was set astride this and forced on his back; his arms and legs were bound at the wrists and ankles with strong cords, called fidiculæ, and these were connected with pulleys and windlasses, which, when turned, tightened the cords and wrenched apart the victim's joints and muscles until either he confessed or died.

While these preparations were being made, Tigellinus

THE TORTURING OF STEPHANUS

and his subordinate, from a corner of the room, looked on, with no more concern for the suffering they were about to inflict than they would have felt over the piecing together of a bit of machinery.

"If we could but drag Marcus into this," Tigellinus whispered.

"Nero will believe no evil of his paragon," said Licinius, with a bitter sneer.

"Excite his fears, he will believe anything," was the reply. "He starts at shadows—shudders at the fall of a leaf. Each bush to him hides an assassin,—poison lurks in every dish,—the very air to him is peopled with the ghosts of those he hath slaughtered. He dare not go on, yet dare not stay. Once rouse his fears——"

"Well?"

"Now, Marcus, I verily believe, doth love this girl Mercia. If that is so, we must arrest her. Marcus' temper will bear no opposing will, not even that of Nero. He will go to any length—run any risk to set her free again. What more simple than to urge him on to some act of folly or disobedience that will bring him into disgrace with Nero? But see, they are ready," he interrupted, making towards the rack, where the prisoner lay bound.

Bending over him, Tigellinus said—

"Now, boy, answer our questions, and save thyself. Refuse again and the jailers shall force those cranks and rend thee limb from limb. Wilt answer?"

Terror assailed the heart of Stephanus, but he fought it back, and stoutly answered—

"No."

THE SIGN OF THE CROSS

Tigellinus signalled to the jailers. They gave two sudden and sharp turns to the windlasses. This tightened up the cords which bound the wrists and ankles of Stephanus, and the muscles of his limbs were stretched and lacerated under horrible tension. The beams were opened, and the body of the boy hung suspended by the cords. The agony was unendurable, and forced from the child a piercing shriek which should have penetrated the most hardened heart; it did not touch these men. Great beads of perspiration covered the body and face of Stephanus; the veins of his forehead stood out like whipcord, and his teeth chattered and rattled together. Servilius looked on with a smile that distorted his face like the snarl of a wolf.

"Wilt answer now?" fiercely demanded Licinius.

"I cannot bear it! Mercy! Mercy!" screamed Stephanus, who had scarcely heard the question.

"Answer, then!" said Tigellinus.

"I dare not!" moaned the tortured boy.

"Again," said Licinius, with a motion of his hand to the jailers. And again the cruel rack was turned until the sinews and muscles of arms and legs were torn, and, with another appalling scream, the child swooned.

Bending over him, Tigellinus, in a hard, callous tone, said—

"He hath fainted. Release him."

Quickly the jailors unbound the boy, and, after dashing some water in his face, followed Tigellinus and Licinius into the other room, bearing the senseless body of Stephanus between them. Placing it upon the floor, they retired.

THE TORTURING OF STEPHANUS

Licinius, kneeling on one knee, lifted the boy's head and felt his heart. Turning to the jailers, he said coldly—

"Some wine."

As he poured some of the liquid down the throat of Stephanus, Tigellinus took the lamp and quietly waited for signs of returning consciousness. A slight shiver of the body, a movement of the head, and a low moan convinced him that the swoon was passing, and he said coldly—

"He recovers."

"Spare me, oh, spare me!" gasped Stephanus wildly.

"Answer, then."

Faintly and mechanically the boy's lips moved, and he gasped out—

"The Grove."

"Where?"

"By the Cestian Bridge."

"The hour?"

"Ten." And Stephanus sank to the floor.

"Ah, my Tigellinus, we have them—we have them!" cried Licinius in triumph. And of Stephanus he asked—

"Their names?"

"I cannot," moaned Stephanus.

"You shall!"

But Stephanus, despite his agony, remembered his promise, and cried passionately—

"I will not! Kill me—kill me!"

"Ah, no! the dead speak not. We want thy answers,

THE SIGN OF THE CROSS

and we will have them. The names of these Christians, give them to us," said Licinius.

"I will not," replied Stephanus, moaning with pain.

Furious at what he considered mere obstinacy, Licinius ordered the jailers to put him again on the rack; but ere they could carry out their orders, a quick step echoed along the stone corridor; the door was opened, and Marcus entered the room.

"The rack for this child!" he said indignantly. "Shame! Set the boy down."

"Obey me, men!" shouted Licinius.

"Obey me," said Marcus quietly, but firmly.

The men hesitated, looking from one to the other, not knowing whom to obey. Tigellinus, scowling at Marcus, asked—

"How darest thou presume?"

"Dare presume?" smiled Marcus scornfully. Then, turning to the jailers, he said, "Set that boy down, or, as Cæsar liveth, thou shalt take his place."

The men placed Stephanus on the floor with more gentleness than they had hitherto shown.

"This is treason against Cæsar, and, as Cæsar liveth, thou shalt answer it to Cæsar!" furiously hissed the Councillor.

"I will answer it. I have Cæsar's orders, and I execute them as I think fit."

"Thou dost not execute them, Marcus. Thou art shielding these Christians, and thou art a traitor!" shouted Licinius.

Going swiftly to him, and half drawing his sword, Marcus said—

THE TORTURING OF STEPHANUS

"Recall that word! Recall it, or, ædile or no ædile, I will cleave thee from thy head to thy heart. Recall the word!"

"Licinius was hasty, he did not mean——" interposed Tigellinus.

"I desire not thy apology, but his. Recall that word 'traitor'!" repeated Marcus.

Tigellinus whispered aside to the ædile, "We shall let them slip. Give way."

"I was too hasty—I regret——" sulkily said Licinius.

With a contemptuous wave of his hand, Marcus dismissed both officers. Enraged as they both were, they could not but yield to Marcus. He was the Prefect, and held Cæsar's mandate for the suppression of this new sect; and they could not dictate to him as to the manner in which that work should be done. Tigellinus plucked the snarling ædile by the sleeve, and said—

"Come, Licinius, we have other work to do. Captain, get thy men and follow me," he called to that officer. "Jailer, see to the boy. Come, come, we shall be late!" and he hurried the ædile away.

Marcus, meantime, had gone quickly to the fainting Stephanus, and, with great gentleness, lifted his head from the ground. Turning to the jailer, he asked—

"Is that wine there?"

"Yes, Prefect."

"Give it to me. Have they had him on the rack?"

"Yes, Prefect."

"The cowards! The wolves!" said Marcus. Then,

THE SIGN OF THE CROSS

with infinite tenderness, he turned to Stephanus, and, offering him the wine, said—

"Come, boy, come; take this."

"Oh, the pain, the pain!" moaned the child.

"Ah, yes, I know, I know!" said Marcus, with gentle sympathy. "But drink this—'twill revive thee."

"Nay, let me die! Kill me, in mercy, kill me! I have betrayed them," sobbed Stephanus.

"What mean you?" wonderingly asked Marcus.

"It was not my heart, but my tongue that spoke. I told them where the brethren meet to-night."

"Who are the brethren?"

"I dare not tell—but if you would save Mercia——"

"Mercia!" Marcus started in surprise and alarm. Could she be in danger? She, whom he had but now left with a warning to escape! Quickly and anxiously he asked—

"Mercia! What of her?"

"She will be there."

"Where?"

"In the Grove by the Cestian Bridge."

"Didst thou tell this to Tigellinus?"

"Not the names, but the meeting-place."

These two then did know, and had probably gone thither to arrest her!

"And Mercia is to be there?" he asked.

"Yes. Kill me, but save her! She is an angel. Save her, and let me die! Save her!" Stephanus sobbed wildly.

Instantly all the soldier was alert in Marcus, and, in ringing, commanding tones, he summoned Viturius—

THE TORTURING OF STEPHANUS

"Meet me with thy men in the Cestian Grove. There is a gathering there of Christians, and amongst them is the girl Mercia," and his voice trembled a little as he spoke the beloved name. "We must save her from Tigellinus, even though we anger Nero himself. Haste, Viturius, haste!"

As Viturius left the room, Marcus lifted the boy gently in his arms, and, bearing him to the door said—

"My poor child! Come."

"But the boy, Prefect?" asked the jailer, remembering the order of Tigellinus that he was to look to him.

"Leave him to me; I will be answerable for him," said Marcus sternly. "Come, my boy."

And, as he went, Stephanus continued to sob, "Kill me! I am not fit to live! Kill me—kill me!"

Great as was his pain of body, the agony of his remorse was greater still. He had betrayed his Master in betraying His people. But the poor little fellow uttered the truth when he said, "It was not my heart, but my tongue that spoke."

CHAPTER XI.

THE DEATH OF FAVIUS

THE gatherings of the band of Christians, of whom Favius was the recognized head, had been held for some time past in a granary in the Palatine, but that had been so closely watched of late that it was determined to nightly change the trysting-place. As Favius had informed Titus, this night they were to meet in a secluded grove near the Cestian Bridge, and hither the brethren were making their several ways, in twos and threes, to ward off suspicion.

Having much matter to discuss, Favius and Titus went together, leaving Mercia to the care of Melos. These two had seen but little of each other of late. Melos was too manly to obtrude himself upon Mercia after her rejection of him; he felt that it pained her to meet him, and he loved the gentle girl too well to cause her needlessly one heart-pang. But it was with a secret joy that he obeyed the commands of Favius to accompany Mercia to the place of meeting, and, as they walked along, he discoursed of Stephanus' arrest, the doings and dangers of the brethren — indeed, upon almost any subject likely to interest Mercia, save that only which was nearest to his heart—his deep and abiding passion for her; but she was silent and absent-minded. At first he was inclined to attribute this to her grief for Stephanus, but, although it was evident

THE DEATH OF FAVIUS

that her tender soul was touched by the boy's arrest, the quick intuition of love told Melos that there was another and a deeper cause for Mercia's abstraction. Several times he spoke to her, and she heeded him not. Their way from the house of Favius in the Palatine lay through some narrow, winding streets, which led to the bridge; across that into the Grove, which grew more dense as they approached the meeting-place. The time was early autumn, but the day had been hot, and the evening was a beautiful reflex of summer. The moon was full, and a soft haze, which arose from the river and the marshes, seemed only to add to the loveliness of the sky.

The city was quiet, save for an occasional distant trumpet-call or strain of music from lutes and pipes, or when some burst of noisy laughter broke upon the stillness of the air. Almost in silence Mercia and Melos walked to the bridge which spanned the Tiber. As they neared the centre of it, a wailing trumpet-call, rather longer than the others, broke upon their ears, and Mercia stopped suddenly and looked back over the city.

"What was that?" she asked.

"The calling together of some of the guards for the night," answered Melos.

Mercia's hand clutched nervously at the bosom of her dress, and she said—

"It sounded like a summons to the grave!"

Melos started, struck more by her manner than her words; it seemed almost prophetic. A chill had fallen upon his heart, too, but he knew not why. After a time he gently touched Mercia's arm; she was standing quite still, looking back over the city, lost to all her surroundings. As she felt the pressure of Melos' hand she gave a little sigh, and, turning to him, said—

"Pardon me, dear Melos. I am not myself to-night. I was thinking—of——"

"What, my sister?"

For answer Mercia blushed, and, in an instant, Melos knew—her thoughts were of Marcus. Ah! it was as if a knife had entered his heart. This was to be the end of all his hopes,—Mercia's love for another. Now he knew,—and Mercia felt that he knew. Her eyes fell before his; he stood looking sadly at her. The old Tiber rolled lazily along under their feet; the splash of the waters against the buttresses of the bridge and the banks could be plainly heard in the silence, and those two, neither able to speak, stood still, while one heart fluttered with strange fears, and the other bled in hopeless agony. A fierce pang of jealous anger swept over Melos. The cause of the visit of the disguised Marcus to Favius was the desire to see Mercia. He knew the character of the Prefect. To him Mercia could be but the toy of an hour; her sweet innocence might inflame his passion for the moment, but it was not in his nature to be constant to a woman. He was without scruple, and, where women were concerned, without conscience. And was all this beauty of face and form, and loveliness of soul, to be made the sport of this heartless patrician? In all the garden the sweetest, tenderest, and most perfect bud had caught the eye of the lordly Marcus, and Melos had little doubt now that his follow-

THE DEATH OF FAVIUS

ing the girl to the house of Favius meant that the flower was to be plucked, let the cost be what it might. Marcus, he knew, was not the man

> "Who, with the choice of all a garden fair,
> Would choose the past month's rose, withered and bare,
> Leaving unplucked the fairest flower that lived,
> To gather that which death had left to moulder there."

Oh, wondrous waywardness of love! Surely these two seemed pre-ordained to love and wed. He, manly, honest, trusting, loving; she, sweet and tender, womanly and true. Their religion, their hopes, their lives, ran side by side, and yet the poles were not more wide apart than Mercia's heart from Melos.

So ran the thoughts of Melos. And Mercia—what of her? The look of Melos had told her what she had not guessed before: that she loved that reckless, bold, unscrupulous patrician, Marcus; and she felt a deep sense of shame and unwomanliness as the thought flashed through her mind. It was as though she had done some unworthy act, committed some great sin. Love this man who, she had been told, was so ignoble, spite of his noble birth! Love this profligate, whose life was a continual offence against the teachings of her childhood and girlhood! Love this persecutor of her faith, this friend of the Antichrist, Nero, who had murdered her parents and her brethren! Oh, the shame of it—the shame of it! She could have covered her face and crept away; but the light touch of the hand of Melos, and his quiet voice, warned her to command her feelings, as he gently said—

THE SIGN OF THE CROSS

"Come, Mercia, we still have far to go; we shall be late."

The old river ran to the sea, inevitably, as always it had flowed, and would for ever flow; and the streams of these two lives ran on, also, swiftly, silently, but surely on and on, fulfilling the will of that Divinity that shapes all ends, "rough-hew them how we will." Mercia loved Marcus. How? Wherefore? *It was to be!*

> "'Twas so decreed—'twas part of nature's plan,
> And all in vain we strive her schemes to scan,
> Each soul had met its soul's affinity;
> She was his woman, made,—he, pre-ordained, her man."

Poor Melos! Go, eat thine heart out in vain longings: Mercia has passed out of thy sphere, never, here, or in eternity, to re-enter it. He knew Marcus was unworthy of her, incapable of appreciating her worth. Should he tell her as much? To what end? No; as well try to stop old Tiber as the course of love. No; he would be silent, and would watch and pray.

And together these two divided souls went on to the meeting-place, with scarcely another word spoken between them.

In the meantime, Marcus—the object of their thoughts—had borne Stephanus in his arms to his chariot, and, bidding the charioteer drive quickly with the boy to his palace and see to his wounds, he went swiftly in the direction of the place where he expected to find Viturius and his troops awaiting him.

Viturius was there, with horses ready. Leaping

THE DEATH OF FAVIUS

into the saddle, Marcus led the way to the Cestian Bridge, his horsemen clattering behind him. His heart was in a tumult of excitement and dread. Would they be in time to save Mercia? Tigellinus would make her the first victim, if only in return for the slight put upon him in the afternoon, when Marcus had protected the girl. No question would be asked by Cæsar—Tigellinus was quite safe. Nero would not punish him for slaughtering these wretches, caught in the very act of plotting against his sacred life. Oh, the horror of the thought, if they should be late! They had still a half-mile or more to go, and Tigellinus had started some minutes before.

"On, men, on!" impatiently called Marcus, and his horse started wildly forward at the prick of the spur. Along the streets they galloped, Marcus feverishly counting the seconds, the strides of his horse, and calculating the distance yet to traverse before he reached the grove.

Suddenly, from a turning to the right of Marcus, appeared a cavalcade of chairs and chariots, in which were seated a party of patrician ladies and gentlemen. So sudden was the meeting, that Marcus had to rein his horse back on to his haunches to prevent him dashing into the foremost chariot. The occupant gave a little scream, and Marcus recognised the Empress Poppæa, who, with her party, was returning from a banquet given in her honour by one of the Court.

With a little laugh of relief, Poppæa said—

"Impetuous Marcus! What love-tryst hast thou to keep, that we are to be ridden down in thy haste, as

THE SIGN OF THE CROSS

though we were some Christian scum starting another fire of Rome?"

Marcus inwardly cursed the untoward chance that had brought about this encounter, but he had to control his anger and impatience, and said—

"Forgive me, Empress; I am indeed in haste, but 'tis no love-tryst I go to keep. I am on a matter of life and death, and must needs press on without delay." And he made as if to ride off. But Poppæa was not minded yet to part with him. She had been devising schemes to meet him, and appoint a time for an interview, but this was not easy: here was an obviously accidental meeting, which could call for no explanation, and she wished to make the most of her opportunity. On the other hand, Marcus' thoughts were with Mercia and her danger, and he could not conceal his eagerness to be gone.

"Whose life or death hangs in the balance, most noble Marcus?" asked the Empress.

"Thou couldst not know the name, even if I told it to thee, Empress; I pray thee, give me leave to go." Without even waiting for permission, he dug spurs into his horse, and, with a wave of his hand, signed for his troop to follow him; and away they galloped towards the Cestian Bridge.

Poppæa was white with fury. Marcus had dared to slight her before these her friends. She must know to whom he was hastening, and if, as she suspected, it proved to be a woman,—woe unto her, for she would be revenged!' Thus, all unwittingly, Mercia had made an enemy of the most powerful woman in Rome, for

THE DEATH OF FAVIUS

Poppæa never rested until Marcus was tracked, and she had discovered that it was to save the life of this Christian girl that he had left her after she had expressly desired him to stay.

The meeting-place was in a hollow or dell in the heart of the Grove. It was most secluded, and could not be seen until one was close upon it. Trees and a dense undergrowth shielded it from the river, while a rise in the ground hid it from the land. The moon shone softly through the autumn leaves and branches, but shed little light. In the dim shadows a hundred and fifty or more men, women, and children had gathered—reverent, devout, earnest, and God-fearing. On a slight eminence stood the reverend Favius; a little lower down was Titus; by the side of Favius knelt Mercia. In her right hand she held a horn lantern, in her left a large cross, made of two branches, broken from the trees before the meeting began, and lashed together with a leathern thong. It had been hurriedly made on the spot, for the emblem of their faith could not be carried with them except at the risk of death.

Melos and other trusty men of the brotherhood had been told off to do duty as scouts, to watch and give warning at the approach of any strangers or enemies.

It was a strange and beautiful scene. The band of faithful followers of the Carpenter of Nazareth were kneeling, facing the aged Favius, in several circles; nearest were the children, then the women, and, on the outer rings, the men. The moonlight fell in patches through the trees, lighting up a face or a form here and there, making the shadows still darker by the contrast.

THE SIGN OF THE CROSS

All were quietly and soberly attired, and the white robes and drapery in which Mercia was wrapped made her figure stand out against the background of green foliage like the glistening form of some angel of light. Softly and reverently all were singing a hymn—

> "Shepherd of souls that stumble by the way,
> Pilot of vessels storm-toss'd in the night;
> Healer of wounds, for help to Thee we pray,
> Guide Thou our footsteps, send the morning light.
> Healer of wounds, for help to Thee we pray,
> Guide Thou our footsteps, lead, oh, lead us home.
>
> All we like sheep have strayed—where is the fold
> That shelters all who seek its loving breast?
> There, where the Cross doth shine like molten gold,
> Emblem of pain, giving eternal rest.
> There, where the Cross doth shine like molten gold,
> Giving eternal rest. Oh, lead us home."

At the end of the hymn, Mercia arose, raising the lantern in her left hand, to enable Favius to read the Epistle which he had unrolled, while with her right she still grasped the cross.

Silently, and with eagerness, the little band of worshippers listened to the blessed message which Favius delivered:—

"And now, brethren, be faithful. Love them that hate you; pray for them that despitefully use you. Love one another. Be patient in sorrow; rejoice with them that do rejoice; weep with those that are in grief. If thy enemy be hungry, feed him; if he thirst, give him drink. Do unto others as ye would they should

THE DEATH OF FAVIUS

do unto you. Love thy neighbour as thyself; for to teach this came the Redeemer into the world. And may the peace He sendeth be with you now and for ever."

"Amen!" all chanted softly.

Then spoke Titus, the messenger of Paulus.

"Brethren, too long have the nations wandered in darkness. The dawn is at hand! But the splendour of the morning gold shall be streaked with blood—the blood of the saints. Yet, though the wicked pursue thee, even unto death, why, death is but the gate to life eternal. Be patient and endure."

All too prophetic were his words. The splendour of the morning gold was all too soon to be streaked with the blood of the saints. The enemy was nearing them; the persecutors were within bow-shot of them. The faithful Melos came running down the bank of the dell, shouting breathlessly—

"Father! Favius! Mercia! Brethren! We are betrayed!"

And some faint-hearted among the women screamed—

"Betrayed!"

"Tigellinus and his soldiers are upon us. Fly! fly! and save yourselves!"

Hurriedly the people were about to fly, some in terror, some with the natural instinct of self-preservation. The children were clinging to their mothers' garments, frightened and helpless; the men were endeavouring to calm them and assist the women to escape; but Mercia saw that flight was impossible, and, raising the cross on high, she cried—

THE SIGN OF THE CROSS

"Stay, brethren! By the Cross, I implore you! Meet your enemies like Christians. Be not afraid!"

Straightway all were calm and reverent once more. Sinking down on their knees, they recommenced their hymn—

> "Shepherd of souls that stumble by the way,
> Pilot of vessels storm-toss'd in the night;
> Healer of wounds, for help to Thee we pray,
> Guide Thou our footsteps, send the morning light.
> Healer of wounds, for help to Thee we pray,
> Guide Thou our footsteps, lead, oh, lead us home."

Down upon these devoted ones dashed Tigellinus, Licinius, and their brutal soldiery. Loudly and fiercely the leaders urged the men to slaughter. "Kill—kill—kill!" roared the bloodthirsty Licinius. "Spare none of the dogs!" shouted his remorseless companion. Not a cry came from the Christians. Strong in their faith, they sang to their Shepherd, until the cruel swords smote them down. When a woman was aimed at, a man would step forward and calmly receive the thrust; mothers threw themselves upon the swords to save their little ones—all in vain, they were ruthlessly murdered with the rest. The aged and the young alike were without fear. There was no panic now; all were prepared to die for their Blessed Master, and die without a murmur. Husbands and wives embraced each other in death; children, who had been spared for the moment, prayed silently over the bodies of their parents. Not one resisted. It was indeed safe sport, as the spy, Servilius, said. He was there, and his

THE DEATH OF FAVIUS

knife sought, and found, the hearts of the women and children, and amongst them the child of the man he had seen struck to the earth by the guards that afternoon, in the street by Dacia's house. It was her only child, and the bereaved woman lifted her hands to God in passionate entreaty to Him to receive its soul.

The ædile seized upon Titus, and remorselessly ran his sword through his heart, and he fell and died without a groan. Tigellinus rushed at Favius, but Mercia threw herself in his way, and entreated him—

"No, no! Kill me, but spare this aged man!"

"No; kill the jade with the rest!" shouted Licinius, as he dragged Mercia away from Favius. Tigellinus stabbed Favius through the lungs, and he fell on the slope, with his face upturned, and his fast-failing eyes fixed upon the sky. Licinius' foot had slipped as he caught Mercia, and, to save himself, he let her go; but her white figure caught the eyes of Tigellinus, and he rushed to her. At the same moment the ædile ran at her; but in an instant their swords were beaten from their hands by Marcus, who, snatching Mercia by the waist, whirled her out of danger, as he struck the weapons from the hands of her would-be murderers.

"In the name of Cæsar, hold!" commanded Marcus. His men rushed between the soldiers of Tigellinus and their victims, and, where they resisted, fiercely fought them into obedience. The mad lust for blood was in the souls of the two officers, and they were furious at the interference of the Prefect. Tigellinus shouted to his men to slay them all, but Marcus' voice rang out like a trumpet—

THE SIGN OF THE CROSS

"Drop your swords, in Cæsar's name! Whoever strikes another blow at these people I swear shall suffer death."

The soldiers knew and feared the Prefect; they sheathed their swords, and the slaughter was stayed.

"Are these miscreants to escape, Prefect?" asked Tigellinus.

"No," said Marcus. "That is my duty; leave it to me. Look to the wounded; take the rest prisoners. Go, all of you," he said to Tigellinus, Licinius, and their men; "I will be answerable to Cæsar for these. Have no fear; justice shall be done."

"See to it," said Tigellinus, "that justice is indeed done. These wretches were plotting the death of our beloved Nero, and he will brook no neglect of precautions to save his sacred life. Look to it, Prefect."

"I will be answerable unto Cæsar, as I have said," replied Marcus.

It was useless for Tigellinus to dispute the authority of Marcus; moreover, he was outnumbered, and so he called upon his soldiers to fall in and march. He left Marcus with his men to look to the living and dying. Amongst the latter was the aged Favius. Mercia had flown to him, and had lifted his reverend head on to her knees, and was wiping the death-dews from his face and forehead. With a heavenly smile he thanked her. He could not speak; his blood was welling into his lungs and choking him, but his eyes were speaking for his tongue, and they were full of a divine love and pity for the child he had cherished so long. With the utmost yearning he gazed upon her, as if to read her

THE DEATH OF FAVIUS

future ere he passed into the everlasting life. Long he looked upon her as his strength waned. Marcus moved towards him as if to help him, and, in so doing, attracted the attention of the dying martyr. For a moment his face clouded, and his eyes darkened with a look of dread. Then he seemed to gaze beyond, steadily and earnestly, and when his look again fell upon these two, it was with a content and happiness beyond all words to express. What had he seen to bring his soul such peace? Had the future opened to his clearing vision? Did he know what it held in store for this man and this woman? If he did, the knowledge gave him a great joy, for he looked upon them both with a perfect peace and happiness, and, seeking the hand of Marcus, who was now kneeling by him, he gently pressed it. His other hand was holding Mercia's, and that, too, felt the last effort of his dying strength. Thus, with his eyes fixed to the last on Mercia, his face growing more and more peaceful, and still more noble and beautiful, the aged saint passed through the portals of death to life eternal, to receive his reward, and to hear his Master's voice utter the joyful greeting: "Well done, thou good and faithful servant! Enter into thy rest."

CHAPTER XII.

THE WOOING OF BERENICE

THE last moments of Favius affected Marcus strangely. There was a grandeur of beauty in his death that he did not understand. The ineffable peace, the radiant joy, which suffused his face were so strange that Marcus wondered. He had been deeply impressed by the dignity of the man in life, but in death he was grand, even glorious. And it was thus that these Christians could die! He had looked upon death often enough, had seen the dread messenger arrive in many guises, but never until now had he appeared as a herald of peace and joy.

Mercia was kneeling beside her dead friend, silently praying. Marcus gave orders for the decent and orderly burial of the dead, and attention to the wounded, who were led or carried away with the rest of the prisoners. They gave no trouble, these strange people: there were no shrieks, cries, nor lamentations —only passive obedience and patient sorrow.

When all was arranged, Marcus gently bade Mercia to go with him; she was his prisoner. Looking, for the last time on earth, upon the face of that dear, true friend and guide, Mercia turned, with heavy heart, back to the city with her captor. In so short a time all who had made her childhood and girlhood bright and happy had been taken from her, but she had been taught not to murmur, only to suffer in patience; and her prayer was, "Thy will be done!"

Marcus watched her with an absorbing interest. His innate manliness prevented him from intruding upon her sorrow, but there was something else that made him hold aloof from her. What was it? The same gracious calm that had marked the passing of Favius was in her eyes; the same peaceful resignation, and, withal, a wondrous depth of feeling that profoundly stirred his better nature. He felt the might of this strange faith, although he knew it not. It surrounded Mercia with an atmosphere through which he felt he could not penetrate. Marcus was sorely troubled. In the presence of this simple girl he felt a self-abasement that hurt him with an almost physical pain. Why should he feel thus? He had not harmed her. On the contrary, he had twice saved her life. He had sought at the risk of his own dignity and place to warn her and her friends to leave the city and save themselves. He could not charge his mind with one action that was not for her welfare; but his thoughts—what of them? As he looked at Mercia, the hot blood surged to his face, and he knew in his heart that he desired her above all other women. But at such a time was it not brutal to yield to such a feeling? The girl was so pure, so innocent; and her deep grief, too, alone demanded his respect. But since his hand had touched hers for that brief moment when he had dragged her out of the reach of Tigellinus, his passion had grown to an extent that made him wonder. It could not be that he loved this Christian, beautiful as she was. The thought was absurd! And yet, what could it be that he felt, if it was not love? So ran his thoughts as he led Mercia back to the city. He could say nothing to her but the merest commonplaces. He felt that in her grief she had some strange help and consolation beside which his attempts at comfort were contemptibly inadequate aud useless. So they returned in silence.

Mercia's grief was not to be measured by her words or manner. Next to her parents she had loved the aged Favius, and her heart was torn with the sorrow of parting from him; but, even in this awful time, her thoughts wandered to the man at her side, and she silently thanked him for his manly consideration for her grief and the gentleness of his manner to the dying Favius and the wounded brethren. Could this be the profligate Marcus, of whose evil deeds she had heard, and against whose wickedness she had been warned? Surely, he could not be the vile thing that she had thought him! There was a nobility about him that she could not fail to understand, all unused as she was to the world and to passing judgment on mankind.

Marcus was pondering on what was to be done with her. Could he leave that tender, white creature in some wretched cell in the public prison? Ah, no! his every instinct of manliness revolted against the thought. And yet—his duty? His duty was to keep her and her friends close prisoners until the will of Nero should be learned. He had full power to exterminate the vermin,—and at the word he had heard used so often to describe these strange people, these Christians, he almost smiled, it seemed so ludicrously inappropriate,—but he need not use that power. Still, he must not release her. He had passed his word to Tigellinus that he would be answerable to Cæsar for their safe keeping, and he must not break that word. His honour was pledged. He would not, however, place her in the cells of the common prison. No; he would lodge her in his own palace until he could see Nero and induce him to grant her pardon.

And so it came to pass that Mercia was bestowed in a portion of the house of Marcus; but across the courtyard only were the cells in which her friends were confined, and, in the stillness of the night, she could hear them chanting their hymns, and in her heart she joined in their praises and their prayers.

The boy, Stephanus, had, by the special orders of Marcus, received every attention, and was fast recovering from the effects of the torture he had undergone; but he still suffered intense pain—he was feverish, and his nerves were terribly shaken. But the elasticity of youth was his, and would assist in his recovery.

After seeing that Mercia was cared and provided for, and delivering the rest of the prisoners up to the guards, Marcus retired to pace his rooms, through the greater part of the night, wondering and pondering over the events of the day and his own surprising change of feelings.

Berenice, too, passed a restless night. Her mind was full of the gossip she had heard of this Christian girl, Mercia. Marcus, she knew only too well, was not overscrupulous where women were concerned, and she was too thoroughly imbued with the manners and morality of the age in which she lived to trouble herself over his intrigues; so long as his heart was not touched, she did not care overmuch. "Men were men," and to look for chastity in them was ridiculous. Indeed, where it existed it did not excite respect—at least in Rome. On the contrary, it was looked upon as a sign of effeminacy and weakness. Therefore, the many escapades so freely attributed to Marcus scarcely affected her; but something in his manner had aroused the suspicion in her mind that his feeling for this Christian girl was not altogether that which he had entertained for the other women with whom he had associated. This troubled and vexed Berenice, and she arose from her couch in the morning in a temper the reverse of amiable.

At times Berenice could be shrewish, and on this particular occasion she was unusually so, as her servants and slaves learned to their cost. She had her spies and agents, who kept her fully aware of all that Marcus did and said, and, in order to appear diligent, they often regaled her with reports of many things which he had not done, and repeated many things he had never even dreamed of saying: they had to earn their wages as best they could.

However, she knew he had gone to the Cestian Grove with the object of saving the girl's life, and had succeeded in so doing. She had heard, too, of the insult to which he had subjected Poppæa; that was another proof of the strength of his regard for the Christian girl. She was burning to see him and judge for herself,

THE WOOING OF BERENICE

by his words and manner, how far he was involved with Mercia; but she knew that he was at the Palace of Justice, and could not leave, even if she sent for him. Still, she sent, and was now anxiously awaiting the return of her messenger.

The apartment which served as a boudoir and reception-room for her special friends was exquisitely, richly, and most tastefully furnished. Refinement and luxury were evident on all sides. The couches, hangings, cushions, and other appointments were all of the most costly materials, and rich in harmony of colour and design.

Berenice herself was a beautiful picture as she lay upon one of the couches, studying her face in a small steel mirror. Her maid, Zona, had been accentuating the delicate curve of her eyebrows. There was but little need for the aid of art to improve the beauty of her face, but there are few women who can deny themselves the delight of trying to elaborate their charms, be they ever so abundant, and Berenice was not one of the few. Evidently, Zona's handiwork did not give Berenice entire satisfaction, for, with a sharpness of tone which her slaves had learned to know boded no peace to them, she said—

"Give me the pencil, Zona. You are careless this morning."

The girl was on her knees by the couch, and, looking up at her mistress, said—

"Nay, lady, I——" But her speech was cut short by a blow on her face administered with no lack of energy by the delicate white hand of her mistress.

THE SIGN OF THE CROSS

The slave sank back on the floor and ruefully rubbed the stinging cheek, as her mistress said—

"Don't dare to answer me! This eyebrow is all askew. What ails the girl? Art sick—in love—or both?"

Zona was still engaged with her smarting face, and did not reply. Her silence provoked her mistress to ask angrily—

"Why do you not speak, fool?"

"Lady, you bade me not to answer," said Zona.

This was too obviously the truth for Berenice to gainsay, and so she changed the subject, and said—

"Well, answer me now. How do I look this morning?"

"Radiantly beautiful, lady!" replied Zona artfully, knowing how best to soothe her mistress's feelings. "The noble Marcus must love you, or he is but a man of stone—not one of flesh and blood."

"Why speak of Marcus?" said Berenice, longing at the same time that the slave should continue to speak of him. "There are scores of others who would give their lives for me."

"That they would, indeed, lady," answered the cunning girl. "There's Metullus——"

"Metullus!" pettishly answered her mistress, deftly adjusting a straying ringlet. "I despise him—he's a fool!"

"He is rich; and a rich husband who is a fool to boot is not a thing to be despised," said the girl sententiously. "Then, there's Tigellinus."

"He's a brute!" was the curt summing-up of that person's character.

THE WOOING OF BERENICE

"Brutes can be tamed, lady," meekly suggested the slave.

"Ah! they all weary me to death! Marcus is worth a score of such." And her voice softened as she mentioned the name of Marcus. Zona was not less swift to catch the passing changes of her mistress's many moods than is a weathercock to obey the changes of the wind, and, in a gush of not altogether feigned admiration, she exclaimed—

"Indeed he is, lady! A score? Nay, a thousand such! He is indeed a god among them all. Would he were here now to see how beautiful you look."

Here was no flattery at least. Berenice did look beautiful indeed; she had no cause to be fretful over her appearance. Her dress was of a creamy white silk; her handsome bust was outlined by a massive band of many-coloured gems which sparkled in the light as her bosom rose and fell; a belt of the same rich character drew the robe together at the waist, while the hem of the garment was wrought so closely with jewels that the material was entirely hidden. A drapery of the most delicate shade of heliotrope bordered with gold, and caught at the side with an immense jewelled clasp, seemed to display rather than hide the beauties of her magnificent figure. On her arms were bracelets of exquisite workmanship; in her hair were entwined gems of the rarest kind, and, as she spoke, she tried the effect of a red rose over an ear. A gong of silver metal was heard ringing outside, and Berenice, with a slight start of expectation, cried, "Enter!"

THE SIGN OF THE CROSS

Another slave-girl—one Catia—came into the room, and, with a low curtsey, awaited permission to speak.

"Well?" asked her mistress eagerly.

"The noble Marcus was at the Palace of Justice, but he sent word he would attend you the moment the causes were tried."

Berenice sank back on the couch in disappointment.

"Enough. Go!" she said, dismissing Catia. "When the causes are tried? That may not be for hours! He avoids me purposely. He must love me—he shall!" And she contemplated the reflection of herself in the steel mirror. The contemplation evidently gave her pleasure, for she smiled as she softly repeated to herself, "Yes, he *shall* love me!"

And indeed she had fair cause to think such a consummation possible, inevitable even. Her eyes glittered with pleasure as she beheld herself. Yes, she was lovely; there could be no doubt of that—and Marcus should soon be at her feet. He was so used to admiration and love that he was careless and thoughtless; that was all. It was not possible that this Christian girl was her equal in beauty any more than in rank; and, as she gazed upon herself, a feeling of contempt for the lowly-born rival steadily took possession of her. This was unwise in her—no woman can afford to despise a rival, however humble. Men are strange creatures, subject to strange whims and emotions that women wot but little of.

So long did she study herself in the mirror that her maid, less absorbed in the subject of her mistress's beauty, had stretched herself out upon the tiger's skin beside the couch, and, nestling her pretty face upon the beast's head, fell into a doze. A sharp ring upon the silver gong startled the slave from her sleep and Berenice from her reflections, and hurriedly and authoritatively she exclaimed—

"That may be Marcus! Put those things away—quick!"

Zona deftly hid the aids to beauty, and Berenice continued—

"Now take thy lute and sing."

Zona sat by the end of the couch upon the floor, took her lute, and struck some chords upon it, while Berenice fell back in a tempting attitude upon the couch, saying—

"Enter! Enter!"

Catia obeyed the summons and entered the room, announcing as she did so—

"The lady Dacia."

With a gesture of angry impatience, Berenice sprang from the couch, saying—

"Dacia! There, get up, girl. I thought it was Marcus. You need not sing for Dacia." And the pretty picture designed for the lordly Marcus was broken up, and gladdened not the eyes of the less important Dacia.

That young and feather-brained lady entered with a smile, and a whirl that stirred to motion the leaves of the plants adorning the room. She was, as ever, bewitchingly dressed. Her robe was of pale rose-pink silk; her draperies, broidered with heavy gold fringe, were crossed over her bosom with bands of rubies and

THE SIGN OF THE CROSS

other precious stones. A string of rubies was entwined in her golden hair, and a pale blush rose was fastened on either side of her head. She seemed the very incarnation of thoughtless, irresponsible gaiety as she fluttered round the couch to salute her friend.

"Ah, my Berenice!"

"Well, my Dacia," replied Berenice languidly, "what brings thee hither?"

"Oh," said the butterfly, dropping her fan, "a fit of depression." This was accompanied by a smile of intense self-content that ill-accorded with her words.

Berenice, who knew her friend's many weaknesses, asked, with but scant interest—

"Have you been gambling and losing again?"

"Worse, Berenice, worse!" said Dacia, restlessly circling the couch on which Berenice reclined; "I would not mind the losing, but that stupid Philodemus tells me he cannot afford to pay my losses."

"Ask thy husband to do so," suggested Berenice quietly.

"I did; but he laughed, and told me that if Philodemus could not afford to pay my debts, I must find another lover who could. That's the disadvantage of being frank enough to let your husband know you have a lover. As for him,—my husband,—he was sore pressed himself. You know what that means, my Berenice. That hook-nosed wife of Vinius is simply ruining him! That woman is a perfect vulture! What the men see in her I can never understand. Vinius is the fourth husband she's had in two years."

"The third," lazily corrected Berenice.

THE WOOING OF BERENICE

"Third? I thought it was four she had had."

"No; only three," said Berenice, with a slight yawn.

"Well, we cannot be particular to one or two when a woman changes her husband as often as she does," said Dacia, dropping a plate of grapes upon the floor. This habit of dropping things was decidedly growing upon the fair Dacia, and the habit boded no good to the accommodating, but partly ruined, Philodemus. It behoved that complacent person to look to his revenues, or submit to pass into the lumber-room of Dacia's dropped, broken, and forgotten trifles.

Berenice, still divided in opinion about a red rose—or no red rose—for her hair, said, as she once more tried the effect in the mirror,—

"There are others quite as bad as she."

"Worse, my Berenice," and the inept Dacia dropped a delicate and costly vase, from which Berenice had just lifted her rose, upon the mosaic floor, where it was shivered into a thousand atoms. Not in the least perturbed in spirit, Dacia remarked, gazing at the fragments,—

"Oh, pardon me, Berenice; I am *afraid* I have broken it."

Indeed she had, but on she rattled, as Berenice sighed over her lost treasure, "Now, there's Adrostia. How that woman dares to show her face is beyond me! She induced her husband, Helladius, to divorce her, that she might marry his friend, Adoncus, and, when she had ruined him, divorced him to marry Symnus,—ruined and divorced him,—re-married her first husband, Helladius, and invited all the divorced ones to the wedding-supper! What do you think of that?"

Here she began to handle a beautiful gold-mounted cup of coloured glass, studded with gems, in her usual reckless fashion; this Berenice, quietly but firmly, rescued from destruction, by taking it out of Dacia's hands and removing it to a place of safety. Not in the least abashed, Dacia repeated her question, "What *do* you think of that, Berenice?"

"That she is a very liberal-minded woman," was the answer. "What has become of your friend Ambascus?" asked Berenice, with slight sarcasm, for this Ambascus was another of Dacia's numerous admirers.

"Oh, don't speak to me of Ambascus!" laughed Dacia.

"Why not speak of him? I thought he really loved you."

"So he does, the mean-spirited creature! But he esteems it a disgrace to have a love affair with a married woman. Pah! Such men are only fit for slave-girls. That reminds me—Marcus——"

"Marcus? What of Marcus?" Berenice was at last roused into an attitude of interest.

"Have you not heard?" innocently asked Dacia.

"Heard what?"

"About this Christian girl that he is so infatuated with? All Rome is talking of it."

Berenice felt her cheeks crimson, but she asked, as carelessly as she could, "About what?"

"Strange that you should not have heard," chattered

Dacia. "But there, thank the gods! lovers and husbands are the last to hear of the pranks their dear ones are practising."

"But what of this Christian girl and Marcus?"

"Tigellinus will tell you."

"I have not seen Tigellinus for two days. What is it?"

"Tigellinus swept down upon a nest of these vipers —these Christians—and would have exterminated them, but, so please you, the noble Marcus steps in, protects one of the wretched females, and has her taken to his palace."

"What?" exclaimed Berenice, in amazement.

"And Tigellinus swears that Nero shall know of it. But then all Rome knows the state Nero is in! Moreover, there's the Empress, Poppæa, she rules the Emperor; and, as she's half in love with Marcus herself——"

"But this Christian girl—what is her name?" interrupted Berenice anxiously.

"Mercia, I think the creature's called."

"The same!" said Berenice, with much trepidation.

"What do you mean?"

"I've heard of her before. What is she like?" Strive as she might, Berenice could not quite steady her voice as she put this question, but Dacia was at the moment too much occupied in admiring herself in her friend's mirror to notice her agitation, and she replied carelessly—

"The *men* think her very beautiful. Philodemus tells

THE SIGN OF THE CROSS

me Marcus is positively foolish over her. But she, forsooth, gives herself virtuous airs, and repulses him."

Berenice felt her heart sink at this evidently scanty appreciation of the beauty of the Christian girl, and she said with uncontrolled bitterness—

"Ah, these men, these men!"

To which the fair Dacia replied, somewhat unreasonably, but with decided emphasis—

"That's exactly what *I* say."

The gong in the atrium sounded once more, and Catia entered.

"Well?" asked her mistress. This might be Marcus! But no, for Catia announced only—"Tigellinus and Licinius."

"Ah! Let them enter," said Berenice. At least, they could give her the latest news of Marcus and Mercia. Throwing herself in a graceful attitude upon the couch, she extended her hand to Tigellinus as he entered with Licinius, and said—

"Welcome, both. Your names were upon our lips but a moment ago."

"Happy names to be so sweetly placed!" gallantly said Tigellinus, kissing her hand. "Would that my lips had lingered where my name did lodge that moment ago!"

"Hast thou left grave State affairs to make pretty speeches upon ladies' lips?" asked Berenice, with a bewitching smile.

"The causes for the day are tried, and, for the time at least, we are free, lady," replied the Councillor.

THE WOOING OF BERENICE

"The causes tried? Hath the Prefect Marcus left the Palace of Justice?" asked Berenice, with an air of indifference which did not mislead the astute and cunning men who were keenly watching her.

"Yes, lady. He left when we did."

"And that was———?" asked Berenice anxiously.

"Half an hour ago," was the seemingly careless reply.

"Oh, indeed! I thought that he———" and Berenice paused.

"That he what, lady?"

"Well, that———. Oh, what matters what I thought?" said Berenice, assuming a gaiety she was far from feeling. "What's the news in Rome to-day?"

"That Marcus has a new toy," sneered Tigellinus, with much meaning.

"Indeed? What might that be?" asked Berenice, knowing full well what the answer would be.

"Have you not heard?" asked the Councillor, with assumed surprise. "And the lady Dacia here! Strange, hath she told thee nothing?"

"Dacia hath told me many things," said Berenice carelessly. "To what do you allude?"

"I hardly like to be the harbinger of evil. If thou dost not already know, why then———"

"Know what? Really, my friend, the evil must be great indeed if thou dost hesitate to give it tongue. Have I to mourn a fortune lost—or a companion dead —or———"

"A faithless lover?" cruelly suggested Tigellinus.

"A faithless lover? Marcus has never been———"

THE SIGN OF THE CROSS

"Did I mention Marcus?" asked her relentless inquisitor, with a smile.

"Of whom else were we speaking?" said Berenice confusedly.

"Ah, yes, of course! How foolish of me to speak of Marcus! Let us talk of something else. The topic of Marcus and his Christian girl can scarcely interest thee, Berenice." And he turned to Dacia.

"Women are always interested in a love-story," continued Berenice.

"And this is a strange one, indeed," interrupted the ædile. "'Tis said that Marcus, the greatest, richest man in Rome, doth madly love and vainly woo some Christian girl—while Berenice doth pine for him in vain."

This brutal speech had the effect that was desired; it roused the anger of Berenice, and on that and her jealousy these two men intended to play.

"Do they dare say that of me?" she asked, and her eyes flashed like polished steel. Your cleverest and strongest woman is the most pliable and ductile weakling if you can but excite her jealousy; there is nothing that she will not believe and accept, provided that it is exactly that of which the acceptance will pain and wound her most.

In imagination Berenice pictured the looks, smiles, nods, and covert sneers of her many female friends, all, as she imagined, busily employed discussing and enjoying her humiliation. Poor Berenice! it was hard indeed for her to bear. Her pride, her vanity, and worse than all, her love, was sorely wounded; and her dear friend, Dacia, femininely and feverishly anxious to let no chance slip of sending the barbed arrow home, said—

"Indeed they do, and for thy devotion they now laugh at thee."

Can anything be sweeter than female friendship in the ordinary realisation of that charming ideal! Poor Berenice! It was certainly hard to be compelled to believe herself an object of compassion and ridicule. She, who had imagined herself the most desired and courted of women! And for whom was she neglected? Not even for one of her own rank, but for a vulgar, nameless Christian—an associate of the vile scum that had burned down Rome; who met in secret to perform their detestable rites and ceremonies; whose crimes were almost unmentionable. No wonder Berenice was furious!

"Didst thou come here to tell me this?" she asked bitterly of Tigellinus.

"No, but to serve thee," he answered with an assumption of extreme solicitude.

"How canst thou serve me?"

"By helping thee to revenge thyself."

"On this girl, Mercia?" said Berenice, with the utmost contempt for her supposed rival.

"And on Marcus," suggested the crafty officer.

"How?" Berenice asked the question, but her heart told her that, angry as she was with Marcus, she could not bring herself to harm him.

"Well, thou knowest that Marcus has full power to judge and punish these Christians. He has chosen to spare this girl, Mercia, and keeps her a prisoner in his own palace."

"Repeat this to Nero, not to me," coldly replied Berenice.

"Eh?"

"Why not?"

"And Poppæa?" asked Tigellinus, exchanging a look with Licinius that conveyed his fear of the consequences of such an act on his part. "If she should learn that I had tried to injure Marcus, the gods be with me!"

"What then do you propose?" quietly asked Berenice.

"That you yourself do visit Poppæa; tell her of Marcus' infatuation, and induce her to influence Nero to send this girl to the lions."

Angry as Berenice was, impatient as she felt to revenge herself for the slight she had suffered, her ideas of honour were high enough to teach her that the part of informer was a degraded and revolting one, and she answered haughtily—

"A contemptible piece of work, that I care not to undertake." Here she rose from her couch and walked away, as if to imply that she wished to discontinue the conversation.

But Tigellinus would not let the matter rest there; he had come for a purpose—that purpose was to use Berenice as his cat's-paw to pluck the chestnuts of the Empress's influence from the Neronian fire; and he did not intend to leave until he had obtained his desire. Again he thrust the poniard of ridicule through the armour of her self-esteem by saying—

THE WOOING OF BERENICE

"Then let Mercia live, and Rome still pity Berenice!" And Tigellinus shrugged his shoulders, and walked to the window, as if to enjoy the spectacle of Rome's sympathy for Berenice.

Dacia had no motive, really, in pressing and urging Berenice on to bring about the separation of Marcus and Mercia, except the essentially feminine one of meddling with all love-affairs, home-made or foreign.

"Berenice," she said, " have more spirit! I should like to see the man who would fling me aside for any Christian girl!"

Berenice was torn with the conflict of love, pride, humiliation, anger, and shame, and she asked herself, aloud—

"What can I do?"

And Tigellinus answered, "Revenge thyself for the slight put upon thee. This man Marcus——" And then he wisely stopped, for the man Marcus had entered the room, and was quietly enjoying his discomfiture. There was a pause, and an uncomfortable one. Dacia was the only unmoved person in the room; she wore her usual placid smile, and munched some grapes, which she took from a dish on the table near her. The two officers were enraged at the interruption, and Berenice regretful that she had been discovered discussing Marcus with his enemies, and by Marcus himself.

Marcus looked from one to the other, and asked, with some irony,—

"Am I in the way, lady?"

Tigellinus answered for her, with a rudeness he

THE SIGN OF THE CROSS

would have hesitated to offer Marcus elsewhere than in a lady's presence, saying—

"Were you eavesdropping, Prefect?"

Marcus controlled himself with some little difficulty; he was too well-bred to create or desire a brawl in a lady's chamber, and he contented himself with answering—

"No. Were you discussing my character?" Then, turning to Berenice, he inquired, "Were Tigellinus and Licinius wearying you with my praises, fair Berenice? I know how dearly they love me. Silent still, my Licinius? Hast thou not yet recovered the breath I knocked out of thy most precious body in that little accident in the Grove?"

The Councillor smiled grimly at the recollection of that "little accident" to his friend, while the ædile scowlingly answered—

"I have breath enough to keep me alive, Excellence."

"Provided thou dost not encounter anything more formidable than a weak boy, or a frail girl, eh?" asked Marcus.

"The boy and the girl were traitors both. I did but my duty," was the surly answer.

"Duty? Ah, duty is responsible for strange crimes in Rome." Then, turning his back upon the two men, he turned to Berenice, who had been a not altogether unamused witness of the confusion and annoyance of the two officers, and asked again—

"Am I intruding, fair Berenice?"

"No, indeed, Marcus," quickly answered the lady. "Pray thee, stay. I wish to speak with thee."

THE WOOING OF BERENICE

Then, turning to Dacia, she gave that lady a look of meaning, and Dacia rose, dropping her fan as she did so, and said—

"I was just about to go when you entered, Marcus. Will you pardon me, Berenice?" Then, looking for Tigellinus and Licinius, she laughed, for they were scowling upon Marcus with an intensity that might have alarmed a less reckless man than he, and said to them—

"Gentlemen, will you accompany me? I think it would be well, for, verily, you both look so fierce that I should fear for Marcus should he be left alone with you."

With unveiled contempt, Marcus said—

"Pray, have no fear for me, lady. The harm they will do me will be in my absence, or when my back is turned. It is not the soldier's sword, but the assassin's knife that thou or Marcus need fear from a Tigellinus or a Licinius."

The insult was so direct and gross that Tigellinus was stung to the quick. Partly drawing his sword, he was about to rush upon Marcus, but Berenice interposed, saying with much disgust—

"You forget this is my house. I will have no quarrelling here. Please go."

Tigellinus was glaring with rage at Marcus, who smiled back with perfect unconcern. Berenice held out her hand to the Councillor as a sign of dismissal, and he had no choice but to bend over it and say—

"Lady, I obey."

"How glad is he to be obedient," laughed Marcus lightly.

Tigellinus made another threatening movement, but Dacia held his arm, and said—

"Come, come, gentlemen; I am in haste. Do you accompany me or no?"

With a shrug of his shoulders, Tigellinus turned towards the entrance to the room, and there awaited Dacia, who was saying to her friend—

"Farewell, dear Berenice." Turning to Marcus, she said—

"Take good care of your fair Christian, Prefect, but do not let her run you into the danger of Nero's anger. A few hours' dallying with a pretty girl is but scant reward for disgrace and a dungeon. Be prudent, Marcus, be prudent."

"I will be prudent, lady, most prudent," answered Marcus quietly, but inwardly chafing at such mention of the lovely Mercia. With a parting smile from Dacia and a scowl from Tigellinus, Marcus was left alone with Berenice.

For what purpose she had sent for him he did not know; indeed, he had scarcely troubled to think. His thoughts had been elsewhere. In the Palace of Justice he had been preoccupied and absent-minded. He scarce heard the causes, barely knew who addressed him.

His thoughts were elsewhere, his soul was perturbed and his mind distracted. The death of Favius had made a deep impression on him. Not a word had the old man uttered; he had scarcely moved after receiving the thrust that so speedily released his spirit, but the unearthly beauty of his face, as his bodily strength failed and his spiritual power seemed to grow, caused Marcus the greatest wonderment. Was this the death of a plotting politician and would-be regicide? That glory of feature and peace of soul the outcome of a life of vile conspiracy and dastard scheming? No; it was impossible! There was in him, as in that sweet girl Mercia, something apart from life as he knew it—as all his friends supposed it. What was that something? This thing they called their Faith? He had almost forgotten where he was.

Meanwhile, his hostess was watching him closely. She had sent for him; he had come. And now, what could she say to him? She felt that he had come unwillingly, as a mere matter of form and courtesy; his manner and attitude proved that. Why, even now he was absent-minded and longing to be gone. Her pride chafed under the knowledge, but she controlled herself, and determined that, come what might, she would continue to do so. He should not see how she suffered.

Marcus lifted his eyes, to find Berenice watching him, and he called back his wandering thoughts, saying with an affectation of lightness that did not mislead or deceive her—

"You sent for me, lady?"

Yes, she had sent for him, but need he remind her of that? Would a lover tell his mistress that he had come by order? She noted the coolness of the greeting, and answered—

"I did; and most unwillingly thou hast come."

THE SIGN OF THE CROSS

Marcus looked at the beautiful creature before him, and some compunction smote him for his callousness. After all, she was a grandly noble woman. Woman in a very high sense of the word indeed, even if not in the highest; and, as he looked, he remembered so many acts of tender thoughtfulness on her part towards himself that he felt something like a little flush of shame at the thought of his churlish response, and he answered with more warmth—

"Unwillingly? Nay, Berenice doth not know Berenice."

Berenice heard, with the quick ear of a woman's love, the pretty intention of the speech, and the lack of depth in the tone in which it was spoken; she answered the tone rather than the words, saying—

"Nay, Berenice doth need no compliments from Marcus."

It was a compliment and nothing more, and Marcus knew it.

When a young, beautiful, and gifted woman begs for something from a man beyond mere compliments, what is that man to do? Given the fact that the woman is worthy, that she is sincere, that her implied or confessed love for a man is honest, the man who receives the confession or the implied avowal of these sentiments in a woman's breast is in a difficult position. How far is he cruel in being kind? How far is he kind in being cruel? Marcus was not unkind naturally: indeed, he was kind to a fault. The yearning, limpid look in Berenice's eyes touched him, and he quickly said—

THE WOOING OF BERENICE

"How can I serve thee, lady!"

Still Berenice felt that here was but kindness,—not what she desired, the great, strong master-passion, love,—and she lightly said—

"Now Marcus is himself. The purse is open,—how much will serve?"

"Nay, Berenice can need no gold of mine," said Marcus.

"But if I did?" she asked, half sitting and half reclining on the couch.

"If thou didst," he answered sincerely, "then I should say—not, How much will serve? but, All that I have is thine,—knowing full well that it would be returned."

Still it was the friend and not the lover who spoke. And Berenice sighed as she replied—

"Ah, so in my heart said I, all that *I* have is thine, —*not* knowing it would be returned."

It was not possible to mistake her meaning. What should he do? What ought he to say? What he did say was not quite the truth.

"I do not understand thee, lady."

"Thou wilt not understand."

"Perhaps it is better that I do not try," was the answer that involuntarily escaped Marcus.

"Am I so very repulsive? Others do not think so."

"Others? Nay, all are agreed patrician Rome can boast no fairer daughter than Berenice."

The emphasis came, unwittingly, rather heavily upon the word "patrician"; the sharp watchfulness of Berenice noted and pounced upon it instantly.

THE SIGN OF THE CROSS

"*Patrician* Rome," she said, with a still heavier emphasis upon the particular word; and then, with a little uplifting of the delicate eyebrows, she continued—

"Marcus could scarce look lower."

This was a home-thrust for Marcus, who knew that Mercia was in her mind as she spoke. He coloured slightly, but with, for him, rare discretion, he remained silent, and Berenice continued, scarcely daring now to look at him—

"We are both rich; indeed, our wealth united might buy an empire."

This was true enough. Had Marcus been ambitious there was but little he might not, with such riches, achieve. A throne had been bought and sold for much less than their joint wealth. Again, what could he say? A woman can refuse an offer from a man,—nay, stop him before he gets to the point of avowal,—but the task is not so easy when the usual position is reversed. There could be no mistaking her meaning; but what could he say or do?

"Berenice!" he began.

Berenice lost control of herself. She had suffered much that morning; her love for Marcus was sincere, and her passion equalled her love. The thought that he might be drifting into a like passion for another was more than the barrier of her womanly reserve could bear, and, with a rush of emotion, it was swept away. Turning to him, she said, with tears in her eyes and voice—

"Marcus, Marcus, canst thou not see what is in my heart? Dost thou not know it is no girlish fancy, but

THE WOOING OF BERENICE

the deep, strong love of a woman who has never loved before—whose whole nature has been held back so long that, unless the floodgates are unbarred, the pent-up tide will burst all bounds and engulf her—body, mind, and soul! Marcus, pity me! forgive me!" And she sank, weeping, with her face hidden in the cushions of the couch.

Marcus was deeply moved—how could he be otherwise? Berenice was no ordinary woman, and this frank avowal touched the better part of his nature. He spoke truly when he said—

"Berenice, thou dost pain and shame me! Thou, all so prodigal of love and I so miserly——"

"Marcus!"

"Believe me, I am honoured, grateful; and if all the respect that man can show for woman, if devotion, friendship——"

"Friendship? I ask for love—you offer friendship!" said Berenice with intense bitterness.

"I offer all I have to give, lady," Marcus answered gravely and respectfully.

So! She had played—and lost! Had staked all, and in vain! She had forgotten her womanhood; had begged and had been refused! Oh, the shame of it! The humiliation! That she should so far forget herself as to throw herself at the feet of any man—even a Marcus—and find herself declined! A sudden rush of indignation swept over her; she sprang to her feet, her eyes blazing with anger, and said—

"All thou hast to give? Ay, all that thou hast to give to *me*—but to *another*, to this girl, this *Christian!*"

And she spoke the word "Christian" with loathing. "Hast thou aught else to give to her?"

Marcus was angry now. Her contempt for the exquisite creature who had been uppermost in his thoughts since his first meeting with her was more than his temper could bear, and he asked with much acerbity—

"Was it for this that you sent for me?"

"No, no!" said Berenice; "I sent for you before I had heard of this girl; but it *is* true? Is it? Thou dost love this *Mercia!* Thou dost! Thou dost! Marcus caught at last, and by the baby face of a miserable Christian girl! Ha, ha, ha!" She burst into a peal of wild and hysterical laughter that was perilously near to sobbing; and, as she spoke, she paced the room. "This worse than beggar, whose life is forfeit to the law! Marcus loves a wretched Christian—a thing despised and loathed—the companion of thieves and murderers—the scum of Rome—a degraded schemer—an outcast—a——"

Marcus, furious that so delicate and lovely a soul should be so miscalled, cried sternly—

"Stop, Berenice! I will not hear you!"

But she was not to be so easily stayed. Her face was crimson with anger. Her eyes ablaze with jealousy, furiously she cried—

"You *shall* hear me!"

"I will not. I take my leave," replied Marcus, going towards the door. But Berenice interposed, saying—

"You shall not go until you've heard me! Love is so near to hate that one step past the boundary line and love is lost in loathing! Have a care, Marcus! Berenice will not be scorned and bear it!"

"Does Berenice stoop to threaten?"

"Stoop? Ye gods! can I stoop lower than I have done?"

"Yes, lady, for true love is no dishonour, but treachery is."

"I care not!" she exclaimed recklessly. She had gone too far to retreat now; she knew her cause was lost. Her hatred for the girl who had come between her and her desires was unbounded, and she went on—

"I will love or hate! Art thou blind? Dost think all Rome does not know this girl is in thy house?"

"I care not!" contemptuously replied Marcus.

"Rome laughs, and swears thou dost plead to her in vain."

"I care not!" again replied Marcus.

"But is it true?" asked the almost frantic woman.

"Lady, it is true," was the frank reply. "I do love Mercia—and I do plead to her in vain."

Womanly pride should have come to her help at such an answer; but woman's weapons are not always at hand when most required. Just now all her pride was swamped in a torrent of mingled rage, hate, jealousy, shame, love, and despair; she threw herself recklessly upon the couch, and burst into a passionate, unrestrained fit of sobbing.

Poor Berenice! Poor Marcus! Is there any position in which a man of heart and feeling can be placed wherein he can feel more helpless than when he is alone with a lovely woman, who is sobbing her heart out for his sake, and he cannot take the suffering one in his arms and kiss and comfort her back to happiness? Probably the wisest course for him to have adopted would have been to have left her to herself; yet that seemed brutal, and he did the most foolish possible thing, instead of the wisest. He went to her and begged her to "be calm," at the same time gently touching the hand which was clutching the head of the couch. The half-pitying tone of his voice completed her rage. She started up, and with intense scorn and contempt, said—

"Marcus, pleading in vain for the caresses of a Christian wanton!"

Berenice was even more indiscreet than Marcus had been. No man cares to have a woman he loves so called, even if there be grounds for the accusation; but, in the case of Mercia, it was an outrage, almost a blasphemy, and he shuddered at what seemed to him a profanation. With much dignity, although white with anger, he turned upon Berenice, and said—

"What Rome may say of me troubles me nothing; what Rome or Berenice may say of this young girl troubles me much. She is no schemer, no degraded woman! She is the purest, sweetest, and most crystal soul that lives in Rome this day. What this Christianity is I know not, but this I know—that if it makes many such women as Mercia, Rome, nay, the whole world will be all the purer for it!"

"You dare speak thus of her to me?" cried Berenice, almost breathless with passion.

THE WOOING OF BERENICE

"Dare? Why not dare, lady?"

"How if I repeat your words?"

"Repeat them if thou wilt!"

"To Nero?"

"To Nero!"

"Yes. What then?"

Ah, what then, indeed? For himself Marcus had no thought, but for Mercia! What evil spirit was it that was ever at work to divert every kind thought, every effort on his part for the girl's good to her hurt and evil? No movement yet that Marcus had made in her behalf had resulted in any real benefit; now he had made an enemy for her in Berenice, while yet another was to come,—and he the most cruel and unrelenting, Nero. No wonder Marcus paused before he answered—

"What then? It is hard to say what then. I can only hope that Berenice will never stoop to turn informer against Marcus."

"Will you give up this girl?" asked Berenice.

"No, lady, no," was the firm reply.

"You shall! I'll force you! Take care! Measure my determination with your own, and add to my advantage the hate I bear her and Nero's power to injure you."

For a moment he surveyed her in silence, then in clear, determined accents he replied—

"Neither Berenice, her anger nor her hate, nor Nero, backed by all his legions, can keep Mercia from me. There is not a nerve in all my body that does not call for her—not a thought in all my brain that does not encompass her. Now the truth is told, I leave you. No good can come of further argument. Lady, farewell."

And he was going in such anger that any future reconciliation was impossible unless he could be induced to soften towards her ere he left; and Berenice made her last pitiable effort to lessen the breach between them, saying—

"Nay, Marcus! Stay—do stay!"

Marcus now did what he should have done sooner—firmly declined to remain.

"No; I have stayed too long. No man should war with women, even with words. Lady, farewell." And with a low, respectful bow, he was gone.

Berenice returned to her couch and to her tears; she sobbed herself hoarse. All was desolation to her now. Her wealth, her beauty, her influence, the flattery of the base, the admiration of the honest—all were as Dead Sea fruit, embittered by the loss of the one thing that made them all sweet—the love of the man she worshipped. It was long before she was roused from the passion of grief and despair to that of revenge, but the moment came at last, and she sprang up saying—

"Reject me! Reject me for this wretched, tawdry, mock-modest Christian! Insult me for her! Scorn Berenice for a Mercia! Oh, for the power to humble him as he has humbled me!"

Then into her mind came the thought of another woman who loved Marcus—the Empress Poppæa. She, too, had come to hate this Christian girl, and

THE WOOING OF BERENICE

she would help her to a joint-revenge. Poppæa's influence with Nero, Berenice knew, was unbounded. Yes, she would go to Poppæa, as Tigellinus had suggested. There was no thought now of the meanness of striking at Mercia through the instrumentality of Nero. Let the low-bred creature go to the lions, or the flames! It could not be greater torture than the humiliation she had endured that day. One more or less of these degraded outcasts done to death—what mattered it? She would be revenged. Marcus, too, should suffer. She would not be scorned, laughed at, made the jest and by-word of the whole city, and bear it tamely! Poppæa and Nero could help her, and they should! Thus, nursing her wrath, Berenice called for her attendants and her chariot, and was driven rapidly to Poppæa.

CHAPTER XIII

SOME PERPLEXITIES

Marcus was in great perplexity when he left Berenice; he was troubled by the power that Mercia had gained over him. Here was a girl, of whose very existence he was ignorant only a few hours ago, occupying his every thought and controlling his every action. For her sake he had gone dangerously near disobeying Nero's commands, been guilty of gross rudeness to the Empress, insulted Tigellinus, and quarrelled with Berenice. Even now, in spite of the difficulties in which he had become enmeshed through her, his one wish was to hasten back to his palace that he might see her again. He was in love with every fibre of his body and all the strength of his soul, and when love comes to a man like Marcus after youth has passed, it comes with the fury of the whirlwind. He could think of nothing but Mercia, see only her lovely face, hear naught save her sweet, gentle voice. The first fierce, overwhelming love of an ardently passionate nature had swept through him with irresistible force. That he desired her more than any other woman he had ever seen, and with a warmth he had never conceived possible, he knew; but that his passion was not to be gratified according to his custom was a possibility that had not as yet presented itself. He had to learn that his love for Mercia possessed a depth and strength

SOME PERPLEXITIES

that had the power to make it the be-all and end-all of his life. Had such a thought come to him he would have derided it. What! Marcus, the wealthiest and most courted man in Rome, to be bound to a mere Christian girl, of whose family and history he knew actually nothing! No, that would be too absurd! Still, as he passed from the house of Berenice to his own, he wondered yet again what it was in Mercia that so moved him. Beautiful as she was, it was not her beauty that held, although it had at first attracted him. It was a stronger, deeper influence than that. What was it? He would go to her and see her again. Perhaps the glamour would pass away on closer acquaintance; it might, after all, be but another feminine trick of manner that had caught him by its freshness. He would go to her at once and learn, if possible, what was the secret of her charm. But he was destined to wait before he could see Mercia again.

Mercia, on her part, was torn by many conflicting emotions and fears. Her task of self-judgment was no easy one. She knew she loved Marcus, and the knowledge was an ever-present reproach and shame to her. For the first time she realized the meaning of all the warnings and counsels she had received from her parents and guides as to the dangers that lurked around her. That which before seemed wildly improbable now began to look dimly possible, and the thought made her shudder.

All the forces were, apparently, ranged on the side of Marcus. He held her captive in his palace, where she was absolutely at his mercy; his wealth, his physical power, his dominant will, his reckless disregard of all authority or moral restraint when his passions were roused (and never had they been so roused as now), were weapons that threatened to decide the contest swiftly and decidedly against Mercia. To all these advantages was to be added her love for him, and with that love she fought, but fought in vain.

On her side were ranged—what? Her purity of soul and her Faith. Would they save her against such odds? Verily, the fight appeared terribly unequal, and Mercia was sore afraid.

All the attentions lavished upon her by the orders of Marcus were so many humiliations, and she refused all the courtesies of the servants with a firmness that nothing could shake. She was a prisoner, not a guest; she had but one favour to ask—that the luxury of her present position should be exchanged for the grim terrors of the prison cell. This desire the servants could not gratify, so Mercia set to work to devise some means of escape. The attendants were all devoted to Marcus, and, knowing the importance he attached to her safe keeping, they would not, even if they dared, help her to gain her liberty.

Wearily she paced round and round in her gilded cage, scanning the doors, the walls,—all to no purpose. Hourly one of the slaves deputed to wait upon her would unlock the door and ask for her commands. If she had none to give, he would retire, fastening the door after him. This door was of solid bronze, and when once locked could not be moved. The walls and floor were of marble. There was but one casement; that was small, and at least eleven feet from the ground.

The hourly visit had been made, and she would now be alone for some time; could she reach the casement? She would try. First she drew one of the couches to the wall beneath it; upon this she placed a small table, with triple legs, that seemed barely strong enough to support her weight. However, she was light and active; it might do. It was difficult to mount, and trembled ominously upon the soft couch. Eventually, she succeeded in climbing upon it, only to find herself still at least a foot below the height required to enable her to reach the embrasure. If she sprang to it, could she keep her hold upon the smooth surface of the marble? No, that would be impossible. But there was an iron bar in the centre of the opening—could she reach that? Should she try? If she should miss it, she would fall back upon the table or marble floor, and be seriously injured. Still, what was the chance of bodily pain and hurt to the danger she feared from the Prefect's evident passion for her? She would attempt it.

Gathering all her strength and energy, she sprang at the bar and reached it. The table was dashed, by the force of her leap, on to the marble floor with a crash. She trembled, fearing this must alarm her jailer. But no thought of an attempted escape on her part had crossed their minds; they would not have been alarmed even had they heard the noise, but they did not do so. Small and lithe of frame, she had no difficulty in creeping through between the bar and the wall; but she found that it was at least fifteen feet from the level of the courtyard outside. To drop this would be sure to result in injury, if not in broken limbs. There was her drapery! This, when unwound from her body, measured quite twelve feet; the half of this and her own length of arm would be sufficient to save her too great a drop to the ground. Taking off the mantle, she wrapped it round the bar of the window, and looked around to see if the place was clear of the guards. Alas, no! There were two, quietly conversing within a few yards of her. Until they went away she did not dare to stir, and it seemed as if they would never go. The minutes seemed hours to the gentle girl, but eventually they moved off in the direction of the palace gates. Quickly throwing the ends of the mantle outside the casement, Mercia lowered herself to within a few feet of the ground; then, letting go of one end of her drapery, she dropped to the pavement, drawing her mantle with her, and quickly sped across the courtyard towards the street. Mercia was free and unharmed.

Marcus arrived at his palace full of sweet and tender thoughts of Mercia. He was to see her again! As yet his opportunities for converse with her had been but scanty. Now she was where he reigned supreme; he had but to command to be obeyed in all things, and he would see her alone where he would be safe from interruption. His mind was full of the many things he would say to her to calm her fears, soothe her sorrows, and build up her confidence in him.

Ordering the attendants on duty to precede him, he went to the room in which Mercia had been kept. His

SOME PERPLEXITIES

pulse quickened as the slave unlocked the door, and he entered the room in, for him, unwonted excitement. The place was empty. In mute astonishment the slave stared about him.

"Where is the lady?" asked Marcus.

"Nay, Excellence, I know not," replied the slave.

"Hast thou let her escape?"

"Nay, Excellence, I barred the door but half an hour ago. She was then safe within."

Marcus looked and saw the overturned table, the couch against the wall, and was furious.

"Idle, careless fools!" he exclaimed; "she hath escaped by that casement. Quick! call Viturius and the guard. Search the courtyard. Haste! or your lives shall answer for it; haste! Viturius!" Calling for that officer, he rushed through the corridor to the gates of the palace, questioning all he met. No one had seen Mercia.

When Viturius appeared, he gave him hurried instructions to send to Mercia's home, the house of Favius, and to all places frequented by the Christians. His anxiety was great, his rage intense, and his mortification bitter indeed. She had flown from him as she might have fled from a Tigellinus or a Licinius; he was her jailer, nothing more,—a being to fear and hate. The thought was gall and wormwood to him; he had fondly believed that his interest in her was reciprocated, while all the time she had been scheming to escape from his hated presence. But he would find her if she were in Rome or out of it; and he rode from place to place seeking news of her. All in vain. No

THE SIGN OF THE CROSS

one had seen or heard of her, and Marcus returned to his palace in anger and despair.

Berenice, in a white heat of anger and with a burning desire for revenge upon Mercia, had driven in her chariot to Nero's palace and requested audience of the Empress. Poppæa had many reasons for keeping on terms of friendship with the handsome patrician. Her wealth and influence were important considerations—too important to be overlooked by a court so prodigal as Nero's. Then, Berenice could be made a useful link between Poppæa and Marcus; an alliance between the latter and her friend would bring Marcus closer to her side. The Empress could not visit the Prefect, but she could visit his wife, and without suspicion. Marcus married to Berenice would be easier of access than Marcus single.

Poppæa was surrounded by her women when Berenice was admitted to her presence. After some commonplaces, charmingly delivered on both sides, the Empress gathered that her visitor desired to be alone with her, and so dismissed her suite, and bade them not return without her summons.

Berenice had not let her anger against Mercia cool. On the contrary, she had fanned it vigorously, and it was at blazing point; but, to look at her handsome face, an ordinary observer would have imagined her to be in a state of beatific calm. What consummate actresses are even ordinary women! What transparent bunglers, compared to them, are even uncommon men in the art of disguising their feelings and desires!

Berenice was inwardly raging with fury; yet out-

SOME PERPLEXITIES

wardly the placidity of a mill-pond was a turbulent stream in comparison. Poppæa was not an ordinary observer, and instinctively knew that her friend was intent on matters of great moment—that her visit was not one of courtesy only, but rather one of much importance to both. Poppæa, too, was a fine mental fencer and diplomatist. It was not necessary to give Berenice a cue to begin; the matter would out. She could wait.

And so these two laughed, chatted, and gossipped upon all imaginable subjects, save the one nearest to both their hearts, until Berenice asked casually whether "it was true that another wholesale arrest of those wretches, the Christians, had been made?"

"Indeed, yes," said Poppæa. "Marcus hath been most zealous in the task assigned him by the Emperor. Last night he surprised and captured a whole gang in the act of holding one of their infamous meetings."

"Is that possible, Empress?" asked Berenice, with a childlike look of wonderment. "Did *Marcus* arrest them, or was it some other?"

"Nay, 'twas Marcus. I met him on his way to the Cestian Grove, and so intent was he upon their capture that he scarcely could be stayed to salute even me."

"Indeed?" asked Berenice, with astonished, uplifted eyebrows. "Was he in such unwonted haste to capture these men—and—um—women?" And the emphasis on the word "women" gave Poppæa whole volumes of information, which to the male listener would have afforded nothing but a blank page.

"Were there many women among the vermin?" quietly asked the Empress.

"Indeed, I cannot say; but there certainly was one, who seemed a person of very great importance—at least, to Marcus."

"So! In what way?"

"Well, probably it might be urged because of her seeming extraordinary influence."

"Over whom? Her own sect?"

"And others, too."

"What others? Surely, none of our own class?"

"Forsooth, yes."

"Whom?"

"Well, Marcus for one. At least, so they have told me."

Oh, that "they"! What would this world be without the "theys"? "They say," "they know," "they impute"! What character is safe—what action unknown—what motive unperceived by "they"? "They" are the lynxes of the world, and, with more than Argus eyes, see through the very stone walls, annihilating space, overleaping all obstacles, penetrating the most reserved chambers of men's minds with an omnipresence as comprehensive as it is marvellous.

Need it be said that Berenice had already achieved the object of her visit? Poppæa's jealousy was afoot, alert and keen to the scent as a bloodhound. She knew all now; Marcus had been fascinated by some girl among these Christian conspirators, and his wild hurry on the previous evening was to save her. So she, the Empress, was insulted, treated with less

SOME PERPLEXITIES

courtesy and ceremony than should be shown to the wife of a tradesman by Marcus, in order that he might be in time to rescue a despicable creature fit only for the gutter or the jail.

The two women looked at each other, and it would be hard to say who was the more furious. Both were ready to consent to any scheme that would result in Mercia's destruction; and all this without one spoken word. Verily, wonderful are the ways of women!

Poor Mercia! A helpless sparrow in the clutches of a hungry hawk would have a greater chance of escape than thou, left to the mercy of either of these thy sisters. And what is thy sin? The most deadly that one woman can commit against another—that of superior attraction for a man beloved.

"Who is the woman?" asked Poppæa.

"Her name is Mercia," replied Berenice.

"What is she like?" the inevitable question followed.

"I have not seen her, Empress."

"But thou hast heard something. Is she young?"

"They say but eighteen; but she must be more than that."

(Why, Berenice? Why *must*?)

"Dark or fair?"

"Dark, Dacia tells me," answered Berenice.

Now, it is an approved fact that women are always more jealous of a complexion the opposite to their own. Had Mercia been as fair as Poppæa she would have aroused less animosity in that lady's breast; it was one more item to her detriment that she was not.

"Where is she?" said the Empress.

THE SIGN OF THE CROSS

"He keeps her in his palace, it is said, while her companions are more fitly lodged in prison."

"He shall not keep her there long. Nero shall know of this."

"Exactly my thought when I did hear of it, and to myself I said, 'I will seek counsel of Poppæa, who will best know how to deal with her; but surely she cannot be allowed to remain in his palace, to the scandal of all Rome.'"

Little Berenice would have rocked of the scandal had she not felt that there must be some stronger sentiment than usual actuating and guiding Marcus' conduct. Here was the sting to both—it looked like a serious passion, not "a passing whim."

"Marcus must be taught a lesson; he has been allowed too much licence," said the Empress. "He knows he is in our favour, but he must not presume upon it. As great as he have fallen ere now. Let him be careful; we are not to be insulted with impunity! This is too much! To be publicly slighted for a Christian girl is more than I feel disposed to bear, even from a Marcus. Come, my Berenice, let us seek Cæsar. We will have this Mercia placed beyond Marcus' power to reach or to deal with." Giving her hand to Berenice, the Empress led her towards Nero's room.

Both had been bitterly insulted by Marcus, and both were intent upon revenging the affront upon the innocent cause thereof, the gentle and lovely Mercia. Whither had she gone?

On leaving the palace, she went straight to the gate of the prison wherein she knew the Christians were confined. A group of guards were at the doors, and among them a young officer, who stopped her, saying—

"What want you here, lady?"

"Admittance to the cells of the Christians," answered Mercia.

"Upon whose authority? whose permission hast thou?"

"I have no authority," answered Mercia.

"Then thou canst not pass, lady," said the officer respectfully, for he, like all men, felt the strange charm of this girl.

"But I too am a prisoner, sir," pleaded Mercia. "And my place is there."

"Prisoner?" smiled the guard; "by Jupiter, thou art free enough, seemingly!"

"I pray thee, let me go to my friends. If they are guilty, so am I. If they have sinned against the laws of Rome, so have I; for the offence they committed I committed too. I was with them when they were surprised and taken captive at the Grove, and what am I that I should not suffer even as they do? I pray thee, let me in to them."

"By the gods!" roared the officer, "this is something new! Oft have I been besought to let a prisoner out, but 'tis the first time man or woman has begged me to let them in. Dost know what kind of place this prison is?"

"That concerns me not. I am young and strong——"

"And exceedingly beautiful too," interjected the officer, with an admiring glance. "And worthy of a beautiful nest, my lovely bird. Let me counsel thee,"

THE SIGN OF THE CROSS

and the officer advanced a step towards Mercia; but she quickly went nearer to the soldiers, so that it was impossible for him to speak to her and not be overheard by the rest of the guard.

"Sir," said Mercia, "either let me in to my friends, or I go."

"What wouldst thou do in yonder?" asked the officer.

"There are many wounded and sick among them; I would be with them, to nurse and comfort them. Ah, sir, I beseech thee to grant my prayer. Indeed and indeed, I am as guilty as they. I can do no harm. I cannot aid them to escape, and I promise thee I will not try. I only desire to be with them, and suffer even as they suffer."

Her beauty, her earnestness, her sweet, pleading voice captivated the young officer, but what was he to do? He had no power to arrest without authority, or grant permission for anyone to visit those already imprisoned. Yet she could do no harm, as she had said. Little would he have hesitated had he the requisite authority, but that he had not.

"It is hard to refuse so sweet a creature anything, but what thou dost ask is beyond my power to grant," he said, after a pause. "What is thy name?"

"Mercia," she replied.

"By Cytherea, a pretty name! Well, gentle Mercia, get thee hence to thy parents; thou wilt be safer with them, I warrant thee—unless, indeed, thy parents are with those thou dost seek within. Is that so?"

"Alas, sir, my parents are dead!"

SOME PERPLEXITIES

"So! Alone, eh?" Then a thought struck the officer—not an unnatural one, either—it was for some lover's sake the girl sought admittance; to be near the man she loved she was ready to sacrifice her own liberty. "Parents dead, and thou art alone, eh?" he said. "Then thou dost seek some lover in the prison! By Jupiter, he is a lucky fellow! But amongst all these rats of Christians I have seen there's none worthy of all that beauty, my girl. Forget him, and take up with some honest Roman soldier. There's many who would take his place, and all too gladly; eh, comrades?"

"Ay, ay," the others agreed, with brutal laughter.

Truly, Mercia had but little bettered her state in flying from the palace of Marcus. Still she pleaded; her tender heart was aching to be with the weak and wounded among the prisoners, that she might tend their hurts and comfort them. But to all her entreaties, jeers and laughter came as answers. It could only be, as the officer thought, some man amongst these Christians was the girl's lover. No, it was hopeless—she could not be admitted. The guards were for driving her away, when something happened which unexpectedly gave her the boon she was craving with so much earnestness and intensity. Licinius came out of the prison. Instantly he recognised Mercia.

"So!" he thought, "this is the way in which the noble Marcus keeps his word; this is the manner in which he holds himself responsible unto Nero for the safe custody of his prisoners." His brutal face had upon it a grim smile as he looked upon Mercia. Here was news for Tigellinus and Nero. The girl who had so infatuated Marcus was free! His course was clear; he would re-arrest her. True, as ædile only he had no power to order arrest, but Tigellinus had commanded that all who were caught at the Grove were to be punished, and he would but be acting in accordance with those commands if he re-imprisoned this girl. His mind was made up; he would do it.

Advancing towards the group at the door, he asked roughly—

"What is the trouble here? Who is this woman?"

Mercia recognised Licinius, and shrank back in alarm. Had he not tried to slay her in the Cestian Grove? Did he not slaughter the good Titus? Were his hands not stained with the blood of many of her friends?

"One of the Christians, ædile," answered the officer.

"What doth she here?" asked Licinius.

"She craves permission to be arrested and placed beside the others of her sect, who lie within."

"Doth she indeed? Let her have her desire."

Then, pretending to recognise her for the first time, he said—

"Ah, now I remember thee! Thou art the girl our Prefect said he would have a care of. By Cæsar, he will have to account for thy freedom! I will see to thy safe keeping for the present. Let her wish be granted, officer, and see that she have little chance to escape again."

Leaving Mercia to the charge of the officer, Licinius strode away, to find and impart the news of her capture to Tigellinus. The officer, attended by a jailer, con-

SOME PERPLEXITIES

ducted Mercia through the hall of the prison along a number of dark and narrow passages, lit at intervals by slits in the masonry. Pausing before a massive iron door, the jailer produced a large, curiously cut key, with which he unlocked it; then, rolling back the heavy bolt, the door was pushed open, and Mercia walked into the general dungeon of the jail, where the prisoners were kept prior to examination or trial.

Some forty or fifty of the Christians were there,—men and women,—and amongst them Stephanus, who was lying upon a heap of straw in one of the corners of the cell. His wounds had been dressed, and he had been carefully attended to, according to the instructions given by Marcus; but he was there with the others, awaiting the decision of the judges.

The brethren received Mercia with mingled feelings of joy and sorrow—joy that they beheld once more her whom they loved and revered so much; sorrow that she was a prisoner like themselves. The cell was a large one, the floor and walls were of stone, and benches of the same material were placed around it. On these and on the ground the Christians sat and reclined in semi-darkness, cheering and comforting each other.

Lovingly Mercia was greeted by all, and, like some sweet ministering angel, she went among them, giving them strength and encouragement. When her eyes became better accustomed to the gloom of the cell, she perceived Stephanus lying on the straw, and seeing that he was ill or wounded, she sprang to his side, and, seating herself upon the ground, lifted his head into

THE SIGN OF THE CROSS

her lap, and besought him to tell her what ailed him.

The child could only sob; he could not find words to tell her the truth, that he it was who had betrayed them into the hands of their enemies. She knew that he was in great pain by the shudder that went through him as she touched him.

"What hath happened, dear Stephanus?" she asked.

But Stephanus could only weep and moan.

"Wilt thou not tell thy friend?" pleaded Mercia.

"He hath been tortured, Mercia," spoke Melos, who was among those imprisoned there.

"Tortured? Oh, the poor Stephanus! How?" asked Mercia. "Tell me how."

"Better not question him yet, Mercia," softly said Melos, not wishing to give the boy the shame of repeating to Mercia the treachery of which he had been guilty. "The physician hath but now left him, and he is weak and feverish still. He had better rest, dear Mercia; another time he will tell thee all."

And so, for a while, at least, they spared the boy the agony of a confession to Mercia. Divining something of the cause of his silence, she asked nothing further, but, dipping her mantle in a large amphora of water, she bathed the feverish, aching brow of the boy, comforting him as much as he could be comforted. Her cool, soft hands upon his forehead and face soothed him presently into a troubled sleep, the first he had known since his torture. After a while, Mercia gently placed him upon the ground,

SOME PERPLEXITIES

fearing to waken him, and went softly among the others, helping and encouraging them in her sweet, tender way, glad to be of service to them in their sorrow and pain, glad, too, to be out of the reach of the man she so loved and feared.

Presently she descried the woman whose child the spy Servilius had slain. The poor creature was crouched motionless on the floor, her heart was well-nigh broken. Her husband had been taken from her and killed, her child too was murdered. She was bereaved of all she loved; she seemed dazed with grief. To her Mercia went, taking her in her arms as though she were but a child, tenderly embracing her, and telling her of the happy meeting that was so soon to come under the protecting glory of Him they all served and loved. Gradually the woman seemed to recover consciousness under the sweet consolation of Mercia's sympathy. Slowly her thoughts were led to Him who had endured such agony for her and her lost ones, and as her vision opened to the sacred figure on the Cross, the memory of His patience and resignation brought a calm to her bruised spirit, and she knelt and prayed silently for strength to endure for His sake. There was not one among the group of persecuted ones in that dark cell who did not feel uplifted and encouraged by Mercia's presence. While she was with them light could not wholly leave them nor peace entirely desert them, and thus it came to pass that the hour which Marcus had hoped Mercia would spend in listening to his words of passion, and perchance submitting to his caresses, was given unto the consoling of the wounded, the sick, and the grief-stricken amongst these poor captives.

And in ministering to their needs Mercia forgot her own perils of body and soul. Not that she failed to realise them, or know that in escaping from Marcus she had fled to almost certain death; but she was not of a nature to dwell upon her own sorrows when surrounded by others who were also grief-stricken, and her training had taught her not to fear death for her Faith's sake, but to embrace it joyfully, if by doing so she glorified her Saviour. Strange chance that had made this sweet girl, whose life up to the time of her parents' death had been so calm and uneventful, the very centre of a vortex of intrigue and passion! Around her revolved rage, hate, jealousy, and lust. Her condition was indeed desperate. With so many powerful foes actively planning her destruction, there were none who could help or serve her, for those who had been her friends were either dead or in prison.

All this Mercia felt and understood, but her nobility of spirit buoyed her up, and she rejoiced that it was still in her power to obey her Lord's commands to help the helpless and comfort the sick and sorrowful, while she gave thanks to God, who had delivered her out of the hands of the man who had sought her soul's destruction. But, even as she prayed, she knew that she loved this man with the whole strength of her constant nature.

After delivering Mercia into the care of the officer of the prison-guard, Licinius hurried off to find Tigellinus and inform him of the capture of Mercia. Li-

SOME PERPLEXITIES

cinius rightly guessed that the intelligence would be gratefully received.

He was admitted to the presence of Tigellinus, who was engaged with a party of engineers upon a scheme of Nero's for the making of a great canal which was to extend from Avernum to Ostia. The length thereof was estimated at 160 miles, while the breadth was to be sufficient to enable vessels with five banks of oars to pass each other. These and other equally great schemes Nero had inaugurated, believing the expense could be met either by the enormous revenues of his empire, or by the recovery of an immense treasure which he had been induced to believe that Queen Dido had taken with her to Africa, after her flight from Tyre, and which he hoped to unearth.

Tigellinus, seeing that his friend and tool Licinius had something of importance to disclose, dismissed the council as soon as it could be done with decency, and then turned eagerly to Licinius—

"Well, my Licinius, what is thy news? Good or bad, eh?"

"Good; if that be good which may help to the undoing of thine enemy."

"Dost thou mean Marcus?"

"Who else is of sufficient power or moment to be dignified or flattered by the name of enemy unto Tigellinus?"

"What is it?"

"The girl Mercia."

"Ah! what of her?" asked Tigellinus, with wolfish interest.

"He promised thee he would be answerable for her safe conduct."

"He did, at the Cestian Grove."

"Well he hath released her."

"Released her? Art sure?"

"Yea, Excellence."

"So, so!" muttered Tigellinus, and a grim smile of pleasure crept over his saturnine features. This was good news indeed! Here was flat disobedience to Nero's injunctions and express commands, a deliberate betrayal of an official trust, and an act of personal favouritism towards an enemy of Cæsar, for which he might be justly expected to feel a deep resentment, and order for the delinquent an exemplary punishment.

"Tell me all that thou dost know, my Licinius," exclaimed Tigellinus.

This Licinius did, embellishing the account with many deft little touches of invention well calculated to enhance the importance of Marcus' neglect of duty and please Tigellinus the more.

"And thou hast her safe under lock and key, my Licinius?"

"Ay, in the prison of my district."

"Where the rest of the gang captured at the Bridge are confined?"

"Yea, Excellence."

"Good! Yet, stay—we must make no mistake in dealing with Marcus. Thou hadst no power under thy authority as ædile to arrest her? How came it?"

"Simply enough. The girl begged to be allowed to

join the other prisoners; this she was doing at the moment I saw her."

"Good!"

"Moreover, thine own orders——" Licinius was continuing, but Tigellinus stopped him, saying—

"Ah, my orders! Let them pass; it is well that I keep clear of all appearance of personal opposition or animosity towards the Prefect. It must not be forgotten that he is a favourite of Cæsar, and Nero will not be easily convinced that he can do aught evil against his state and sacred person. His fears for his personal safety can alone do that." Here Tigellinus began to pace the room in deep thought, Licinius quietly waiting for his chief to speak. Presently he did so.

"My Licinius, of this we may now be sure: Marcus loves this girl, or he would not have released her. Still, to Nero he may aver that her release was but a ruse to entrap yet more of her companions, so that we had best not trade upon that alone. If we can bring the girl to some dire harm that will tempt and lead Marcus to an open and palpable breach of discipline or revolt against Cæsar's commands, we shall have him in the hollow of our hands."

"What are we to do, Excellence?"

"There is the torture-chamber, my good Licinius," said Tigellinus, with a cruel leer.

"True, Excellence," leered back Licinius.

"Women are more easily moved by terror and pain than even that imp of a boy that Marcus wrested from us. It will be an easy task to wring from the girl all she knows concerning her associates, and, at the same time, force her to confess that, out of lust or love for her, he—Marcus—Rome's Prefect and guardian of the sacred person of our august master—hath let her, an avowed enemy of the State and Cæsar, go free. Eh! what sayest thou, my Licinius?"

"Excellent! excellent!" And the two friends laughed sardonically at the prospect of the girl's sufferings and the undoing of Marcus. There could be but little danger in torturing her. She had been caught at the meeting, was evidently of great importance to the brethren, and must know much of this conspiracy. The torturing of women at that time was no rare thing, nor was it confined entirely to the Christian prisoners. The case of the freedwoman, Epicharis, proves to what hideous lengths those in authority would go to gain information. So horrible were the cruelties practised upon her that, to escape from them, she strangled herself. In some cases the flesh was torn from the bodies of the victims with hot pincers, while, as has been said, many of the innocent and pure young girls of the Christian faith were submitted to such foul and revolting outrages that any detailed account of them is impossible. And it was upon such an exquisite creature as Mercia that these two men contemplated inflicting horrors such as these.

"Come, my Licinius," said Tigellinus, "let us to the prison; we will talk as we go." And the twain set out for the jail into which Mercia had voluntarily entered in order that she might escape the dreaded violence of Marcus' passion for her.

SOME PERPLEXITIES

Marcus, in the meantime, was helplessly raging at the futility of his quest for her. The city had been scoured in every direction, but no news could be gained of her. No one thought of inquiring at the prison over the way; and so it was that, while leagues were covered in pursuit of her, Mercia was actually within speaking distance of Marcus, who was striding about his room, looking pale and worn. He had scarcely slept for the twenty-four hours, and his food had remained untasted. When the slaves besought him to eat, he ordered them angrily away; but he drank freely of wine, which served to heighten both his rage and passion. He loved this girl almost to the point of hatred; now that she had escaped from him he felt incensed against her to an absolutely ferocious degree. He who had been so sought for, whose every caress was prized by so many beautiful women of rank, to be scorned by this girl, who had risked her life to escape from his loathsome presence! The thought was maddening to him. It choked and smothered all his nobler feelings, bringing uppermost all that was most brutally degrading. Find her he must, if only to repay her scorn with scorn! But whither had she fled?

What was that? A sweet, clear, mellow, silvery, ringing voice, singing from the prison yonder—

> "O Father, let Thy loving hand
> Guide us through death's dark way."

He could not be mistaken—it was Mercia's voice; In an instant all his resentment vanished in the ecstasy

THE SIGN OF THE CROSS

of having found her once again. Then she had not fled from him after all! She had gone to the help and comfort of her suffering friends, he thought; and in that belief hot tears of relief and joy sprang to his eyes. Rushing to the entrance-hall of the palace, he called upon some of his guards to follow him, and crossed at once to the prison opposite, and, presenting himself at its portals, demanded to be admitted to the cell where the Christians were confined. Knowing his supreme authority, the keeper of the jail respectfully conducted him to the dungeon.

It was with a strange tremor at his heart that Marcus passed through the opened door and saw again the beautiful girl who had so enthralled him. She was upon her knees, facing the little light that struggled through the narrow embrasure in the massive walls, her hands clasped, her eyes upturned, pouring forth in a stream of rich melody, with no more effort than a bird makes in full song, the hymn of supplication—

> "O Father, let Thy loving hand
> Guide us through death's dark way."

And again he felt that thrill of awe, respect, and wonderment which had so moved him at the death of Favius. The feeling was indescribable. It was as though some unseen, unknown spiritual power swept through his very soul.

Mercia ceased singing, and turned, impelled by the magnetism of Marcus' presence, to find herself face to face again with him whom she so loved and feared. Gently, but firmly, he bade her accompany him.

SOME PERPLEXITIES

"I pray thee, let me stay with these my brethren," pleaded Mercia.

"That may not be, lady," quietly said Marcus. "Thou must hence with me."

What purpose could be served by refusal? She knew that she could not resist the force he would employ to compel her to obey him, so she turned to her friends, who were regarding her with tearful sympathy, and said—

"Be not afraid, oh, my people! He will not suffer harm to come to me, and, though we may not meet again here, in this land of pain and persecution, yet there are many mansions in our Father's house, and there we shall be reunited—we, who have taken up the Cross to follow Him whom we do love. Let not your hearts fail you, though death's dark waters threaten to overwhelm you, for hath not He promised that 'whosoever will save his life shall lose it, but whosoever will lose his life for My sake, the same shall save it. For what is a man advantaged if he gain the whole world and lose his own soul—and be utterly cast away?' Farewell, dear brethren," she murmured softly to her comrades. Then, turning to Marcus, who stood silent and abashed, she said, "Sir, I am ready."

Marcus felt his face and brow flush with shame as this calm, dignified woman passed by him from the dungeon with head erect and eyes uplifted, eyes that did not deign to notice him even with a single glance. Quietly she followed the guards back to the palace of Marcus, to be this time locked in a room from which there could be no escape.

THE SIGN OF THE CROSS

When Tigellinus and Licinius arrived at the prison, full of their schemes for Mercia's torture, it was but to learn that she had again been given up to the keeping of Marcus.

At first disposed to rage at this discovery, they saw, upon reflection, that this second rescue of Mercia from their custody was another weapon in their hands for the assault they intended to make upon Marcus before Cæsar; and, consoling themselves with this thought, Tigellinus went with Licinius to request audience of the Emperor.

CHAPTER XIV

POPPÆA WINS

When Tigellinus and Licinius arrived at the palace of Nero, they were requested to wait in the audience-chamber. A crowd of courtiers and officers were already in attendance, who fawned obsequiously upon the favoured Tigellinus, and greeted even the ædile with courtesy, because of his propinquity to his more powerful friend.

An officer entered and, in a loud voice, said—

"His Sacred Majesty the Emperor will give audience here at once."

All those assembled bowed low at the mention of the Emperor's name, and Tigellinus turned to his friend and said—

"If we do but win the Emperor, the sun of Marcus will quickly set."

"Would it were quenched in everlasting midnight!" replied Licinius. "His arrogance hath long been past endurance."

Now great shouts were heard of "Ave, Cæsar!" "Hail, all hail!" "The mighty Nero!" "Our god-like Emperor!"

Nearer and nearer the volume of sound swelled, and first there entered a file of Ethiopian guards, giant-like in size and strength, clad in parti-coloured skirts reaching from the waist to within an inch of the knee, wearing slung across their bare breasts and shoulders the skins of huge leopards (the heads thereof being brought over their own foreheads, thus lending them an appearance of savage ferocity); with brawny arms and legs unclothed; carrying in their right hands long spears with heads of polished bronze, and bearing over their left arms stout shields of the tanned hides of lions. These guards were followed by splendidly dressed heralds, with long trumpets of gold, upon which they blew a rude blare of harmonised chords, as a signal of the approach of Nero. After them came a crowd of nobles, walking backwards, with bowed heads, grovelling almost to the ground in adoration of the bloated, sensual being whom they professed to worship—that wonder of distorted genius, Nero, the Roman Emperor. He was leaning upon the necks of two feminine-looking boys of some fourteen years of age; they were garbed in short white tunics, their golden hair bound with fillets of gold; their legs were bare to the sandals, and they minced and smirked with all the airs and graces of girlhood. To these favourites of the detestable brute the courtiers cringed and crawled with a sycophancy as transparent as it was degrading.

Nero was gorgeously dressed, but there was a suggestion of effeminacy in his attire, the outcome of deliberate design, which robbed it of all dignity. The under dress was soft, cream-coloured silk, richly embroidered with gold, scarcely reaching to the knee. The toga was of Tyrian purple, studded with amethysts and emeralds. Of the amethyst and Tyrian purple

POPPÆA WINS

he was extremely fond; indeed, so anxious was he to make them peculiar and personal to himself that he rigorously forbade the use of them by any of his subjects. It was said that, as he was singing in the theatre, observing a lady of rank among the audience dressed in the colour he had prohibited, he stopped the performance until she was dragged from her seat. He afterwards gave orders that she was to be stripped not only of her garments, but of her property, which he appropriated. On another occasion, he privately sent a spy to sell a few ounces of the forbidden colours upon the day of the Nundinæ, and then shut up all the merchants' shops, on the pretext that his edict had been violated.

As Nero met with a slight inclination of the head the salutations of the courtiers who, on their knees, awaited him, his eyes fell upon Tigellinus and Licinius, who were at that moment exchanging a few words in an undertone. Sharply, and half in jest and half in earnest, he said—

"Ah, Tigellinus, Licinius, ye are whispering! What is it—eh? What treason's toward—eh?" And his quick, furtive, frightened gaze shifted uneasily from one to the other, while his heavy, double chin shook with a nervous dread.

"Treason? Nay, Cæsar," replied Tigellinus, on his knees, with lowered head; "I did but say that, had thy august mother not made thee Emperor of Rome, thy god-like voice had given thee empire o'er the world."

At the mention of the mother whom he had murdered Nero started and slightly shivered, but his vanity was tickled at the flattery so lavishly bestowed upon his voice, and he said—

"Ah, yes, yes! I can sing! Even my detractors admit that. An artist—eh?"

"In sooth, yes. Apollo must lay aside his lyre when Nero sings," was the fulsome answer.

Gross as was this exaggeration, it was not too much for Nero, who flung himself into a grotesque attitude, which he intended to be one of extreme grace, and exclaimed—

"Apollo! Ah, yes! A statue of myself in gold—all gold, as Apollo! I'll have it done. See to it, Tigellinus." Then his mind wandered quickly off in an entirely new direction, and he said venomously—

"Tigellinus, that wife of Garamantes hath insulted our Empress, our beloved Poppæa."

"Hath she dared?" asked Tigellinus, with assumed horror, while all the court gazed into each others' faces with pretended astonishment.

"Refused to attend her feast—called it an orgie," continued Nero. "Her delicate health forbade her attendance. We'll physic her delicacy! See that Garamantes is warned that his absence from this world can alone atone for his wife's absence from Poppæa's feast. Request that he open his veins to-night; if he is alive when dawns to-morrow's sun, not he alone, but he and all his brood shall die ere it doth set. See to it, Tigellinus, see to it."

A slight shiver ran through the cowardly crowd of courtiers at this command. Such orders had been only too rife of late, and no man knew when, under some equally flimsy pretext, his own time might not come to receive this hint to die. Even Tigellinus felt a slight sensation of dread as he answered—

"I will, great Cæsar, and gladly. It is but justice. How could she dare so to insult thy omnipotence?"

Nero shrugged his shoulders with what would, were it not for the tragedy of the circumstance, have been a comical gesture, and said—

"It is madness—veritable madness! But, Tigellinus, we'll make his wife a widow—eh? And warn her to give a strict account of all her husband's wealth, and render a full half to Cæsar, or, by Pluto, she shall lose the whole, and her brats with it. See to it, Tigellinus, see to it."

"I will, mighty Cæsar," answered Tigellinus, while the crowd mutely pantomimed their approval of the horrible orders Nero had so calmly issued. Then, with another quick turn of his abnormally active brain, he dismissed entirely the subject of this latest murder, and asked, with a smile of egregious self-complacency,—

"And how liked you that last epic of mine—eh? It is good—eh? Strong——"

The answer came deftly from the lips of Tigellinus, ever ready to feed, if never able to satisfy, his monstrous egotism.

"Strong? 'Tis mighty, Cæsar! Thou art indeed a marvel! Soldier—poet—actor—singer—athlete—Emperor—a god among gods!" And every craven among the crowd re-echoed the profanity.

THE SIGN OF THE CROSS

For once Nero was mildly pleased at their adulation, and smiled approvingly as he said to Tigellinus—

"Well said! Well expressed—very well! But posterity alone can do me justice; my contemporaries are all too jealous—eh? That is a fine verse—eh? that one commencing—

> "And Jove's great thunder, rattling around the vast, empyrean vault, spoke of a god's great wrath in mighty tones."

And the vain-glorious tyrant declaimed his turgid stuff with all the exaggeration of the amphitheatre, with a voice hoarse with bellowing and dissipation; and the chorus of flatterers applauded with wild enthusiasm, a compliment which Nero acknowledged with a bow as theatrical as the effort that had provoked it.

And thus all State business stood still, while Rome's mighty Emperor played the fool. There were among the crowd ministers of state, waiting to receive commands; rulers of provinces, with details of revenues and general government; heads of departments, civil and military, awaiting orders and instructions; yet none dared to hint their business until desired by Nero to do so.

Now his mind wandered off at a tangent to the Circus, and he said abruptly—

"We want new games in the Circus. I weary of the old eternal round of trained gladiator against gladiator. We must devise something fresh—eh? eh? What shall it be?"

Here Philodemus was emboldened to ask—

"Wilt thou race at the festival, great Cæsar?"

"Race?" said Cæsar, moving with extreme difficulty. "I have not yet decided. But even if I race or sing or act not myself, we'll yet have rare sport, I promise thee. Ah! now I bethink me, what of this Christian conspiracy—eh?"

This was an opening for Tigellinus that he had scarce dared hope for. Here was the chance to approach the subject which was the main purpose of his coming hither! And he replied, with an air of horror,—

"Alas, mighty Cæsar, the vermin still plot against thy sacred life——"

Nero shook with terror, and blanched to the lips as he spluttered forth—

"What—what—sayest thou—eh? Thou knowest this, and yet two of the reptiles are left alive to conspire! What doth it mean—eh? Is Cæsar's life valueless? Is such an Emperor, such an artist to perish— eh? Answer, answer!" he roared, his eyes blazing with anger and terror.

Almost as terrified himself, Tigellinus said—

"Licinius and thy servant have done all that was in their power, but——"

"But what—what?" asked Nero. "Our sacred person in danger and our orders not obeyed! Who dares hesitate when Cæsar commands?" And here, for a moment, he towered above the kneeling, cowering crowd with all the grandeur of real majesty. For this buffoon could, when roused, be at times terrible in his wrath.

THE SIGN OF THE CROSS

"Who is to blame?" he asked, as no one had dared to speak.

"Not thy devoted servant Tigellinus," said that person, grovelling on the mosaic pavement at Nero's feet and kissing the hem of his toga.

"Who, then? What are the ædiles doing? Where are the spies—eh?"

"Indeed, neither the ædiles nor their officers are at fault, mighty Emperor; but if, when they have performed their duty, their work is undone, their authority resisted, their commands set at naught, what are they to do?" said Tigellinus, with a crafty simulation of helpless indignation.

"Whom dost thou mean? Who hath done these things?" asked Nero furiously.

"Nay, Emperor, ask me not. I would rather not betray——"

"Ha! Then Cæsar's life must be in peril because thou wouldst rather not betray some cowardly associate? Thou wouldst betray me—eh? Who is it? I command thee!"

"Since thou dost command, thy servant must obey. Thy Prefect, Marcus——"

Nero hastily interrupted Tigellinus, crying—

"Marcus? No, no! not Marcus! Have a care! If thou dost belie our Marcus, the best officer we have——"

"Licinius knows I speak the truth," persisted Tigellinus, mutely appealing to his friend. "Marcus it was who stayed my hand when, for the sake of thy sacred life, I put one of these Christians—a boy—to the torture, to force him to reveal the meeting-place of the conspirators; and a girl who is one of the most trusted among them was taken out of our hands by him and released. Yet again did we arrest her, and but an hour ago thy Prefect, charged by thee with the safe keeping of these wretches, did again set her free. Marcus, too, it was who, regardless of thy safety, did——" And here the glib tongue of Tigellinus was silenced, for the Empress had quietly entered with Berenice, and was listening, unobserved by Cæsar, to this accusation. Poppæa's eyes were fixed upon Tigellinus with an expression of such menace that he saw he had gone too far in his denunciation of Marcus for her approval. He stammered and hesitated, staring in confusion at the Empress. Nero, following the direction of his gaze, beheld Poppæa, and, with a hoarse cry of relief, staggered into her arms. The slightest hint of a design upon his life was sufficient to spur him into the wildest frenzy of fear and anger, in the throes of which he would scatter half-inarticulate commands for the wholesale murder of all who fell under his suspicion. The mere thought that Marcus could be guilty of neglecting any possible precautions seemed to Nero monstrous, and he might instantly have been moved to some stern, if not disastrous, measures against him but for the tact and courage of the Empress.

"Ah, my Poppæa," he murmured, "thou hast come in time. Here's treason, foul treason, towards our sacred selves."

"Treason?" questioned Poppæa. "Who says this?" Her gaze was fixed upon Tigellinus with an expression of threatening wrath that somewhat disconcerted the wily Councillor.

"Tigellinus. He hath accused Marcus——"

"Of treason?" asked the Empress, and she dwelt on the word with such scornful contempt of the possibility of such faithlessness on the part of the Prefect that Tigellinus made an effort to remove, to a certain extent, the impression which his words, and still more subtle insinuations, had left upon Cæsar's mind. Stammeringly he explained—

"Treason! Nay, Emperor, not exactly that—but——"

"But what—eh?" fiercely demanded Nero. "What else than treason to Cæsar is it if he protects those who scheme against Cæsar's life?"

"There has been some exaggeration here," said Poppæa calmly, gazing fixedly at Tigellinus. "I know the whole story, Cæsar. Berenice hath confided it to me, and I was even now seeking thee to ask for thy authority to set the matter right. Possibly, zeal for thy safety"—and a cold, cruel smile of contempt played momentarily round her lips—"hath induced your faithful servant to overestimate the importance of Marcus' error."

"What is it, then—eh? What hath he done?" asked Nero, his wild suspicions not yet allayed.

"Marcus is a man, and, lacking thy constancy, great Cæsar, is too easily caught by a pretty face." And she placed her arms around Cæsar's neck, with an expression of such intense love and trustfulness in his loyalty to her that he was almost led to believe himself the model of marital faith that her words were intended to imply. "Of all these hordes of Christians that we hear of, he hath spared but one—and that one a mere girl, who, for the moment, hath caught his wayward fancy."

"Is that all? Only one girl—eh?" gasped Nero, with intense relief.

"I do not think that any here can name another. How say you, Tigellinus?" The question came from Poppæa more in the form of a threat and command, and as such Tigellinus understood it, and hastily he replied—

"No, Emperor, no."

"Only one girl! Oh, that matters but little. A girl—but even a girl——" And again Nero looked fearfully and furtively around, as if searching for evidence of this new peril.

"May be dangerous. And so it were wise in thee, my love, to give power to Tigellinus to take this girl out of the hands of Marcus, and leave thee to deal with her thyself," urged Poppæa, cunningly achieving the task she had set herself. Marcus was not to be punished, but Mercia was to be taken from him and placed in her hands, to be done with as, in her judgment, might seem best. For was not her will Cæsar's?

Gladly did Nero acquiesce in this arrangement, and he pressed Poppæa's hand with damp and trembling fingers as he answered—

"Yes, yes; of course. Deal with her myself. Thou shalt have power. Accursed be the whole race of these murderous Christians! Seek our sacred lives? I'll throw them to the beasts! I'll dress them in skins of wolves and set the bloodhounds on them! Ha! That will be sport! I'll soak them in oil and tallow, as I did before, and set them blazing! I'll light all Rome with them!" Nero looked more devil than man; his face was distorted with passion, his eyes glaring with insane ferocity; foam flecked the corners of his mouth, and his whole body quivered in the grip of the fury which possessed him, while the skin of his forehead worked up and down with the flexibility of that of an enraged monkey. Even Poppæa, used as she was to his paroxysms of fury, involuntarily shrank from him, while the parasites who watched him shivered with apprehension. He had utterly forgotten the business of the day in his rage and terror.

With a wave of the hand he dismissed the whole Court, save only Tigellinus, to whom he cried—

"Tigellinus, come thou with me. I will give thee power to arrest this girl. Plot against Cæsar's life? Look to it that not these Christians alone, but all who trade or traffic with them, or house or countenance them, or hold converse with them, be punished too. Double the guards round my palace, good Tigellinus. Search every house suspected. Show no mercy. Let Fenius Rufus organise a troop of German horse to ride from street to street and arrest all who are suspected of harbouring these vile regicides. He is a good man, our Fenius; he will show no mercy. Wretches! Have they forgotten that Nero is immortal, and that all who attempt to harm his sacred person are doomed to death by the wrath of the gods themselves? Come, they have yet to learn my power, my Tigellinus. I—I—I——" But speech failed the imperial craven, and he staggered away, muttering, mouthing, shivering and inarticulate, his villainous Councillor following.

Poppæa paid but little apparent attention to Nero's insane ravings, but she felt deeply the danger to which all who came under his notice were constantly exposed; perhaps some presentiment of her own fate overshadowed her. The time was not so far distant when her influence over the mad tyrant was to decline; when she was to plead in vain for mercy, and meet her death by his brutality. But, meantime, it was for her to hide his weaknesses from the people, to magnify his power and genius; for in his greatness she flourished and thrived.

Turning to Berenice, who stood, pale and trembling, affrighted at Nero's brutal violence, Poppæa reassuringly placed her hand upon the shoulder of her friend, saying—

"I have kept my word, and thou hast thy desire. This Christian girl shall trouble thee no more."

Berenice was now fearful for the safety of Marcus. She saw how narrow was the plank on which he stood in Nero's favour, how insecure his position in the goodwill of the fickle tyrant, and she began almost to regret the haste with which she had sought for Poppæa's aid. Should this whirlwind of hate and anger shift in the direction of Marcus, his life was not worth an obolus. It hung by the frail thread of Nero's whims and temper.

With these thoughts crowding in upon her mind her

THE SIGN OF THE CROSS

thanks were but stammering and half-hearted. Kneeling, she answered Poppæa, saying—

"I thank thee, Empress, but—but——"

"What now? Dost thou regret?"

"Not for this wretched girl, but for Marcus. Should any evil come to him through fault of mine or——"

"Or Cæsar's anger? Have no fear, my friend; no harm shall come to Marcus through Cæsar. I will protect him from Nero, but I cannot always be on the watch to safeguard him from others. Tigellinus is cunning, and, hating Marcus as he does, will spare neither gold nor labour to bring about his ruin. What I know, I can provide for, but I must be forewarned; so keep me well informed of all that concerns Marcus. He must be cautious too."

Berenice, whose anger had subsided, was now all fear and apprehension. Her eyes were filled with tears; she could scarce restrain her sobs; the clouds of rage and hate were dissolving in this rain of dread and pity. Poppæa took her by the hand, saying, half smilingly, half soothingly,—

"Poor Berenice! Thou art already sorry for thy eagerness for revenge. There, take courage! Marcus shall not be harmed. The girl shall be taken from him, and he will forget her soon enough when once she is out of his sight. Thou shalt have thy heart's dearest wishes gratified. Marcus dare not disobey Cæsar's commands, and Cæsar shall command that he wed thee."

"How can I thank thee enough, dear Empress?" softly exclaimed Berenice.

POPPÆA WINS

"Do not thank me at all—at least, until thou hast tried Marcus as a husband. It is best to wait. Now, what I am about to do must seem a blessing; it may prove a curse. Thy lover now seems all that thou desirest; but wait, my Berenice, wait! We poor, weak women never know these men until we have married them." And, with a look in which a rallying humour was not altogether unmixed with regret for her own precarious position with her husband, Poppæa led her friend to her own apartments in a distant part of the palace.

CHAPTER XV

ANCARIA

THIS was the day for which Marcus had arranged the supper at his palace, to which, before he had met Mercia, he had invited his boon-companions and acquaintances. Glabrio was to be there; so, too, were Philodemus and many others of the reckless young patricians, all ever eager to share with Marcus his banquets or adventures. Marcus had spoken truly when he told Berenice that no ladies would be present at this feast. The women invited to minister to the delectation of his male guests were the most beautiful and amusing among the courtesans of Rome. First in favour with the patrician youths was a woman named Ancaria, a magnificent creature. Superbly moulded in form and feature, cunning, clever, passionate, gifted with an exquisite voice, she had become immensely popular as a singer at the feasts given by the rich of the city, who paid her almost fabulous prices for her services. Her songs and odes were not such as would be chosen for the edification of the young. Love, and the passion which served as such among the profligate, were the themes of her verses, and she sang them with an abandonment, coupled with a dramatic vivid pantomime that proved to those who composed her audience exciting in the highest—or lowest—degree. Her face was finely shaped, the lips suggesting the bacchante that she was; the eyes, of dusky bronze, large, lustrous, now half-closed with sensuous languor, anon blazing with passion, were of the species fitly named "speaking." They spoke indeed, and spoke whole volumes, though it must be confessed the scope of the matter was confined to what was frankest and coarsest in her vigorous nature. She could be seductive as Circe herself when she desired, or when it paid her to appear so, but a perfect fury when aroused to anger; and, in truth, it needed but a very tiny spark with her to cause a portentous and startling conflagration. No man had dared to break the chains which she had wound about him until she gave the signal, and seldom did she give that before the ruin of her captive was complete. No man could flatter himself that he had ever won her affection, save, perhaps, her present patron, Marcus. Whatever was possible for her debased nature to feel in the way of love she felt for him. He, on his part, was lazily amused by her vagaries and her talents, and mildly fascinated by the physical glory of her person. This was the woman who was the chief guest as well as the principal entertainer at the feast that night.

Marcus, under the stress of excitement, roused by the stirring adventures of the past two days, had partly forgotten his banquet; but his household was too well managed and controlled for his absence of mind to affect the necessary extensive preparations, which went forward as smoothly as though he superintended them himself. When he remembered that he had to meet Ancaria and her companions that night, he was angry

THE SIGN OF THE CROSS

with himself for having invited them to come. It was too late to postpone the supper, and, even if it were not, he had no reasonable grounds for doing so. He would, at least, see Mercia once again before his guests arrived. From that reflection he drew some consolation.

Summoning his attendants, he went to the room in which she was detained, and, when the door was unlocked, he dismissed them, and asked to be allowed to speak with her. Quietly she assented, saying—

"Thou art my jailer; thou hast a right to speak."

There was no anger in her tones. He could have wished there had been; this dignified calm perplexed him sorely. He felt ill at ease; for all his thoughts and wishes seemed, as he gazed upon her, but profanation, degrading to himself and leaving her untouched.

"Jailer?" he answered at last. "Nay, not quite that."

"What else? At least, I am thy prisoner," said Mercia.

"Ay, true; but not by any choice of mine, gentle lady."

"Why then not leave me with those who need me yonder?" asked Mercia.

"I could not bear to do so; thou art so fair, so young, so sweet, and——"

"My youth is better able to suffer the hardships of that prison than is the age of many who are there. I am content to bear whatever burden is placed upon me, for His sake."

"*His* sake? Of whom dost thou speak?"

"Of Him who came into the world to save the world, and died that men might live," answered Mercia.

All this was so much jingling of words to the ears of Marcus, who knew but little of the foundation of the Christian faith, and he said—

"Lady, I understand thee not. Tell me of this—superstition." He paused before the word, but could find no better substitute.

"Dost thou indeed wish to hear?" asked Mercia gently.

"Yea, indeed," he answered, glad only to keep silence in her presence, to look upon her and listen to the sweet, rich music of her voice.

"Then I will tell thee the noblest, greatest story ever told to ears of man,—a tale so sad, so glorious, so grand, that imagination cannot equal nor invention surpass it. Hearken to it, Prefect, full of the world and its faithlessness, proud in thy strength of power and place, proud of thy birth and wealth! Hearken to it, and pray to be led to the true understanding of it, which, alas! I cannot impart."

And then she told the story of the "Man of Sorrows," picturing, with an unconscious vividness, the lonely night-watch of the shepherds; the coming of the great white light; the terror and wonderment of those lowly men, to whom the heavens opened as the angel of the Lord came down, saying unto them, "Fear not; for, behold, I bring you good tidings of great joy, which shall be to all people. For unto you is born this day in the city of David a Saviour, which is Christ the Lord." "And suddenly there was with the angel a

THE SIGN OF THE CROSS

multitude of the heavenly host praising God, and saying, Glory to God in the highest, and on earth peace, good will toward men."

As Mercia proceeded with the divine story her manner seemed inspired; her face shone with the glory of conviction; her eyes were lit with the fire of belief and faith.

Marcus sat in rapt, silent entrancement as she told of the coming of the Lord; of the strange star shining over the humble stable in Bethlehem, where He was born; of the going of the shepherds thither; of the wise men from the East, who, led by the star, found Him cradled in the manger, and knelt in adoration before Him; of the youth and glorious manhood of the Messiah; His miracles, teachings; His agony and bloody sweat in the Garden of Gethsemane; His betrayal, His crucifixion; His last cry, "Forgive them, Father, for they know not what they do." So exquisitely pathetic were the tones of Mercia's voice, as she recited the last events of that wondrous sacrifice, that Marcus was moved to the soul, and his silent tears paid tribute to the story and the absolute belief of the narrator—a belief that was evident in every word she uttered.

When she ended, both were for a time silent, Mercia thinking with prayerful gratitude of His martyrdom, Marcus of the strange fable he had listened to. Mentally he contrasted the clear simplicity of this new faith with the old Roman worship of the almost countless gods of the mythology; of their mundane weaknesses, vices, and follies; the prayers to one deity for this favour, to another for that; of the sacrifices to Jupiter, Juno, Ceres, Neptune, Venus, Vulcan, Mars, and the others. How puny, how unworthy they all seemed, compared to the Divine Being this girl had so eloquently described. Fables all, of course,—his gods and this new one of the Christians,—all myths; but how noble was the God of these Nazarenes, how ignoble his own!

As he raised his eyes to her face, he found that her gaze was fixed upon him with a look of strange, yearning sadness, that went straight to his heart. Where were the glib, swift, pretty compliments, the quick, ready jests with which he was wont to flatter and amuse other women? The compliments withered and shrank in his brain, unspoken; the jests never left his tongue. He coloured with shame at the thought of the feeling with which he regarded this innocent girl. His evil thoughts and desires were thrust back, beaten and humiliated. Sin appeared utterly powerless in her presence. As Mercia looked upon him, his nobler self rose above the mere lusts of the flesh, and real love, born of respect bordering on reverence, grew stronger and deeper.

So engrossed had he been, that he started with astonishment when Viturius came to warn him that his guests were arriving, and that he was required to receive them. Commending Mercia to the supervision of the faithful captain, Marcus left her, inwardly raging at the thought of the contrast of her purity with the reckless licence of those he was about to welcome and entertain.

THE SIGN OF THE CROSS

Mercia, left alone, pondered on the character of the man she had learned to love. In it she recognised great merits and greater possibilities. Quickly intuitive and extremely sensitive, she felt the good that was underlying the crust of evil which, she saw, was the effect of training and custom rather than the outcome of natural inborn depravity. She longed for the wellbeing of this man's soul,—yearned for the coming of the eternal truth to him. What power for good to the world would such a man as Marcus become if imbued with the true faith! She thought of Saul, his persecutions, his hatred of the followers and disciples of Jesus of Nazareth; of his sudden conversion, his ministerings, his teachings, his readiness to testify to the truth, even unto death. Inwardly she prayed for the light to come to the young Prefect, as it had, in days gone by, shone upon the now revered disciple. More of Marcus than of herself and her fate did Mercia think, albeit her condition was perilous in the extreme. She knew that, if given up to the law, her life would be forfeited; she shuddered to think of the death she might be called upon to die, but she never wavered or thought of saving herself by renouncing her faith. Nothing could shake her constancy to her Master,—not even the overwhelming earthly love that had come to her for one who knew Him not, nor followed His precepts.

Marcus went to receive his guests, many of whom had already arrived. Daones and Cyrene, two of Rome's most famous dancers, had come with Dardanus and Cusus. Daones was a tall, beautiful girl, with large brown eyes and a profusion of gold-tinted auburn hair, which fell in clustering ringlets to her waist. Her figure was splendid, lithe and supple; her movements were grace itself; her temper was placid,—as easy as her morals. Cyrene was less tall than her companion; swarthy of complexion, quick of temper, tongue, and limb; pretty in face and figure. Their escorts, Cusus and Dardanus, were both wealthy, young, extravagant; both, too, already well filled with wine. The whole four were noisily laughing over some coarse jest just uttered by Daones.

It was not without difficulty that Marcus contrived to meet these and others of his guests with the cordiality that is demanded of a host. As he was bidding them welcome, there was a laugh in the prothyrum, or entrance-hall, and Glabrio entered, leaning somewhat heavily upon the arms of two women who were respectively named Thea and Julia; both dark, handsome, sensuous-looking creatures. The cause of the mirth was a tipsy stumble made by Glabrio, who, missing one of the steps, had been barely saved from a heavy fall by the outstretched arms of Thea and Julia.

"Thou art not hurt?" lisped Philodemus, who was following.

"Hurt?" echoed Glabrio, with a leer at the two women who were still upholding him. "Hurt? Ay, hurt to the heart; stabbed nigh to death by two pairs of bewitching eyes; pressed to suffocation by four of the loveliest arms man ever trusted, to his own undoing. Didst thou think, O Philodemus mine, that the little stumble made by me was accidental? Nay, my undiscerning friend, it was by design and cunning. For, look where that almost shipwreck hath landed, thy friend! Into what haven of joy hath this barque of mine been steered!" And the tipsy old reprobate bestowed his embraces with strict impartiality upon Julia and Thea alike.

The guests were arriving rapidly. The chariots rattled up to the gates of the palace incessantly, and the cries of the charioteers, the tramping of the horses, the laughter and chatter of the women and their partners, the sensuous music played by an unseen band, the lamps, the braziers of incense, the sweet-smelling flowers (of which there was an endless profusion), the rich and varied hues of the bejewelled costumes, the white arms and busts of the women, their beauty, and the splendour of the palace,—all tended to make the scene one of magnificence and luxury remarkable even in those days. And from all this pomp and grandeur the thoughts of Marcus wandered to the simple, white-clad figure of Mercia, whom he had but now parted from. Over the laughter and the rattle of these scores of gabbling tongues he heard, in thought, the sweet, tender voice of the Christian girl reciting that strange story of Jesus of Nazareth, "who came into the world to save the world." Gladly would he have exchanged all the glare, the luxury, and homage by which he was surrounded for that quiet room, illumined only by Mercia's dear presence. As one woman after another smiled and beamed upon him, he mentally compared them to her, and turned shudderingly away.

ANCARIA

The most varied of entertainments were now in progress in the large atrium and the surrounding rooms: troupes of posturers and acrobats, performers with trained dogs and monkeys, and bevies of girls dancing to accompaniments of pipes and tambourines. Everywhere was light, mirth, gaiety, brilliancy, beauty, save in the heart of the giver of the feast, and there gloomy unrest, indefinable longings, unshaped desires, were torturing and perplexing him.

Ancaria had, as was her wont, left her coming until late. The spoilt beauty, who loved to be in a constant whirl of excitement, was never happy unless she was the centre of attraction. Admiration was as necessary to her existence as food and rest. Not that she valued it when she received it, still, she could not live without it. So she had purposely delayed her arrival in order that attention might be focussed upon her when she did come. As her chariot dashed up to the gates of the palace the idlers gathered about them recognised her and shouted loud welcomes, a compliment which Ancaria rewarded, as was her custom, with handfuls of coins, which she scattered recklessly among the crowd who were cheering her. As she entered the atrium, and the lights from the lamps fell upon her, she looked even more than usually radiant and handsome. Marcus had been won to her side, but he had to be kept there, and so to-night she was effulgent in beauty, radiant and splendid. She might have spared her pains, for Marcus scarcely noticed her, much to her annoyance and surprise. She found him with some of the more seriously inclined among the male guests, languidly discussing matters of the State, paying no heed whatever to the constant and assertive blandishments of the fair ones around him. With womanly and pardonable weakness, Ancaria ascribed this to his pique at her tardy arrival. In this she grievously erred; Marcus would have been better pleased had she remained away altogether.

"After vainly endeavouring, by many little feminine lures and devices, to draw him to her side, all utterly thrown away upon and unheeded by Marcus, Ancaria was compelled to go to him. This she did in a far from amiable frame of mind.

"Since when hath the host refrained from welcoming his guests?" she asked, interrupting, with cool effrontery, the conversation in which Marcus was engaged.

"Some two hours ago, when all who respected his invitation and wishes had arrived," was the icy rejoinder to her unfortunately impertinent inquiry.

There are some women who never know when it is most politic to leave a man alone. Ancaria was one of this class. Had she been possessed of less beauty and more wit she might have been warned by the cold glitter in the eyes of Marcus that at another time, with other weapons,—with whimperings and tears, for example,—she might have induced him, with many caresses, to request her pardon for his present rudeness. But this was destined to be one of Ancaria's least triumphant nights; and she unfortunately detected so much resentment in the tones of Marcus' voice, that she was impelled to try what effect an even more bitter reply would have upon him, and she flashed back—

"Ah, all are not slaves to the lordly Marcus! There are some who have the fortune and the freedom to be desired and worshipped by others who are even as great as he."

"Doubtless," was the quick retort; "he must be indeed a stranger to Rome and Roman doings who would suspect Ancaria of allegiance to any one, or any score of masters." A sufficiently brutal speech, and one not softened by the manner in which it was uttered.

Now was Ancaria's opportunity. A little dignity, a quiet appeal to his manliness, would have moved Marcus to immediate, if somewhat reluctant apology; but most unwisely she essayed to send another arrow home, exclaiming—

"Or Marcus of constancy to those who love him."

"Among whom Ancaria can scarce be numbered, for, to her, constancy is but another word for perpetual payment," was the still more unmannerly rejoinder made by Marcus.

Ancaria was astounded. Careless, even callous she had known Marcus to be often, but ever considerate and polite. What could this burst of unrestrained rudeness mean? What had provoked it? Ancaria was guilty of yet another error; she attributed it to jealousy on the part of Marcus. Erroneously imputing this jealousy to a fresh access of love on his part, she determined to heighten the passion in order that she might strengthen her hold upon him when it

THE SIGN OF THE CROSS

should please her to heal, with tender asseverations of devotion, his wounded vanity. But she could not even now have done with him, and exclaimed with asperity—

"Ancaria at least is fortunate enough to receive from those who admire and seek her other payments than those made in gold; respect, deference, and love being not the least of her rewards."

"But by many degrees the least valued," replied Marcus, and, taking one of his friends by the arm, he strolled carelessly away, leaving Ancaria in a whirl of wonder and rage. What could such behaviour on the part of Marcus mean or portend? She must learn, and that quickly.

To that end she determined to seek those who would be able to inform her of the movements of Marcus during the few days that had intervened since her last meeting with him. Good or evil fortune steered her to a little group of men and women to whom Glabrio was detailing, with much unction, an account of the meeting of Marcus and the beautiful Christian girl. Glabrio's description did not err on the side of underrating the charms of Mercia, nor the effect created by her beauty upon the heart of the Prefect. With a few rapid, cleverly-put questions Ancaria placed herself in complete possession of the whole of the facts of this encounter, and perhaps a little more. This was the cause of the change in Marcus—a fresh face! Some low-bred Christian girl had dethroned her in his favour! In her burning curiosity to know what this woman was like she kept Glabrio and Philodemus fully occupied in replying to her questions until the signal was given for the adjournment to the banqueting hall.

Sumptuous as the reception rooms were, their splendour paled before the magnificence of this apartment. The walls were exquisitely frescoed with panels representing mythological subjects, the drawing and colour all being in the highest degree artistic and elaborate. The columns that supported the roof were twined with roses, and garlands of the same flowers hung in festoons from pillar to pillar; lamps were everywhere gleaming from huge banks of blossoms; the tables were almost obscured by roses, in the midst of which were bejewelled gold cups and flagons. Amphoræ of the choicest wines stood or leaned against the walls. The divans were composed of cushions covered with the richest silks, delicately embroidered and luxuriously stuffed. Perfumed fountains plashed musically in various corners of the room; at once cooling and scenting the atmosphere. Hosts of slaves, richly attired, stood round the guests, ready to obey their smallest order, or slightest desire. The banquet was a marvel of culinary skill, and during the whole of the feast a band of lutes and harps discoursed the most delightful music.

As the wine circulated, such restraint as had existed began rapidly to vanish. Draperies were cast aside, peplums and pallas were loosened—the heat of the room being a sufficient excuse, if any excuse were needed in such company. Long before the repast was concluded most of the male guests and many of the female were strongly under the influence of the wine, of which all had partaken without stint.

THE SIGN OF THE CROSS

Glabrio was in his element. His bacchanalian proclivities were indulged to the full. The more he drank the more witty and humorous he became. His face, nose, and bald crown, on which the roses seemed to wither from the excess of heat within, literally glowed a ruby red. Not only did he take care that his own emptied cup was immediately refilled, but he kept a wary, if somewhat tipsy eye upon all in his vicinity, roundly denouncing those who failed to keep pace with his own inordinate thirst. His eyes beamed and twinkled with good-tempered fun.

"Drink, my Dardanus, drink! By Bacchus! but this Falernian is ambrosia fit for Jove's own table. Slave, fill another cup for Dardanus. Where's—where's—Philodemus—the most ess—esselent Philodemus—where is he? Is he still quite drunk? Or is he able to pledge with me in this nectar to the bright eyes and silvery laugh of the fair Dacia? Would she were here! Philodemus, hail! Daones, hand that cup to my friend, my ess—esselent friend, Philodemus."

"But he sleeps, my Glabrio," answered Daones.

"Then awake him. Asleep thus early! Unpardonable! What an is—isult to our host! Awake the slumberer! Ho, my Philodemus! A libation to the goddess Dacia!"

"Verily, I will," quoth the vacuous Philodemus, who was with much difficulty partly aroused; "a goddess she—the fair Dacia is a goddess. A cup to Dacia!" And with some difficulty Philodemus contrived, with the aid of Daones, to guide the cup to his mouth.

Marcus was still moody, silent and abstracted.

ANCARIA

Edonia, a fair, voluptuous, and beautiful girl, was leaning over him, flashing her steel-blue eyes at him in vain endeavour to attract his attention. His thoughts were still with Mercia. He was impatient with himself and all his surroundings. He loathed the drunkenness around him, yet continued to drink himself, heavily, silently, morosely. As yet the wine had created no effect upon him save to deaden and benumb his faculties. He was ashamed, and sought to drown his shame in intoxication. The air reeked with licentiousness; every word he heard seemed to him, in his present frame of mind, debasing and degrading. The jests were coarse, pointless, vapid; but his guests laughed at them with tipsy exaggeration. Their laughter served still further to enrage and disgust him.

Suddenly a cry was raised for Ancaria. A desire expressed for one of her songs was received with shouts of approval. Ancaria was delighted at this diversion in her favour; she had been in a fever of anger at the want of attention bestowed upon her by Marcus, and this appeal to her was exactly what she desired.

She declined—feebly—to exhibit her undoubted talent, but cleverly insinuated that a very little urging would induce her to comply with the request. The shouts were redoubled, and, after some further hesitation, she begged the guests to choose what they wished her to perform.

The song they selected was called " Eros and the Vestal." Ancaria smiled slightly at the acclamation with which the men received the name of the ballad chosen, and said under her breath to Glabrio—

THE SIGN OF THE CROSS

"Why not re-name it 'Marcus and the Christian'?"

Glabrio laughed, but, with a look towards Marcus, said warningly—

"Have a care, my nightingale. Our good Prefect loves not to jest upon that subject."

"Doth he not indeed?" laughed Ancaria. "I jest as I please, nor choose my shafts to fit the bow of any man."

But, in spite of her assertion, Ancaria glanced a little uneasily in the direction of Marcus, fearing that he had overheard her. But he was at that moment listening to Edonia, and Ancaria's spiteful remark had not reached his ears.

Silence was called, and Ancaria began her performance.

Wrapping her draperies about her head and face, she assumed a manner so modest and demure that the men shouted with delight even before she had sung a word. When the uproar had subsided, she continued in a voice well under control, low and exquisitely musical. In soft and cooing tones she sang of the Vestal's modesty, and of her exceeding care to keep her beauties hidden from the gaze of all mankind; no eye was to behold even her face unveiled. In this phase of the character the singer seemed to shiver with the iciness of her own chastity. Next, she described the coming of Eros. How, at his first approach, the Vestal drew her veil still closer over her face; but, as the god of Love gazed upon her, curiosity impelled her to draw it a little aside to peep upon him. Then, as she began to feel the warmth of his breath upon her face, she gradually let her hood and veil fall from her head and neck. As Eros drew closer, her face burned with the heat of his presence, her breath came in short gasps, and her bosom heaved. All this Ancaria pantomimed with skill and subtlety. Eros became more importunate, and the Vestal shrank in a terror which the singer contrived to pourtray as half-feigned, half-real. Love still advanced and clamoured, while the Vestal's resistance became more feeble; she appeared nigh unto swooning under his attacks. Her drapery seemed to stifle her. She threw it from her, and her magnificent figure was fully revealed by the diaphanous and filmy gauze that clung about her while she sang, writhed, and twisted, as she reproduced, with wonderful simulation, the yielding up of the last barriers of reserve to the assaults of Love.

Marcus, for whom the warmth and passion of Ancaria's singing had been especially devised, had scarcely noticed her, but at the finish he cast at her a look of profound contempt, which fortunately she did not see, and, taking advantage of the applause and commotion that attended the termination of her performance, he strode from the room.

CHAPTER XVI

MERCIA'S PERIL

MARCUS was angry with Ancaria, his guests, and himself. In his heart was a dull, leaden pain, born of regret and remorse. Regret for neglected opportunities of doing good, remorse for acts of evil,—committed thoughtlessly enough, it is true, but the remembrance of them brought the hot blood in crimson flushes of shame to his face and brow.

He sought the quiet of a room away from the banqueting-hall—the same from which he had looked over the city the night before, while waiting for news of Mercia. "The night before!" Was it possible that only four-and-twenty hours had passed since then? It seemed as though half his life had been lived in that one little day. He walked to the casement, and, looking out into the quiet night, wondered at the change that had taken place in him. What was it made the feast he had quitted so abhorrent? The men whom he had thought his honest friends but one short week ago, now seemed to him fawning, self-seeking, flattering sycophants. The women he had esteemed as careless, happy, merry companions, he now saw as leering, hollow, false-hearted jades, whose charms were regarded by themselves as so much merchandise for which was to be exacted every obolus possible from those who trafficked in them. And these were his friends! Friends? Yes, friends all for what he had, not one for what he was.

A peal of drunken laughter from the supper-room broke in upon his thoughts, and, guessing at the jest which provoked it, he wondered how he could possibly have found amusement in such coarse ribaldry. He thought of their mirthless gibes, their hollow laughter, and wonderingly asked himself whether they had changed? Was it possible that the drunken indecency, the lewd licence of to-night could have brought him any pleasure but a few nights ago? Were those brazen, immodest, unsexed women, reeking with sensuality and unbridled lust, or, what was even worse, the paid-for simulation of these vices—were they, *could* they be, his chosen companions of yesterday? No, they had not changed; there was not much variety in such women as these. Their tricks of trade were but few, and old as the hills bathed in the moonlight out yonder. The change was in himself. Like some life-long prisoner in a darkened cell, he had learned to look upon his feeble, flickering lamp as the only light; being released, he had seen for the first time the sun, and, for the first time, knew what light and darkness meant. Yes, light had come; not in the full, but bright enough to show the darkness he was leaving behind him. What had brought him light? He looked at the prison across the way, picturing Mercia upon her knees, as he had found her when he entered her dungeon. In fancy he saw her again in the room in his own palace; and he felt that the sunshine of her

THE SIGN OF THE CROSS

purity had illumined the dark void in which he had lived till now.

Yes, it was Mercia who had wrought this change in him. How? By what magic or sorcery had she transformed the whole of his desires, tastes, and wishes? Was it her beauty? At the supper-table within there were others as beautiful as she. Her virtues? Not she alone was virtuous. He had met and known other virtuous women. Berenice, who so loved him, he believed to be pure and true. Had he not surrounded Mercia with the halo of his own romance? Would not possession dispel the illusion conjured up by his all too vivid imagination? After all, it might be but a passing fancy, a mere infatuation that would vanish in a night. Why should he hesitate? Mercia was there, alone, his prisoner,—if he so willed, his slave. Who could or would step between him and his will? No one. Why should he not go to her now? She would yield—she must.

Thus Marcus argued with himself, and, as the rich wine he had drunk so feverishly began to flow more freely through his veins, his passion rose, and the better part of his nature was obscured again. Surely he was but a timid, hesitating fool to let this girl so master him, so enthral and defy him. But that sweet face and voice, that fable of the Nazarene, told so exquisitely!

Again were his thoughts interrupted by a drunken shout from the banqueting-hall, and Glabrio, with unsteady feet and waggling head, came reeling up to Marcus, asking with hiccoughing reproach—

MERCIA'S PERIL

"Why are we thus dis—deserted, Marcus mine?"

Marcus looked at Glabrio with an expression in which a certain liking for the old bacchanalian was mingled with undisguised anger at the intrusion upon his reverie. Glabrio was quite unconscious of offence, and rambled on—

"I have been sent to bid thee return. Why hast thou left the table?"

"I—the heat stifled me," answered Marcus evasively.

"I tell thee I have been sent to beg thee to return. The fun lags without thee—the wine no longer cheers—the song enlivens not—and the jest falls flat. Ancaria sighs like the bellows of a smithy. Return to her."

"Ancaria?" queried Marcus, with a look of disdain.

"Ay, Ancaria. By Venus, she is fair! Doth she not content thee?"

"Content me?" Marcus turned towards the window, from which could be seen the wing of the palace in which Mercia was imprisoned, and mentally he compared her with Ancaria; then, with an impatient shrug of his shoulders, he continued, "Contentment is for the gods, good Glabrio. Nay, even they seek for that pearl in vain."

"Yes, I know," said Glabrio, who did not in the least understand what was the drift of his friend's remark. "But Ancaria—a flower—a rose—the very rose of roses!"

"Yea," answered Marcus, with a gesture of contempt, "but plucked the day before yesterday, and swiftly fading."

THE SIGN OF THE CROSS

"Fading? Nay, in her first bloom rather. Fading? Ancaria? She is divine! Her beauty Cytherean, and her temper—her temper!" (this with a cautious look over his shoulder, for Ancaria might be within hearing). "Oh, my Marcus, thou art a bold man to risk the rousing of that temper. Juno herself is dove-like, in comparison. Return to her in time."

"Return to her? Ancaria? I begin to hate and loathe Ancaria and all her kind! Go back to them—tell them I——" What was Glabrio to tell them? That he longed with all his heart to be rid of them all, at once and for ever? That his yearning to be with the Christian girl was almost uncontrollable? No, he could not tell them that! And he lamely added, "Tell them I am busy—tell them any lie—tell them the truth—only leave me to myself!" And he flung himself impatiently on a couch, and rested his head upon his folded arms.

Glabrio staggered towards him with tipsy gravity, saying—

"Here's a change indeed! Has this Christian bewitched thee? Is it possible thou art turning Christian too?"

The question startled Marcus. Christian! Was it possible that this girl had so much power over him that even the drunken carelessness of a Glabrio could not fail to perceive it? Had he so little command over himself that all who saw him could see his infatuation? And was the feeling he possessed for her influenced by her religion? Could it be that he was so easily swayed by a pretty face, a pretty fable?

These questions passed rapidly through his mind, but he remembered that not only these questions required answers—Glabrio was also waiting a reply. How could he make him understand, or expect him to sympathise with his feelings? Better be rid of him, he thought, and so he cried impatiently—

"I—I Christian? Leave me, Glabrio, leave me. Go!"

"Marcus, Marcus, thou art in a bad way. Something is out of order with thee." And Glabrio shook his head with so much energy that the rapidly wilting rose-wreath tumbled on to his nose. "Is it the heart or the stomach? If 'tis the latter, send for the leech—if the former, send for the woman. Women and physicians resemble each other in this—'tis kill or cure with both of them." And, in the endeavour to emphasise his speech with an imposing and dignified gesture, he lost his balance, and sat down all too suddenly upon the couch.

"To what avail?" asked Marcus. "She is unlike all other women I have ever met. Her innocence inflames, even while it baffles me, and, for the first time in my life, I find myself baulked. I can neither conquer nor forget her. If I start some jest and look into her pure eyes, it dies upon my lips in very shame. Between my desire and Mercia, her innocence rises like a rock of adamant—I may beat my heart out dashing myself against it, but I can never move it. And yet I feel I must, or else go mad! Glabrio, I fear that girl's purity, absolutely fear it." And, rising from the couch, Marcus strode fiercely about the room, Glabrio watching him from under his disordered vine-leaves and roses.

"Yes, I have felt that way myself" (this he said

with maudlin sentimentality) "when I've been too sober" (this with an accent of deep regret for ever having been in such an undesirable condition). "But a full cup of wine soon cured that complaint with me. Send for this Mercia. What if she did deny thee yesterday? 'Twas but to whet thy appetite for her consent to-day. Let her but think she'll lose thee, and she'll yield—and yield in haste, be sure."

Marcus was looking from the window, seemingly not heeding the counsel of this tipsy philosopher, but, in reality, carefully weighing every word he uttered. Was it not more than possible that Glabrio was right? Might not this innocence and purity, after all, be a snare, a cleverly-devised trick to draw him into some serious entanglement? Was she prompted to act thus by a desire to enmesh him in some of the plots or schemes of her associates? Women were cunning—full of wiles, adepts at deception. Yet, no! Not this gentle creature; it could not be. Turning to Glabrio, he exclaimed—

"Ah! thou dost not know Mercia."

"No, I do not—but I know her sex," was the sententious reply.

"But Mercia is virtuous."

"Virtuous? Virtue is as saleable and pursh-pursh-purshasable as most commodities," chuckled Glabrio. "Every woman has her price. It is all a question of marketable value. Thou hast made thy bid—she hath declined. Bid again, my friend, and bid higher. Thou art rich, and, as it is more than evident that thou dost desire this par-tic—partic-lar piece of merchandise, be content to pay for it. Only, here I do solemnly beseech thee to hearken to me, whatever thou dost offer, let it not include thyself, my Marcus; thou art too precious for a score of Mercias." And Glabrio, fatigued with so much talking, reached round mechanically for the wine-cup, which, unhappily for his desires, was not within reach.

Marcus was only too eager to see Mercia again, and the advice given by Glabrio jumped too closely with his own inclinations for him to decline it. He struck the gong upon the table by his side, saying to Glabrio—

"Glabrio, thou art a fool—but with thy folly is ever a smattering of wisdom. I will send for Mercia."

The black slave glided quickly into the room, in answer to the summons made by Marcus, who, in quick, hard tones, ordered him to bring the lady Mercia. As the slave left the room, Marcus moved to the casement. From the dungeon, across the courtyard, came the sound of singing; it was the captive Christians chanting this hymn—

"Glory, Glory, Glory, hail to Thee, O Father,
We, Thy children, crave Thy hand to guide our steps aright.
Glory, Glory, Glory, Thou Who sent the Saviour,
Lead us through the darkness to Eternal Light.

"Glory, Glory, Glory, Thou Who died to save us,
By Thy Cross of Calvary, we kneel in trust this night;
Glory, Glory, Glory, Thou wilt walk beside us,
Guide us through death's valley to Eternal Light."

The night was still, and the words of the simple hymn came clearly and plainly to the ears of Marcus, who felt strangely moved. Another revulsion of feeling perplexed him. He almost regretted having sent for Mercia. No such tender sentiment disturbed Glabrio, who, with admonishing and didactic gravity, again addressed his friend—

"The woman is sent for. Now, hearken to my folly. That which a man hath he seldom longs for. Longing makes a man sick. Thou art hungry with longing; if thou wouldst be well, long no longer. A good full meal, my Marcus, is what my folly counsels—a good——." Here he paused for a moment, listening to the chant of the captives. "How those Christian prisoners of yours sing, Marcus! Are they always at worship, night and day? Hath death no terrors for these Christians?"

Marcus had gone to the entrance to the room, not heeding Glabrio's loquacity. He was eagerly and impatiently awaiting Mercia.

At last the slave appeared, followed by Mercia. The thought that she should encounter the tipsy leers of Glabrio was so repugnant to Marcus that he turned to him, and, in urgent tones, said—

"Go, Glabrio. Return to thy friends."

But Glabrio, ever alive to the charms of women, pleaded—

"Let me see this beauty. Send me not hence, I beg of thee, without one embrace."

Marcus shuddered at the thought of Mercia in the arms of such a man as Glabrio, and cried indignantly—

"Thou? Thou embrace her? Go! Why, thy very look would pollute her."

MERCIA'S PERIL

This was too much even for Glabrio's equanimity; he felt as nearly angry as was possible for a man of his easy disposition. He staggered to his feet with all the dignity that his tipsiness would admit of, and, vainly trying to straighten the vine-leaves on his slippery pate, he protested—

"Come, come, Marcus! I am fairly good-tempered, drunk or sober, but this is more than I can bear. Pollute is a harsh word—ess—esseedingly harsh. I am not the plague!" And he drew himself up almost straight, with such a grotesque attempt at dignity that, had Marcus been less engrossed in the coming of Mercia, he must have laughed outright. However, his present desire was to get Glabrio out of the room, and he answered quickly—

"Well, well, I was hasty; but go, Glabrio."

"But pollute?" echoed Glabrio, with tipsy pathos in his voice.

"I was wrong. Forgive me, Glabrio."

At this plea for pardon all Glabrio's mild resentment vanished; a broad smile of content widened his capacious mouth, and, chuckling to himself, he murmured—

"Well, well, I bear no man ill-will, least of all my Marcus. Such wines! . . . such wome . . . ! Oh! ah, yes! . . . reminds me . . . Ancaria—temper . . . do not forget Ancar——"

An impatient gesture from Marcus interrupted him, and he went on, knowingly,—

"'Tis well. I understand. I am no spoil-sport. I am going."

"Then go. But say nothing of Mercia," urged Marcus.

THE SIGN OF THE CROSS

"No, no; discress—discression itself. Do not fear your Glabrio." And, with many a wink and nod, he waddled away to the banqueting-hall, from which an uproarious burst of laughter was heard, announcing his return.

Marcus gave a quick sigh of relief, for Mercia was close at hand. As she entered, he saw, to his astonishment, that she had chains upon her wrists. Turning to the slave, he demanded—

"Who has dared to do this?"

"The guard, Excellence, fearing that she might again escape."

"Take off those chains instantly!"

The slave, taking a key from his girdle, unlocked and removed the manacles.

"Send the guard to Viturius. He shall repent his officiousness."

The slave made his salaam, and went noiselessly away.

Marcus bowed with grave respect to Mercia, saying, with much regret,—

"Lady, I grieve that thou hast been thus insulted. I did not know of it, believe me. 'Twas done against my direct commands."

Mercia replied, quietly and sadly,—

"I desire no favour, sir. What my companions suffer I would suffer too."

"But they are so different," urged Marcus.

"Indeed, yes; and most of them less able to endure the chains than I," was the gentle response.

With difficulty Marcus restrained the inclination to

take the beautiful creature in his arms. The brutal advice given by Glabrio had borne some fruit. For the time, his evil propensities were strongly in the ascendant. The sight of her beauty tempted him into forgetfulness of her purity. He glided quietly to her side, murmuring—

"That lovely form—those tender wrists were made for other chains—the chains of love." And he moved still nearer to her. But Mercia gently retreated from him, and, with calm dignity, asked—

"Why didst thou send for me?"

"To feast upon thy beauty; to hear the music of thy voice; to see the light that beams from those bright eyes; and watch the roses chase the lilies from thy cheeks." Marcus spoke in deep, low tones, his eyes hungrily taking note of all her loveliness. Mercia shrank from him, and said—

"Wouldst thou indeed do me a service?"

"Gladly!" replied Marcus eagerly. "Command: I obey. Thou hast but to name thy wishes."

"Send me back to my fellow-prisoners."

"Ask anything but that," urged Marcus, with a slight touch of resentment in his accents.

"That and their freedom is all I wish."

"I cannot grant thee either request."

"Why? Thou art all-powerful."

"I cannot give them freedom, because the law is stronger than I, its officer. I cannot send thee back to them, because my love for thee is greater even than my desire to serve thee."

Mercia shrank yet farther from him. His eyes were

flaming with wine and passion. She was alone with the absolute lord of her liberty and life. She began to dread the consequences of her coming thither. She had wished to see him again, but she had never seen him as he appeared to her now. The manly solicitude for her safety had given place to undisguised admiration. Mercia felt a quick pang of regret clutch at her heart as she measured the fall of this man in her esteem. Her intuition bade her escape from him if she could, and she said, with great dignity,—

"Sir, I am a prisoner of the law. If I have transgressed that law, punish me. I have been taught to suffer without murmuring."

"Punish thee?" he echoed. "Suffer? I would not have thee suffer a single pang. Come, let us be friends." And again he moved nearer to her, endeavouring to take her hand. Mercia quietly avoided him as she answered—

"Friendship with the good cannot exist without respect."

Marcus bit his lip in anger. Who was this girl that she should so repulse him? His caresses, so sought after by all other women, declined by this strange girl, with almost a shudder! He controlled a feeling of resentment and asked—

"And thou hast no respect for me? Is it not so?"

"How can I respect one who has no respect for himself?" was the gentle reproof.

"And have I no respect for myself?" he questioned.

"No man respecteth himself who hath no respect for woman. For the Teacher hath said that woman is the fount of all that is good and beautiful in man." Mercia said this with such firm, though sweet dignity, and with so much conviction, that Marcus paused to gaze upon her in wonder. Never had woman so spoken to him before. He was perplexed beyond measure. With him was all the might and force of unrestrained manhood, power of place, strength of will; and yet this physically frail girl, alone, seemingly unprotected, dominated and controlled him, yea, even against his will and desires; lessened and weakened the evil, prompted and strengthened the good in him. Involuntarily he submitted to her virtue and acknowledged her goodness as he uttered—

"Ah, I have met few such women, lady."

Softly, yet firmly, came the answer—

"Women are too often what men desire them to be. What man desires that a woman, other than his own kin, should be good?"

"Good?" Marcus laughed. "Good? Right, wrong, virtue, vice, goodness, sin,—what are they? The accidents of habits and conditions; a mass of contradictions amongst which we men grope blindly, raking and scratching for that which is not there—happiness. Ah! happiness is a rare thing, lady,—most rare,—and is seldom found when sought for. If it comes my way unsought, why should I reject it?"

With earnest conviction came the gentle answer—

"Happiness is seldom found, because men seek it in pleasure. Pleasure and happiness are not always akin. Pleasure is too often of the world; true happiness comes from God."

THE SIGN OF THE CROSS

"What God do you mean?"

"The only God—the Everlasting."

"So we consider all gods. Are they not all immortal?"

"There are no gods save One."

"To avow that is to admit thyself a Christian."

Mercia remained silent, and, after a moment, Marcus proceeded—

"Thou art a Christian? Have no fear. I promise thee I will not use thy confession to thy detriment, but it is true, is it not? Thou *art* a Christian?"

"I will not deny it."

"Why didst thou become one?" Marcus asked, almost contemptuously.

"Why does the sun shine, the flowers bloom, the birds sing? Because He willed it." Her eyes, upturned, beamed with celestial light. A smile of intense joy was upon her lips. Filled with the rapture of belief, she appeared less a thing of earth than heaven. But, for the time, her influence for good on Marcus was gone; he was blind to all but his passion for her. He could not think or reason; he could only look upon Mercia with the eyes of mad, unholy longing. Moving closer to her, his voice coarsened and hoarse with the intensity of his desires, he said—

"Lady, we stand here arguing like two parchment-dried philosophers; we, who are young, and feel youth's hot blood galloping through full veins. We are not musty pedants, but warm, passionate children on the very threshold of life. Let us leave philosophy and doctrine to grizzled greybeards, and let us love."

And with that he caught her in his arms and pressed her passionately to his breast. Mercia was terrified. Involuntarily, a slight scream escaped her, and she cried, struggling to release herself,—

"Pray, let me go hence: I fear thee!"

But Marcus held her fast, and with his face bent down close to hers, he whispered—

"Fear me? Nay, love is soft and kind and gentle. What is there to fear?"

Still she strove to free herself, and still he held her close; and again she pleaded—

"I beg of thee, let me go hence, even though it be to death."

Marcus grew furious. To be thrust away from this girl with such loathing and horror—for there was no mistaking the expression upon Mercia's face—was so wounding to his vanity that, for the moment, he almost hated her. Now all his pity for her helpless condition was gone; she could not protect herself, it was most evident. He had been too submissive, he thought, too gentle, too considerate. No man ever yet profited by yielding too completely to the whims of women. He would cease to plead—he would command. Death preferable to his embraces? This proud or cunning Christian girl had yet something to learn of his character; he was not all submission, not quite altogether weak and docile—as she would find!

"Death?" he repeated. "Let us to-morrow welcome grisly death; to-day thou shalt taste some of the joys of living."

He went to a table, and pouring out a full goblet of strong wine, he exclaimed—

"By Venus! my blood must be half-frozen in my veins that I have let thee waste that beauty in solitude so long." He emptied the cup, drinking to the last drop. "Glabrio was right," he thought. He had been "too sober." "A cup of good wine" would dispel the sickly sentimentality of his feelings towards this obdurate or calculating girl. The wine was powerful, and surged through his body like liquid fire. He flung down the cup upon the table, and turned towards Mercia.

But quickly Ancaria entered the room, and, not observing Mercia, went straight to Marcus, saying, as she threw her arms around his neck,—

"Ah, thou truant! Have I found thee at last?"

Thus evil wrought for good; the intervention of the brazen Ancaria unwittingly preserved her purer sister from insult.

Still ignorant that she was not alone with Marcus (for Mercia was at the other end of the room, partly hidden in the shadow), Ancaria continued—

"Why hast thou forsaken us? Glabrio, sent to woo thee back, returned without thee, and would not tell us why. Come, return to thy friends. The wine lacks flavour, and the feast its zest, while thou art absent."

Almost fiercely Marcus disengaged himself from Ancaria's embrace. Half in wonderment, half in anger, she asked—

"What means this sudden change in thee? Dost thou no longer love Ancaria?"

MERCIA'S PERIL

Marcus turned and looked towards Mercia, who was gazing through the casement into the night, in apparent indifference to the presence of Ancaria or himself. "Love Ancaria!" The thought sickened him. Love this shameless creature! With a swift glance he compared the two women, and for the courtesan he felt a loathing unutterable. With a struggle he conquered the feeling sufficiently to enable him to say, with comparative steadiness of voice,—

"Go back to thy friends. Go, and leave me here alone."

"Alone? But, Marcus——"

A slight movement on the part of Mercia caused Ancaria to look in her direction. Seeing her, she assumed a look of disdainful inquiry, and, with raised eyebrows, she said—

"Oh, I understand! This is the cause of thy absence. Who is this—lady?"

"My guest," was the brief, cold answer.

"Then let her join the others."

"She is not here at thy command."

"But I am here at thy desire."

"Then, at my desire, go hence."

"Oh, no! I came for thy pleasure; I remain for my own!" cried the enraged and partly intoxicated Ancaria, throwing herself upon the couch in an attitude as remarkable for its grace as it was for its absence of decorum.

Marcus looked at her in helpless disgust. Had it been a man who had dared to defy him thus, he could, and probably would, have thrown him bodily from the

THE SIGN OF THE CROSS

room, but with a woman—and withal, such a woman as Ancaria—what could he do?

Mercia was anxious only to be gone, and she pleaded, almost tearfully, to Marcus—

"I pray thee, let me return to my prison!"

"Prison?" echoed Ancaria. "Prison? Ah! now I know. This, then, is the Christian we have heard so much about! So, this is the witch who hath enchanted thee!" Then she burst forth into a shout of derisive, half-tipsy laughter that incensed Marcus still further. "Here's sport indeed!" continued the furious woman. Running to the entrance of the room, she screamed out vehemently—"Glabrio! Daones! Thea! Dardanus! Come hither! Come, and come quickly! Come, and learn the cause of our dear host's desertion! Slaves there! bring lights, that we may see her, and wine, that we may drink to her. Come, friends! Come, all of you! Come!"

Shrieking, laughing, staggering, jeering, the whole of the semi-drunken guests who were able to stand or move from the table came flocking into the room. When the lights were lit, they saw the pure, white figure of Mercia, unconsciously following the example of her divine Master in her sorrowful pity for the misguided beings around her. She stood alone and unfriended amidst all the glare of gaudy colour, glint of jewels, coarse jesting, crackling, mirthless laughter, reeling women, and staggering men. Calmly she awaited the orders of her jailer. With eyes uplifted, and in silent prayer, she was no more touched by the foulness that surrounded her than is the Christian faith by the dirt that may bespatter the walls of one of its cathedrals.

At the first sight of her beauty and unconscious innocence a slight hush fell upon the revellers, but it was but momentary; their finer faculties—such as they possessed—had long since been obscured by the wine they had drunk, and their tipsy jeers, jests, and laughter went on as before.

"Here's new sport, friends!" shouted Ancaria.

"What sport?" queried Glabrio, who had not yet caught sight of Mercia. "Why are we brought hither? We were so merry yonder, and there's no one sober save myself. Look at our ess—essellent Philodemus, already in his second drunk!"

"Nay, nay," piped that candid, if somewhat feeble creature. "Not my second. Let us be honest—this is my third."

"What is it we are—— Oh! Ah!" chuckled Glabrio, as he observed Mercia. "Now I see exactly!" And, noting Ancaria's blazing cheeks and fiery eyes, he added under his breath to Edonia, "Now we shall see some sport!"

"What sport?" asked Cyrene.

"Look yonder," answered Glabrio, indicating Mercia.

"And who is she? What can she do? A pantomime? A dance?" said Cyrene.

"A dance?" cried Daones. "What dance? Who is she, I pray? Why, I will dance her for my life!" And Daones whirled quickly round, and, finishing, struck an attitude at which those sober enough to do it, applauded.

THE SIGN OF THE CROSS

"Who is the girl?" inquired Julia.

"Who?" sneeringly replied Ancaria. "Who but the Christian?"

"The Christian?" the revellers shouted. "Let us see her!"

"Ay, pray look upon her, ladies," continued Ancaria, "and learn for what you are deserted. This is the enchantress who hath bewitched our Marcus. This is the Christian—this piece of lifeless marble! By Venus! ladies, we must learn to distil the charms these Christians brew, or we shall be left loverless."

"Nay," lisped Philodemus, "I will never leave thee, my Ancaria." Whereon he embraced Julia.

During all this revilement of the lovely girl Marcus stood apart, quiescent, motionless. His first natural instincts were to rescue Mercia from the insults levelled at her, but his anger, fanned by his wounded self-respect, betrayed him into another act of brutality. He determined to humble the pride of this coldly contemptuous Christian. Let her suffer a little indignity! It would do her no harm. He would see that it did not go beyond that. Meanwhile, a glimpse into a side of life different to that in which she had been schooled might induce her to think a little more leniently of those who indulged in its pleasures. Let her see that there was another, merrier, brighter side to existence than that she had known. No, he would not interfere yet. Let the stream of banter flow on; time enough to dam or divert it when it tended to injure physically the woman who was the innocent cause of it.

"Well, ladies," said Ancaria, tearing in pieces the

wreath of roses she had girdled about her, "what think you? Is this the star that is to outshine us all?"

"She outshine us?" queried Daones. "In what, I pray? Can she sing as well, or dance as nimbly, or pantomime as well as I?"

"Perchance not," replied Glabrio; "but," with an unctuous smacking of his lips, "she's very lovely."

"Lovely?" laughed Daones. "Perhaps. But I care not for that style of loveliness,—if loveliness it be."

"Nor I. She is too tall for my taste," cried Thea.

"And too cold for mine," said the sensuous Julia.

"And a statue hath more animation," exclaimed the volatile Mytelene.

"In what lies her attraction for such a man as Marcus?" asked Daones.

"She has a fresh face," answered Edonia.

"She has bewitched him. She is a sorceress!" said Ancaria spitefully. "They say these Christians can perform miracles." Then the angry woman stalked up to Mercia, and, with arms akimbo, said derisively, "Perform one now."

"She hath performed one already, if she hath made Marcus really love her," laughed Daones.

"Marcus love her?" venomously retorted Ancaria. "Oh, yes, for an hour—perchance for two—assuredly not for a day. Poor fool! the cast-off sandal of a year ago will not be more forgotten than she will be to-morrow. Marcus love her? Oh, yes! with a love that will live as long as a snowflake in the noonday sun."

A roar of laughter followed this sally, and Marcus, seizing Ancaria by the wrist, hissed in her ear—

"Keep thy tongue quiet, mistress."

"Keep my tongue quiet?" shrieked the courtesan. "Was it for that you brought us hither?" Wrenching herself from the grasp of Marcus, and turning to the guests, she added, "Ladies, here's a change indeed! Marcus would have us still our tongues!"

"Impossible!" sapiently murmured Glabrio.

"Quite," retorted Ancaria, "unless he first seal our lips." And she offered her mouth to be kissed. But Marcus turned from her.

"His present seal should be the ass's head," said the lively Daones; and all shouted—

"Ay, ay! Anakoites!"

When the shouts and laughter had subsided, Ancaria sprang into the centre of the room, crying—

"Let the girl join us! She is asleep—awaken her! Let her be as one of ourselves, or let her go. She hath spoiled the feast—ruined our pleasure. What dost thou say, friends? Shall I sing thee a song of love? A new one?"

"Yea, yea!" all the guests shouted. And Ancaria answered, "I'll rouse this statue, if anyone can. Pass thou the wine." And, with consummate skill, she sang—

> "What though to-morrow cometh grisly Death?
> To-day the roses bloom, the wine runs red.
> Red wine to red lips, hot breath to hot breath!
> Love's kiss would waken me e'en were I dead.
>
> Elysium is but fulfilled desire,
> And Hades but desire still unfulfilled.
> Then let—then let——"

MERCIA'S PERIL

The singer hesitated—tried to begin again—then broke down utterly, for, far above the tones of her voice, rang out in tones of devout belief and supplication the hymn of the imprisoned Christians—

> "Shepherd of souls that stumble by the way,
> Pilot of vessels storm-tossed in the night,
> Healer of wounds, for help to thee we pray;
> Guide thou our footsteps, send the morning light.
> Oh, lead us home!"

At the sound of the beloved words, so often sung by her at the feet of her parents and Favius in the happy bygone days, Mercia, whose power of endurance had been waning, lifted her head and, with glowing face and glistening eyes, seemed to drink in renewed life, fresh hope, new strength, under this appeal to the Shepherd. The drunken revellers, like foul, noisome reptiles, crouching in darkness, suddenly startled by a flood of sunshine, shrank back into uneasy and, to them, inexplicable silence. Daones was the first to recover herself.

"Who are those singers?"

"The Christian prisoners," replied Glabrio.

"This girl's associates? Stop them!" screamed Ancaria.

"Stop them! stop them!" repeated the rest.

"They chill, they freeze me!" shivered Ancaria. "I cannot sing against these crazy fanatics, Marcus. Send to them and bid them cease."

"No, indeed—not I!" cried Marcus sternly. "'Tis a battle of the gods—Christus against Pluto. Let the fight rage on!"

THE SIGN OF THE CROSS

"We'll drown their howlings! On with the song!" shouted the guests.

"Ay. Shall I be beaten by these wretches?" said Ancaria. And again she essayed to sing the words—

> "Elysium is but fulfilled desire,
> And Hades—but desire——"

Again, in its simple strength, the hymn rose above the sensual song of the courtesan, who stopped, glaring at Mercia for a moment, and then cried loudly—

"I cannot—I cannot sing!"

"By Venus! I'm freezing! What ails me?" said one of the men.

"I feel that I could weep," whimpered one of the women.

"'Tis this girl's witchcraft. Smite her! smite her! smite her! She is a sorceress!" yelled the infuriated Ancaria.

"Make her drink!" exclaimed Daones. "Give her wine, Glabrio."

"Ay, come, drink," urged Glabrio. "Drink and be merry, for to-morrow we die."

Then, for the first time, did Mercia turn and look upon them, and, with a simple dignity that was majestic, she called in her sweet, clear tones—

"No! to-morrow we live. To-day thou art dead in unrighteousness."

"Drink, girl, drink!" they shouted.

"I will not," replied the faithful Mercia; "and woe unto you who would tempt me, for ye are lost! Ah, turn from the ways of darkness—seek the light; 'tis shining there to guide thee."

Mercia stood with arms extended, her pure face, her white-clad figure standing out among the rest of the glittering, sensual, drunken throng like a messenger of Heaven.

"Stop the witch's mouth! Give her wine!" cried Ancaria.

"Make her drink!" shouted the others.

"I have said I will not," was the calm reply.

Glabrio, with drunken insistence, exclaimed—

"By the gods, thou shalt!" And, going towards her, he would have forced the wine upon her, had not Marcus suddenly seized him, and, hurling the easily yielding Glabrio in one direction and the wine-cup in another, confronted the whole of the assemblage with angry defiance, saying—

"Let no man touch her!"

"A pretty host, forsooth!" exclaimed Ancaria. "Insult us for this new-found toy—this inanimate piece of bloodless whiteness! He must be mad!"

"Perchance I am mad, for my brain is reeling and my veins run fire! Hence, all of you! You are not fit to breathe the same air with her, for your breath reeks of wine and in your kisses lurks the pestilence, and in your bartered love lies ruin—misery—madness —despair and death! Hence! hence! hence! I command thee!"

With mirth and astonishment on the part of some, and indignation on that of others, the medley crew of patrician men, courtesans, and dancers hurried from

THE SIGN OF THE CROSS

the room, laughing, scowling, jeering, and cursing. While the sound of their voices could be heard Marcus stood still, his arms tightly folded across his breast, his gaze fixed upon Mercia. When the last echo of the cries of the tipsy crowd had died away in the distance, he spoke.

"See, I have driven those who reviled thee hence. Art thou content?"

Mercia saw the wine-inflamed face, the bloodshot eyes of Marcus, and heard the hoarse accents in which he addressed her, and she trembled with apprehension. Controlling her voice as best she could, she answered—

"Now, let me go hence." And she moved towards the door. But Marcus barred the way. He was breathing heavily; his eyes were glaring with passion; his chest heaved; he was trembling violently; his fingers clutched at his arms until the nails tore the flesh to bleeding. He had lost all control over himself; the excitement of the past two days, the want of food, the wine, his lust, anger, wounded self-esteem, all were at work within him; his brain was clouded; he could think of nothing but the mad desire to control this girl who had so enthralled, so scorned him.

As Mercia stood watching him, she shuddered. Could this be the same man who, but a few hours ago, was so full of gentleness and sympathy? He was transformed; all trace of nobility, even manliness, had left his face. The girl's position was terrible indeed, and yet, through it all, she loved and pitied the man with all her heart. After a moment, he cried, in hoarse rage,—

"Go? No! you sorceress or witch! No, you beautiful statue—you cold, glittering star! You have driven them hence, but you remain. Your icy chastity burns into my heart! I never knew desire until I knew you, and, if your touch were poison, I'd possess you! If death lurked in your kisses, I'd feast upon them! Come to me! come to me!" Rushing to her, he seized her in his arms. Struggling with his greater strength, Mercia was almost breathless, but she fought him still, exclaiming—

"For shame! Are you a man or a brute?"

His face, burning with lust, was close to hers, his hot breath upon her cheek, his eyes blazing as he answered—

"Both! All the brute in the man is roused by your disdain—all the man in the brute is fired by your glorious beauty."

Mercia slipped from his arms, but he ran swiftly to the door, calling loudly—

"Slaves, enter! Quick! Quench those lamps! Fasten the doors! Let no one enter—man or woman—without my orders!"

Instantly his commands were obeyed, and before Mercia had exclaimed, "Mercy! Do not leave me, men, if you have sisters, mothers, wives!" they had extinguished the lamps, and the grinding of bolts and locks in the distant doors told her that she was alone, —absolutely alone with the mad, uncontrolled being who was intent upon her destruction.

When her eyes became accustomed to the sudden darkening of the room, she saw that he was near the door. The casement was but a few feet from her—she rushed towards it, intent upon throwing herself from it, whatever the cost to limb or life. But Marcus was too quick for her, and dragged her back, crying—

"No, no; there is no escape! We are alone, and you are mine—body and soul!"

But even now the brave girl's faith was unshaken, and she answered—

"No, you cannot defile my soul. That is inviolate. He who gave me that soul will keep it pure, unstained; and unto His mercy and into His hands I commit it."

He heard the words, but recked not of the meaning and, still holding her in his arms, he cried—

"No, no; into mine! It is not enough that you should be mine; I must have your very soul! Mercia, love me, and thou shalt be worshipped as never woman was worshipped yet. See, here I grovel at your feet," and, as he said this, he fell on the floor, clutching her robes, "I kiss the hem of your garment! Only love me! I'll load you with gold—cover your beauty with the rarest gems—only love me! I'll give thee wealth, power, empire—only love me!"

"Mercy, mercy!" called the half-fainting girl.

"Have thou mercy! I love thee so! Have mercy upon that love—upon me!"

With a last piteous effort of waning strength, Mercia pushed him from her and ran towards the door. What use? It was locked, and she could only beat her tender hands vainly upon its brazen panels. He caught her in his arms once more.

"Art thou man or devil?" she moaned.

"Man or devil, thou shalt love me!" he hissed back, kissing her passionately.

Her senses were reeling, her strength exhausted, her voice powerless. The earth seemed receding, the marble floor appeared to rock like waves in a storm; utter darkness was falling. . . . And then—was it a miracle that happened? The darkened room was illumined by a soft, white light; the hymn of the Christians rang through the still air of the night—

> "Shepherd of souls that stumble by the way,
> Pilot of vessels storm-tossed in the night;——"

A tide of strength superhuman surged through her whole being. With a swift movement she threw Marcus from her as easily as though the strong man had been a weak child; as she did so, she held the wooden cross, the emblem of her faith, aloft, crying with ecstatic joy—

"A sign! A sign! The Master hath spoken! You cannot harm me now!"

Marcus staggered from her, trembling, amazed, sobered, and sane, all his anger, lust, passion, gone from him. A daughter of heaven, an angel of light, this radiant being was a thing to worship, not to profane. The scales had fallen from his eyes. Virtue was not a myth, purity not a delusion, faith not a pretence. He fell upon his knees and buried his face in his hands as a loud knocking was heard at the door, and the voice of Tigellinus called—

"Open, in the name of Cæsar! Make way, slaves; open the door!"

THE SIGN OF THE CROSS

The bolts rolled back, the locks were turned. Tigellinus, followed by armed guards, and servants bearing torches, swiftly entered the room. Holding in his hand the Emperor's mandate, and showing a seal set in a ring upon his finger, Tigellinus exclaimed—

"Prefect, by Cæsar's command, I come to take from your custody the Christian girl, Mercia. See here the mandate of the Emperor, and this his signet."

Mercia's peril, for that night at least, had passed.

CHAPTER XVII

MERCIA'S CONDEMNATION

BEFORE the might of Nero's mandate Marcus was helpless. He would have flung himself upon Tigellinus and his guard without a thought of the consequence, but, fresh from the banquet-table, he was unarmed; the soldiers, armour-clad, with drawn swords, stood between him and Mercia, and she welcomed them as friends, heaven-sent to succour her.

He raved in his impotency, but all to no purpose—the hour of Tigellinus had come. The game had been craftily played; he had won. The force and cunning arrayed against Mercia were overpowering. The subtle cleverness of two revengeful women, backed by the strongest authority in Rome, was not to be combated by her guilelessness or the courage and impetuosity of Marcus. He begged and prayed for but one word from her, as the guards drew her away. She turned for a moment, looked him full in the eyes, and asked—

"What wouldst thou have of me?"

"Forgiveness," he murmured in broken accents.

"Ask for that of Him," replied Mercia sadly. "Him thou hast defied. He alone can grant forgiveness."

"Thou shalt be rescued—have no fear," cried Marcus.

THE SIGN OF THE CROSS

"Rescued from what? What should I fear?"

"Death."

"I have no fear of death, when death is the saviour from sin. There is no more to say. Sir," she said, turning to Tigellinus, "I pray thee take me hence."

Giving the soldiers the signal to march, Tigellinus, with a look of triumph, but without a single word, left the palace with his prisoner, and Marcus was alone—alone with despair.

Bitterly he reproached himself for his neglect in not suing to Nero for her pardon before the quarrel had gone too far with Tigellinus. He had no need to be told that her re-arrest by Nero's special command meant for him at least temporary disfavour, if not disgrace, with Cæsar. He had been given absolute authority to deal with the Christians, and suddenly, without hint or warning, that authority had been overridden by the Emperor's own mandate and signet—a proceeding no less significant than it was unusual.

Little he cared to inquire into the cause of this; he could too easily guess. Berenice had carried out her threat, had gone to Nero, told him all, and the result was the re-arrest of Mercia. He had no hope of saving her—or even of seeing her again—without the intervention of Cæsar himself. Was it possible to gain that? Nero was fickle, changeable, vacillating; but behind him was Poppæa. Marcus knew full well, by intuition, that she was, with Berenice, the instigator of this attack, and knowing it, he felt his utter helplessness. The whole Court was against him, for Nero,

MERCIA'S CONDEMNATION

Poppæa, and Tigellinus were the Court. The rest were nonentities, to be swayed by every whim of these all-powerful three.

To appeal to Tigellinus were surely to waste time and breath.

To solicit the help of Berenice or Poppæa were worse than useless.

There remained but the Emperor—what hope had he of success with him? None. The task was hopeless; the difficulties insurmountable. Still, he would try—must try. Mercia should not be done to death without a struggle on his part to save her. He would seek Cæsar at the earliest moment on the morrow; nothing could be done until then. Would Nero give him audience? Surely he dared not deny him that? But Nero!—who could rely on such a broken reed? Still, his vacillation told for, as well as against, Mercia. He who had turned and changed so often, might change again.

Thus Marcus argued with himself until, utterly exhausted, he flung himself upon a couch and waited for the dawn. Sleep refused to visit him; he was overwrought, overstrung, and burning with fever. Alternately he tossed upon the couch, and paced the marble floor. The night seemed never-ending. There rung in his ears Mercia's last words, "Ask forgiveness of Him." "Him"? Whom did she mean? This Nazarene? This Jesus she had told him of? This lowly-born martyr? Could he pray to Him? And, if he did, what then? Could He hear? Would he answer? What was that that Mercia cried? "A sign! The Master hath spoken! He is here! You cannot harm me now!"

Oh, the shame of it! A young, innocent girl at his mercy, alone and helpless, whom every instinct of manhood should have prompted him to protect, whom he had called his guest, forced to defend her honour against his brutal passion, and cry upon her God to save her! His face burned with the hot flush of shame that swept over it. He was racked by remorse for what he had done, horrified at his own degradation.

"Pray to Him for forgiveness." "Him, the Master." Forgiveness! Sorely he needed it; for he felt he could never forgive himself. He had railed against the vices of his late guests, driven them from his house with scorn. But in what was he better than they? They trafficked with vice—he had sought to violate virtue. All the hideous scene came back upon his memory—every cry of Mercia, every movement, each look of horror and terror that had flashed into her face and eyes during that brief struggle with him; and her beauty, innocence, and utter helplessness appealed to his sobered senses in such irresistible force and with such pathos that he fell upon his face and sobbed with shame and regret. Forgiveness! Ah, yes! "Nazarene! Jesus! Master! Thou who art her God, help me! pity me! Forgive me!"

For the first time in his life Marcus prayed, and prayed to Him who never turned deaf ears to the call of the repentant or the prayers of those who were heavily laden with sorrow or distress.

The rosy glintings of the morning shot in bright

MERCIA'S CONDEMNATION

flashes through the casement, to find Marcus still prone upon the floor. His long vigil had brought him some composure, but no peace. His course of action was clear. He must learn whether Mercia and her associates were to be tried or executed without trial by Nero's mandate. To-day was fixed for the performances in the Circus; scores, yea, hundreds of these Christians were to be butchered in public. Ingenuity was to be taxed to the utmost to devise new means of slaughter. The male victims were to be burned, crucified, devoured by wild beasts; and the women and girls subjected to horrors not to be described.

And Mercia! to escape from him only to encounter such a fate! How could he save her? For save her he must.

The hours crept slowly by; the sun had risen, shining in glory over his palace—over the dungeon in which she was again imprisoned—over the Hall of Justice in which she might presently be tried—over the Amphitheatre, where, before it sank again, she might have met a shameful, brutal death.

Oh, how slowly the moments sped! But the hour for the opening of the Hall of Justice came at last, and the first man to pass the portals on that eventful day was Marcus, the Prefect of Rome.

The officers of the Court scarcely recognised him; the anguish of the preceding hours had so changed his look. His face was an ashen grey, his eyes sunken and bloodshot, his lips colourless—he seemed to have aged in a night.

On inquiry he learned that all the prisoners taken at

THE SIGN OF THE CROSS

the Grove were to be tried together, and that Mercia was among them. There was no need to tell him that, under such circumstances, she was already doomed. The trial would be the merest form. And so it proved.

All the prisoners were assembled. The Prætor named the judices, who were in waiting to be called, having received orders to be in attendance. The drawing of lots for the office was dispensed with, nor were the prisoners permitted to challenge any of the jury.

The Prætor and the Judex Quæstionis directly charged the accused, Tigellinus and the ædile gave evidence on their "honour." The spy was sworn in the ordinary way, holding in his right hand a flint stone, and saying—

"*Si sciens fallo, tum me Diespiter salva urbe arceque bonis ejiciat ut ego hunc lapidem.*" The evidence was to the effect that the accused had been caught in the act of conspiring against the Emperor and the State, and, furthermore, of practising a new and prohibited religion. Marcus was not permitted to address the Court. By his faith and honour he was sworn as a witness. The few questions asked concerned his interruption of the punishment that Tigellinus and his soldiers were inflicting on the unlawful and treasonable assembly in the Grove. None of the prisoners were allowed to speak for themselves. No advocates appeared for them. The law for the giving of judgment after midday (*post meridiem præsenti*) was ignored, the verdict given, and sentence of immediate death, in manner to be decreed by the beloved Emperor, instantly pronounced, and then without delay the prisoners were

MERCIA'S COMDEMNATION

conducted, chained and guarded, to the dungeons beneath the Amphitheatre.

The laws were suspended, outraged, and defied that the arena should be drenched, and the vampire appetite of the people glutted with the blood of the prisoners.

Marcus had stood in an agony of grief listening to the mock trial. His eyes, fixed upon the pale, calm face of Mercia, had vainly sought to win one look from her. She scarcely listened to the proceedings; her arm was wound about the fainting, crippled form of Stephanus, her gaze upturned in silent abstraction. Only once did she turn her head—at the moment when the dread death-sentence was pronounced. Then she gave one long, earnest, steady look straight into the eyes of Marcus, and in that glance he read forgiveness and fervent exhortation to repent. No bitterness was in her face, no shadow of reproach,—only the divine light of martyrdom cheerfully to be endured. Marcus shivered as one with an ague when he saw her depart to her doom, and dashing from the Hall he sprang into his chariot, and drove at impetuous speed to the palace of Nero.

CHAPTER XVIII

THE REMORSE OF MARCUS

WITH Marcus, ever, to think was to act. His resolve was taken—his plan of action clear. He would demand audience of Cæsar, and plead in person for the life of Mercia. Nothing that he could urge or do to save her life should be left unsaid, undone. Saved she must be—the mere doubt could not be tolerated.

His heart almost stopped beating at the very thought of such a possibility as Nero's refusal of pardon. It should not be. He had many claims upon the Emperor's regard, and the life of this one girl could not be denied him. If Cæsar could but be approached alone,—if Poppæa and Tigellinus were but absent,—he felt assured that his petition would be granted. But would they be absent? That was the one momentous question he asked himself as he entered the palace and requested audience of the Emperor.

Nero was holding a reception in one of the smaller chambers, thronged by a crowd of courtiers and officers of State. He was reclining on a throne raised upon a marble platform, approached by marble steps. Over the steps and platform were flung magnificent draperies; cushions, skins of tigers, leopards, and wolves were strewn everywhere.

THE REMORSE OF MARCUS

Nero's negro guards, heavily armed, stood in statuesque silence around the throne. At his feet knelt the cup-bearer and taster, the officer charged with the safety of his monarch's life, his preservative from treachery by poison. On his right hand sat Poppæa, at her feet was Berenice. Among the crowd were officers of all ranks and governors of the provinces.

Nero fingered on the table by his side a huge programme on parchment of the performances in the Circus for that day. As the officers and governors handed in their reports, he listened with unconcealed impatience to the details, turning with absorption to the catalogue of the sports, and, from time to time requesting the opinion or soliciting the approval of the Empress, who was at work, assisted by Berenice, upon the embroidering of a silken scarf for the protection of Nero's throat. Of this he always took the most assiduous care, lest his voice might be injured by exposure.

Ignoring the remarks of one of the officers, Nero said to the Empress—

"The games in the Circus to-day, Poppæa, will eclipse all we have yet seen. Here's sport indeed. The chariot and the foot races, the gladiators, the Masque of Venus, and then the lions and tigers and two hundred Christians!" With a mirthless chuckle of enjoyment he beckoned to Metullus, and asked, "The beasts have been well starved, Metullus?"

"Ay, Cæsar," answered Metullus.

"And they are strong and fierce?" Eagerly and savagely was the question put.

THE SIGN OF THE CROSS

"Rome hath never seen such beasts, Cæsar."

"Good, good!" gloatingly responded Nero. "When the sun goes down, we'll have the living torches all round the Amphitheatre, at a distance of twenty paces. Let those Christians be bound, soaked in pitch and oil, and, at my signal, let the vermin burn. Yes, yes! And see that stakes are placed beneath their chins that they do not too easily suffocate, and so die too soon. Moreover, that way I can the better see their faces as they roast—eh?"

As the Emperor lingered lovingly over the details of the torture, Tigellinus entered and knelt at his feet.

"Well, Tigellinus, well?" queried Nero impatiently.

"The girl is arrested, as thou didst command, great Cæsar," said the Councillor, with a look of triumph which he did not endeavour to conceal.

"Good, good!" cried Cæsar exultingly; "make a torch of her, and place her near to Marcus' seat. They say she was cold to him—we'll see her afire to-night! Ha, ha! What said he—eh? What said Marcus?"

This question, though eagerly put by Nero, was uttered in a tone suggestive of much nervousness and trepidation. He regarded with a wholesome dread the courage and impetuosity of his Prefect. Tigellinus knew this, and worked upon the fear, replying—

"He raved against Rome, the laws and thee, great Cæsar."

"Ah! did he dare?" exclaimed Nero, half in anger, half in terror.

Poppæa saw the intention of Tigellinus, and en-

THE REMORSE OF MARCUS

deavoured to minimise the effect of his words by soothingly interposing—

"Forgive him that, Cæsar. This choice morsel of his, this Christian beauty, has been snatched from his lips; he may rave for a time, and not without some reason, but he will be faithful."

"Dost think so—eh, eh?" tremblingly questioned the cowardly tyrant.

"I do know it," answered Poppæa, reassuring by word and gesture her royal husband, who breathed a heavy sigh of relief as he said—

"Well, well, I'm glad. We cannot well afford to part with Marcus." Then, with renewed ferocity, he turned to Tigellinus and asked, "But the girl—eh? Did she scream and faint and plead for mercy?"

"No, Cæsar; she was calm, and said that she was ready," answered Tigellinus, with an expression of puzzled bewilderment.

Nero, too, was at a loss.

"Strange, eh?—the obstinacy of these fanatics," he muttered reflectively. "They die so calmly, it robs the killing of half the joy." Then, more hopefully, he added, "Well, well, perhaps some of the rats may squeak to-day—eh? Ha, ha, ha!" And in grim enjoyment of his own fiendish humour he broke into a laugh.

He was revelling in the anticipation of the horrors he was to witness, of the torture and suffering he was about to inflict. No other thought ever entered his mind, no glimmer of pity or compassion found its way into his heart. On the anguish of others he battened

THE SIGN OF THE CROSS

and thrived. As he turned once more to his programme of the "sports," a slave entered and prostrated himself on the ground, crying—

"The Prefect Marcus would have audience of Cæsar."

"Eh, eh?" ejaculated Cæsar, startled. "Marcus? Audience? What? What? Eh, Poppæa? We will not see him now—eh? Not now!"

"Better see him at once, Cæsar, or he may suspect that thou dost fear him," cunningly suggested Poppæa, who was anxious, for her own reasons, to see Marcus once again.

"Fear him?" cried Cæsar, indignantly, but at the same time trembling violently. "Fear him? A Nero fear a Marcus? Preposterous! Absurd! A god does not tremble at presence of any mortal. Admit him," he said to the slave, who bowed, and with many obeisances retired from the room.

Nero gazed around him, anxious, nervous, frightened. At his feet the cup-bearer still knelt. Beckoning him to pour out some wine, he wiped the sweat from his clammy forehead. As the wine was handed to him, his hand shook so violently that the liquor was spilled upon his robes and the floor. Eagerly he raised the cup to his lips, and then, with a new fear, a fresh dread, the miserable monster looked doubtfully at the wine, not daring to drink, lest it should be poisoned.

With shaking hands he gave it back to the officer, with a gesture of command that it should first be tasted by him. Then anxiously he waited, watching its effect, and assuring himself that no antidote was taken by the cup-bearer. Finding that no evil had resulted from the draught, he raised the vessel to his own lips and greedily drank its contents. As he was handing back the goblet to the officer, Marcus entered.

Throwing a hasty glance round the room, he saw, to his despair, that Poppæa, Berenice, and Tigellinus were present, and the chilling silence which met his appearance struck icy forebodings to his heart.

Already he felt that his errand was useless; the boon he had come to crave was refused before he uttered it.

From the quivering face of Nero to the impassive features of Poppæa, from the guilty consciousness of the look of Berenice to the unconcealed smile of victory on the lips of Tigellinus, Marcus turned, and his hopes were crushed.

Mercia must die! Still, he would plead, urge, yea, threaten even, before he would accept the defeat that so obviously awaited him.

Kneeling before Cæsar, he saluted him, saying—

"Hail, mighty Cæsar!" Then, with another obeisance to the Empress, he added, "And hail to thee, lady."

Nero, with a transparent simulation of attention to the programme of the Circus, said, with a coldness that sounded another knell to the hopes of Marcus—

"Well, Prefect, what wouldst thou with us?"

"Mercy, great Cæsar," pleaded Marcus.

With a look of well-feigned surprise, Nero asked—

"For whom—eh? For whom does Marcus crave mercy? Not for himself, surely? Our trusted Marcus hath no need of mercy, having done no wrong, neglected no duty? Faithful and true, our Marcus hath no need to pray for mercy, surely?"

"No, Cæsar; I plead not for myself, but for an innocent girl."

"Dost thou mean Mercia, the Christian?" questioned Cæsar, with a craftily assumed look of astonishment.

"Yea, great Cæsar," replied Marcus, noting the look in Nero's face and the menacing inflection of his voice.

"Ah! she is not innocent," was the cold and curt reply, and Nero turned from Marcus with studied indifference.

At this intentional slight Marcus' anger flashed into his eyes, but he curbed his rage for the sake of the cause he had come to plead, and, though he rose to his feet, he asked submissively enough the question—

"Of what is she guilty?"

Nero started slightly at the tone of Marcus' voice, which, though respectful, had in it a certain ring of determination that he did not like. After a pause, he said—

"Guilty? Thou knowest well. She is accused of being a Christian."

"By whom is she accused, Cæsar?"

"Well, by —— " He was about to mention Berenice, but a warning look from Poppæa made him substitute another name. He continued, "By Tigellinus and—others."

"The others being Berenice and——?" Here Marcus paused. He would have added "Poppæa," but he hesitated, if it could be avoided, to add to her enmity,

THE REMORSE OF MARCUS

and refrained. After a moment, he continued, "A jealous woman is not always a reliable witness, Cæsar."

"Ah, but there is other proof," exclaimed Tigellinus, bowing cringingly to Cæsar and facing Marcus. "Thou knowest, Marcus, she was captured at one of their secret meetings, caught in the very act of——"

"Act of what, Tigellinus?" demanded Marcus quietly but sternly. "Act of worship, prayer, and praise? What harm is there in these? I am firmly convinced that Cæsar has no more virtuous subjects in all his dominions than these Christians."

"And thou hadst to fall in love with a Christian to gain that conviction—eh, Marcus?" asked Poppæa, with a smile of contempt.

Marcus made no answer to this sneer, and Nero said—

"Even if true, their virtue is hardly a recommendation to my mercy. Virtue would smother half the joys and pleasures of this world." And he leered sensually into the face of his Empress.

"Vice hath already smothered the other half, Cæsar," interposed Marcus. Nero looked for a moment as though he would resent this speech, but, changing his mind, he said—

"Eh? Well, well, but these Christians are gloomy, austere fanatics who worship a wretched Jew whom Pontius Pilate crucified between two thieves—eh?"

To this Marcus quietly and calmly replied—

"And testified he could find no sin in Him."

"There Pontius was wrong," angrily retorted Nero.

THE SIGN OF THE CROSS

"I would be King of the East, and they set up this Nazarene as king."

"Not as temporal king, Cæsar," pleaded Marcus.

"Yes, as temporal king. 'Twas testified that he did endeavour to stir up the people of Judea to revolt, in order that he might be proclaimed King of the Jews."

"'Twas falsely testified, Cæsar, by spies and informers, bribed by Pontius Pilatus himself. He sought no temporal power, but preached alone the kingdom of heaven," urged Marcus, recalling the teachings of Mercia, "and bade His followers render unto Cæsar the things that were Cæsar's, but unto God the things that were God's. Again and again did He tell the people that His kingdom was not of earth."

"Eh? Come, enough of this! I am Cæsar! I have power over life and death—eh? I have decided. This Mercia dies with the others this very day." And again Cæsar turned away from Marcus.

But Marcus was not to be denied. "Hear me, Cæsar," he cried. "Thou dost know me to be faithful—and thou hast many flatterers, but few friends——"

"How—how? Eh?" stuttered Nero.

"I dare to tell thee truths, Cæsar, that others tremble to speak of. Around thy throne are many who serve for greed—for fear—but scarcely one for love. The people groan beneath the burthen of taxation—the army is restless, discontented—while the families of those whom thou hast punished hate thee."

These honest truths angered and alarmed the tyrant. He knew they were truths, but dared not admit as much even to himself. He turned upon Marcus and, with rage, exclaimed—

"By Jupiter, thou art going too far, Marcus! Have a care——"

"Of what, Cæsar? Thine anger? Has it come to this, then, that to be faithful to thee is to incur thy displeasure, thy resentment?" calmly asked Marcus.

"Nay, but to insult me thus," petulantly muttered Nero.

Marcus turned to Poppæa and, with a look of meaning that almost brought a blush to her cheek, said—

"Lady, I appeal to thee. Dost thou believe me faithful unto Cæsar?"

Poppæa understood the meaning of the glance that Marcus had given her, too well. Had she not vainly endeavoured herself to induce Marcus to dishonour her lord? She answered quietly, but with decision—

"I *know* that thou art faithful, Marcus."

Then once more Marcus pleaded with Cæsar, crying—

"The hour of darkness looms close to thee, Cæsar, and to Rome. In that dread hour at least one faithful hand to guide thee and protect thee, even unto death, shall be thine if thou wilt but grant me this maiden's life. Cæsar, I never asked of thee a boon before. Wilt thou refuse this little thing—the life of one weak girl?"

Cæsar was troubled and sore afraid. He looked round at the crowd of courtiers and officers of the Court, and felt in his heart that, of the whole number, not one was as true and honest as the man now pleading for the life of this Christian girl. After all, what could it matter whether she lived or died? Why should he not spare her? He would! He turned to the Empress and said—

"Poppæa, let us grant her life—eh? eh? What sayest thou?"

But Poppæa, in her jealousy, was relentless, and replied—

"NO."

Turning from her to Marcus, Nero cried—

"It cannot be, Marcus. The whole of the vile horde are not only enemies to Cæsar, but enemies to the public weal. She is a Christian, and she must die with the rest."

Marcus saw that Poppæa had influenced Nero against him, and, with a look of hatred at her, he exclaimed—

"Christianity is not a crime, great Cæsar."

Poppæa returned the look Marcus gave her with one of contempt, as she sneered—

"Marcus pleads strongly. Can it be possible that he is to turn Christian too?"

This was a cruel question for Marcus. To answer yes was to seal his death-warrant—this he knew; but he felt some power impelling him not altogether to deny this Christ, and he answered—

"Lady, I am almost persuaded to follow where I see such angels lead."

At this the Empress laughed in derision, but her laughter did not conceal her anger. With an affectation of contemptuous pity she said—

THE REMORSE OF MARCUS

"Poor Marcus! Thou art very much in love indeed!"

Her sneer moved Marcus to make the fatal avowal—

"With all my heart and soul, Empress."

"These Christians must be sorcerers, in truth, so easily to enmesh thee, Marcus," angrily exclaimed Poppæa.

Marcus, incensed in his turn, gave full rein to his tongue, and, fixing on the Empress a look of the most intense scorn, he retorted—

"Mercia's sorceries are the most potent, her spells the most powerful weaved by magician since the world began—the charm of innocent and virtuous womanhood."

Poppæa was silenced. She coloured violently and then turned deadly pale. Berenice sank her head upon her hands, dreading the consequence of the storm she had evoked, while the courtiers stared in amazement at the audacity of Marcus. Nero broke the temporary silence by saying—

"But she is a Christian."

"Even if she be, give me her life, Cæsar," implored Marcus. "It is so small a thing for thee to grant—'twill cost thee but one little word, and that one little word gives me a world. I will serve thee as never man served thee yet. Give me her life! I pray thee, give me her life!"

Again was Nero moved to grant the boon, but again did Poppæa restrain him, and reluctantly he refused, answering—

"I cannot, Marcus."

THE SIGN OF THE CROSS

With a vehemence that would have caused the immediate arrest of any less trusted or important man than he, Marcus cried—

"Thou canst, Cæsar! Think!—have I ever hesitated to risk either treasure or life in thy service? To me the wish of Cæsar hath been law; to obey that law scores of these Christians have suffered—wives have been torn from their husbands—children from their fathers—and the arena hath been swamped with their blood. Until now, all this hath seemed just and necessary, even if harsh and cruel. But now, this simple girl hath opened mine eyes. I see that even if sedition and rebellion do exist in the Christian ranks, they are not Christian deeds; for Christianity is not murder, lust, treason, or sin of any kind—it is love and peace, self-sacrifice and charity. Cæsar, for my sake, for the sake of Rome, for the sake of thine own welfare, give me this girl's life—only her life!"

And, with clasped hands and bowed head, Marcus threw himself in supplication at Nero's feet. His agony of mind was terrible, the suspense almost beyond endurance.

Every look, the faintest indication of relenting on the face of Cæsar, was watched and at once checked by Poppæa. She was absolutely merciless. She had sworn to Berenice and to herself that Mercia should die; even though she earned the everlasting hatred of Marcus he should never possess the girl for whom he had shown this extraordinary and reckless passion. Firmly she exclaimed—

"Marcus, you, of all men, know that these Christians are all alike condemned. To spare one and destroy another is not justice. No man or *woman*"—this word she emphasised strongly, staring straight at Marcus; then, after a slight pause, she continued—" or woman can profess Christianity in Rome and live. The decree of Cæsar hath gone forth."

"Then, must she die?" hopelessly asked Marcus, with a hard, cold ring in his voice.

"Let her renounce, publicly renounce her faith—then she may live," was the cunning and pitiless rejoinder.

At this alternative Nero clutched eagerly. That would throw the onus of her death upon the girl herself. With a nod of approval to Poppæa, he said—

"Eh?—yes, yes—then she may live."

"And if she will not?" asked Marcus.

"Then let her die, and die this day."

Marcus made a gesture of entreaty, but Nero waved him aside and went on—

"Cæsar hath spoken. Come, friends, come; the games await our presence. Let us to the arena. We'll have rare sport to-day! Ha, ha, ha!" And, leaning heavily upon the arm of the Empress, he gladly left the room, followed by his whole Court, Berenice alone remaining, unseen by Marcus.

Marcus was frantic with anger and despair. He knew the alternative would never be accepted by Mercia. Renounce her faith? Mercia renounce her faith? Never! And yet, to die! Mercia to die—to-day! She must not! But how to save her? She knew no fear, and would be faithful even unto death.

Mercia and death! The thought was horrible—and he cursed the women who had plotted her destruction.

Berenice watched him in terror, scarcely venturing to speak. At last she did so, breathing softly his name—

"Marcus."

Swiftly he turned upon her, and, with a dangerous glitter in his eyes, he cried—

"Ah! Thou art here! Art thou content?"

"With what?"

"Content with the evil thou hast wrought? Mercia is to die—and die this day."

"'Tis well," answered Berenice.

Marcus seemed scarce to comprehend, and he echoed—

"'Tis well? With whom is it well?"

"With thee, at least, it should be well; when she is dead thy senses may return to thee."

"When she is dead? When Mercia is dead, then Marcus will die too," firmly replied Marcus.

"What?"

"When Mercia is dead—" he continued, as if thinking aloud, "methinks the world will lose its light; the flowers will bloom no more; no more the birds will sing; the stars and moon will veil their beams in sorrow; the glorious dawn will never come again; the sun will set in darkness everlasting, when Mercia is dead."

"Others will live, though Mercia be dead," pleaded Berenice softly.

"Others will live though Mercia be dead?" he re-

THE REMORSE OF MARCUS

peated. "Hearken, woman! Not one of those who have sought her death shall live when Mercia is dead —neither thou, nor Tigellinus, Licinius, Poppæa,—no, nor Nero himself shall live when Mercia is dead! Dost hear? Dost hear?" He was frantic with rage and desperation.

"Marcus, thou art mad! She was no mate for thee," cried Berenice.

"She was my mate!" he exclaimed. "The gods ordained it so from the beginning of all time. My very mate!—the better part of me, that killed the worser moiety, lifted my soul from filth and degradation, made me abhor evil and yearn for good, opened mine eyes to light and truth. Woman, Mercia is still so much my mate, so much the very breath and soul of me, that when she dies she will take with her the very breath and soul whereby I live!"

This served to enrage Berenice still further. All her pity was gone, and she cried—

"Then let her die—and die thou too! I'd sooner see thee dead than alive with Mercia."

"She shall not die!" exclaimed Marcus wildly. "She shall not die! I will pluck her from her cell! There are no guards—no bars—no laws—no power that can keep Mercia from me. Tell that to Nero, and tell it now! Tell it!"

He moved towards her threateningly, but, controlling himself, he cast upon her a look of unutterable hatred and strode from the room.

Berenice was alone. This, then, was the end of all her scheming and treachery. She had not parted him from Mercia after all; rather, had she not united them to all eternity in the bonds of death? Her punishment had come. Never had she so loved Marcus as now; his courage, manliness, devotion, recklessness of danger, self-sacrifice in the interview with Nero, had moved her profoundly.

If she loved him before, she idolised him now, and gladly would she have exchanged her wealth, liberty, power for the love that this Christian girl had aroused in him. Joyfully would she meet even death for such a prize. What now was left to live for? She was constant—she could never love another. The world was empty to her, her heart was broken, her life a void. Death! Death, for his sake, would be a release gladly to be welcomed.

Slowly and sadly she returned to her home. She hardly spoke when addressed by her slaves, but retired to her private rooms, giving orders that she was not to be disturbed or wakened, for she needed rest.

Her orders were obeyed; never was she disturbed again.

When, alarmed by her long hours of silence, the faithful slave crept softly into the room, she thought her mistress was quietly sleeping. She was still attired as when she returned home; her right hand was clutching her drapery, her left lay lightly on her breast. When that hand was moved, the golden and jewelled handle of a tiny dagger was discovered; the point of that little weapon was sheathed in her heart.

Berenice, the haughty, luckless, passionate beauty, was calm enough now; her tempest-tossed soul had

THE REMORSE OF MARCUS

foundered in the dark. But a few days before the world had seemed so golden bright to her. With wealth exceeding that of any other woman in Rome, beautiful and talented beyond the common, with every desire gratified, every wish anticipated (save that without which all the rest were as nought to her), with apparently nothing to step between her and a prolonged and happy life,—there she was lying cold and still, done to death by her own hand, self-murdered, rashly gone to the unknown, wrecked by a love despised. Poor, loving, impetuous, headstrong Berenice! Not all thy beauty could win the love that was thy life, nor all thy wealth purchase the heart that made up thy world. May the All-Merciful show mercy unto thee! Thy sin was love,—if love can e'er be sin,—and, for that thou didst love truly, may He, the source of all true love, grant thee His peace, and give thee indeed—rest.

CHAPTER XIX

A ROMAN FESTIVAL

It was a festival day in Rome. Nero had decreed it.

In the Circus was to be given a performance the like of which had never before been witnessed. All the most notable gladiators, singers, and pantomimists were to appear; but the greatest attraction expected was the promised slaughtering of the Christians. The whole city was excited by the rumours of the numbers doomed to die, and of the ferocity of the beasts they were to encounter. The public appetite was whetted by the stories circulated of the new devices for torturing and murdering the prisoners, and all who could provide the means or spare the time were on their way to the arena.

The streets were thronged with the expectant crowds. Gaily dressed and carrying flowers, women and children as well as men were hurrying on, eager to see their fellow-creatures encounter the most horrible and shameful deaths. Among the number was the heartless gadfly, Dacia, attended by the ever-useful Philodemus. Near the gates of the arena she encountered Glabrio, who saluted her, saying—

"Hail, Dacia! Whither goest thou?"

A ROMAN FESTIVAL

"To the Circus, of course. Dost thou not go too?" inquired Dacia, dropping her fan, which was immediately recovered and returned by the attentive Philodemus.

"I do not know; I doubt it," answered Glabrio, shaking his head gravely.

"Why?"

"Well, I am ever tender-hearted, and this slaughtering of Christians pleaseth me but little."

"Art growing effeminate in thine old age, Glabrio?"

"Effeminate? By Vulcan, no!" he replied. "It is no longer feminine to pity or to be tender. The sexes are changing—women do all the wooing nowadays; men are no longer the hunters, they are the hunted! The wounded gladiator looks up to the circles for mercy, and 'tis the women's thumbs that are turned for his death. Bah! There is nothing left for us poor men but the wine-cup, and even at that game some of the—ahem!—weaker sex are our masters."

"All the better for thee. Men are only fit to be women's slaves," said Dacia. And Philodemus nodded his head approvingly.

"Ah! Umph!—and pretty tame puppies they become when enslaved, do they not? Look at poor Philodemus—he is thy slave. I had hopes of him until he met thee, and now!—well, I have done. Get thee a silken cord and tie it round his willing neck, and make him caper as thou wilt. I have done."

"Nay, friend Glabrio, one must humour the weaker sex," lisped the complaisant Philodemus.

"Weaker? If there exists aught weaker than a

tame man, it is the spider's slender thread that a puff of the west wind bears away," rejoined Glabrio, with a look of regretful regard at his friend.

"So sour, Glabrio? Canst get no woman to love thee?" asked Dacia.

"I can get scores to say they do, while my money doth last. Women are cheap enough in Rome—which doth remind me that that pretty Christian, Mercia, over whom Marcus hath lost his wits, is to die to-night. You had some hand in her arrest, I hear."

"Why not? She was in the way," said Dacia, with a cheerful smile.

"Whose way?" asked Glabrio.

"That of Berenice—and we women do *sometimes* help each other," laughed Dacia, little guessing that her friend was lying at her palace dead and alone.

"Willingly, to pull some fairer woman down! Poor Marcus! Poor Mercia!"

"Oh! thy head is sore from last night's drinking," good-humouredly responded Dacia. "Philodemus, let us leave him, for to-day he is not even amusing."

"Farewell, friend Glabrio," exclaimed Philodemus; and, picking up a rose that had fallen from the hair of the fair Dacia, he accompanied that lady to the Circus.

"Well, the gods keep me in love with wine!" thought Glabrio. "He who loves wine may have his senses sometimes—he who loves woman, never! What have we here?" he asked mentally, as a crowd came surging along the street, following an officer and a guard of soldiers who were dragging with them the

A ROMAN FESTIVAL

spy, Servilius. His face was grey with fear, his clothes were torn, he was trembling and shrieking in his terror. With the utmost contempt, the officer said to him—

"Come on, thou coward!"

"I beg of thee to let me go! I am no Christian—I swear by all the gods!" cried Servilius.

"This man doth swear he hath seen thee at a score of their meetings," exclaimed the officer.

The man alluded to was his accomplice, Strabo, who had denounced him, after a quarrel between the two as to the share Strabo should have received of the blood-money earned by the denouncing of Favius and Stephanus.

"But as a spy. I went to denounce them; I am well known as an informer. Let me go! I have sent scores of Christians to their deaths! I have denounced hundreds!"

"Ah, well," grimly retorted the officer, "now comes thy turn. Thou wilt feel what it is to be denounced thyself."

"Ah, no, no! Spare me, good Viturius!" screamed the wretched coward. "This man is a liar—he hath accused me because he wanted more of the rewards than I could give him. He is forsworn. Release me, and I will get thee a score of Christians before the sun goes down. Have mercy!" And the spy grovelled in the dust at the officer's feet.

"Bah! you sicken me, you crawling thing! you wolf without its courage! I would willingly pay to see thee meet the lions in the Circus." And, with an

THE SIGN OF THE CROSS

expression of deep disgust, he threw Servilius from him.

"Spare me! Mercy, mercy!" entreated Servilius.

"On with him!" said the officer to the guard.

Now the shrieking, trembling Servilius recognised Glabrio, and, with the strength of mad terror, he threw off the guards who had gripped him, and flung himself at Glabrio's feet, crying—

"Ah, good Glabrio, thou knowest me; thou didst see me denounce the girl Mercia, and the old man Favius, when thou wert with the lady Dacia at her house."

"Did I? Well, and if I did, what then?" drily questioned Glabrio.

"Plead for me! I am a good Roman."

"An thou art, I forswear my country," answered Glabrio, with great disdain. "Now hearken, good officer. If thou wouldst serve me, Rome, Cæsar, and Marcus, if thou wouldst help to cleanse this somewhat dirty world, take that carrion to the beasts; and all Rome will thank thee for the deed. Farewell!" And with a gesture of the most profound contempt, Glabrio departed.

Frantic with terror, Servilius now turned, as a last resource, to his late friend and present denouncer, crying—

"Strabo, good Strabo, recall thy accusation! I have money—thou shalt have it all."

"Nay, I'll not go back on my word. I have said thou art a Christian, and I will abide by my saying."

"On with him! We have lingered long enough," commanded the officer.

A ROMAN FESTIVAL

"Mercy! Rescue me, friends! Mercy! Do not let them take me!" Thus, screaming, struggling, imploring, and cursing, the guilty wretch went to the death to which he had devoted so many who were innocent.

CHAPTER XX

THE GATES AJAR

THE dungeon beneath the Amphitheatre, in which Mercia and her companions were imprisoned, was a large, gloomy stone vault, destitute of furniture of any kind save a rude, wooden bier dragged in by a jailer, at Mercia's earnest entreaty, to serve as a couch for the suffering Stephanus. At each end of the cell were doors leading to the corridors. In the centre, approached by a few stone steps, were sliding doors which opened into the arena. They were of iron, and ran in oiled grooves; when opened, the arena could be seen, and with it a section of the first mænianum and its occupants.

Great was the contrast between the dark, dank cell and the sunlit Circus, crowded with eager, gaily-dressed patricians. In the dungeon were scores of men and women waiting for the signal to pass forth to a cruel and certain death; in the auditorium was a seething mass of humanity, thousands upon thousands impatiently awaiting their coming forth, and gloating already, in imagination, upon the horrors they must undergo.

The roars of the hungry beasts could be faintly heard even when the doors were closed; so could the equally merciless howls of the bloodthirsty populace.

At intervals the trumpet-calls, summoning the different performers, rang round the arena and warned the martyrs that yet another item of the entertainment had been concluded, bringing them so much nearer to their share in the amusement of the day. How they were to die had not been told to them—only this they knew, that they were to die, and that every endeavour would be made to make their deaths as horrible, revolting, and cruel as possible. They knew, too, that not a vestige of sympathy would be given to them, that even a cup of water was denied them. They were there to be slaughtered for the amusement of Rome, and the more they suffered, the greater would be the enjoyment of the audience. If given to the gladiators, they would be stabbed to death amidst the hisses and howls of the people, enraged at their refusal to defend themselves, for had not their Redeemer enjoined them to "pray for their persecutors, to love them that hatefully and despitefully used them."

Among them were a few that trembled and felt sick with physical fear, but not one murmured. Their eyes were mentally fixed upon the Cross, and His anguish, His sufferings, His endurance for their sakes was their courage, their hope, their strength. O wondrous faith! O glorious belief! Forerunners of freedom, founders of civilisation and of a religion destined to endure unto the end of all things earthly were these despised, lowly people, who, in their martyrdom, made the world wonder what could this faith be that gave such endurance and brought such peace. Hail to them, the noble army of martyrs, who have so long entered on their well-earned rest!

Mercia was by Stephanus, exhorting him to courage. Suddenly a blare of trumpets smote upon their ears. The iron doors flew back—a roar of delight was heard from the assembled multitudes in the Amphitheatre. A file of armoured guards lined either side of the steps and the passage, and Tigellinus, attended by the ædile and other officers, entered the cell. At a gesture given by the Councillor, the doors were closed. In harsh and unfeeling tones, Tigellinus exclaimed to the prisoners, who, at the moment of his entrance, were all kneeling in prayer—

"Stand up, there! Up, you vermin! Up!" (Pointing to the younger men, among whom was Melos) "Stand on this side, you! These are for the gladiators," he added to the ædile.

"They'll not give the gladiators much trouble—they're a puny lot," sneered that officer.

"Stand here, you!" cried Tigellinus to the older men. "These old rats we'll give to the tigers to toy with. These women to the lions, with the boy there." Then, recognising Mercia, he laughed sardonically, saying, "Ha! *thou* here? This is the wench Marcus made so much ado about. Where's thy lover, girl? Is he not here to save thee? Answer!"

"I have no lover," was the quiet and dignified answer.

"Marcus Superbus—where is he?"

"I do nothing know of him," replied Mercia.

But Tigellinus had turned to an officer of the guards,

asking the names of the men, and writing them down upon his tablets.

"Ah! that is like Marcus," said Licinius, approaching Mercia. "Little he cares what befalls his cast-off strumpets."

This was more than the devoted Melos could bear, and his manliness overcame his patience. Springing forward towards Licinius, he cried—

"You lie, you tyrant! Unsay those words!"

In his wrath he would have struck the ædile, but Mercia imploringly cried—

"Hush, Melos! Answer not. His words do not move me." Her calmness angered Licinius still more, and he sneeringly exclaimed—

"No? Well, perhaps the flames—or the lions—will shake thy obstinacy. Dost know 'twill be either the beasts or the fire for thee to-night?"

Sweetly and resignedly came the reply from Mercia—

"The Master will be with me."

Finding his shafts were powerless to move Mercia, the brutal ædile turned to the shivering Stephanus, and growled out—

"And you, you young scorpion! Call on thy God to help thee—thy sun sets this night too."

The child could not control himself, and he trembled violently; a weakness that Licinius noted and gloated over. He continued—

"Ah! You tremble—eh?"

"He will not tremble when the hour doth come," said Mercia, enfolding the hapless boy in her arms.

THE SIGN OF THE CROSS

Again there was a loud call of the trumpets, and Tigellinus cried—

"The gladiators are ready. Open the doors!"

The doors were thrown open, and the arena beyond could be seen by the prisoners, flooded with golden sunshine.

"Now then, march!"

For a moment there was a pause, but, almost before it could be realised, Mercia's clear, sweet voice rang out the first words of their beloved hymn—

"Shepherd of souls that stumble by the way."

Instantly all save Stephanus took up the strain, and, with uplifted eyes and undaunted hearts, these noble martyrs went calmly and resignedly through the dark Valley of the Shadow of Death to the everlasting peace that awaited them beyond.

Melos was the last to leave. He turned and looked at Mercia, who, pointing to Heaven, encouraged him to endure.

With a smile of love that transfigured his face, he bowed his head, as if in obedience to her injunctions, and went to his death.

With a little sob, Mercia sank on her knees by the couch, crying—

"O Father, give them strength to endure!"

Stephanus was sobbing violently. Mercia forgot her own grief, and, turning to him, asked—

"Stephanus what is this?"

"I am sore afraid, Mercia," tremblingly replied the boy.

"I am so young to die. Think!—to die! to die to-night! to leave this bright and beautiful world to-night!"

"For one more bright, more beautiful," was the soothing rejoinder, "where pain and sorrow is not, nor persecution, nor parting; where happiness is, and purity, and holiness evermore."

But the boy had suffered so terribly that his courage failed him, and he cried—

"But the pain, Mercia! The pain!"

"Think of His agony who died for thee," implored the faithful girl. "Thou wilt not faint again. Fix thine eyes on the Cross when the hour doth come."

"Shall I dare?" he asked tremblingly. "Have I not betrayed you all?" And he broke into sobs of remorse.

In gentle, soothing accents, Mercia said—

"Thy soul was true; the weak body only proved false."

"Yes, yes! But, Mercia, I am a coward—I have not thy courage." And he buried his face in his hands and wept bitterly.

Mercia was wrung to the heart by pity. In her grief for others her own fate was forgotten; utterly unselfish, her every thought was for her suffering companion. Taking Stephanus in her arms as a tender mother might take her child, she answered—

"My courage is not my own. It comes from Him, the Master. Look to Him; He will give thee strength."

Great shouts were now heard from the arena.

THE SIGN OF THE CROSS

Trumpets sounded; the doors were again thrown open, and an officer entered the cell followed by a file of soldiers. With a gesture, their leader signified that Stephanus was to accompany him.

The poor child stood half-dazed with terror, but Mercia, by look and caress, urged him to be calm. With faltering feet he made for the arena; tottering and hardly conscious, he ascended the steps.

As he passed the threshold, the scene of horror which met his gaze terrified him beyond control, and, with a piercing shriek, he dashed back into the cell; and falling upon his knees and burying his face in Mercia's garments, cried—

"Mercia, Mercia, I cannot, I cannot! Save me! Save me!"

Mercia had need of great effort to retain her own self-control, but she succeeded, exclaiming—

"Stephanus, Stephanus, thou wilt not falter? Thou didst ever say that thou didst love me. If that is true, by all the love thou bearest me, by all the love I bear thee—by all the love the Master bears to all, be true! Promise that thou wilt not shrink! Promise!" And the noble girl held the shrinking child to her heart, and looked lovingly and imploringly into his eyes.

Her courage seemed to inspire him at last, and, with a deep breath, he uttered—

"I promise, Mercia. Ah! the dread, the fear hath gone! Lay thy hand upon my heart, Mercia; 'tis all calm now. He hath come to guide me—He doth walk beside me. I see the Cross! I fear nothing now!"

Clenching his hands and crossing them rigidly over

his breast, the boy walked firmly to the door. The grim, stern soldiers, accustomed as they were to horrors of all kinds, felt a clutching at the throat as the child passed out to his horrible death.

As Stephanus appeared in the arena, there went up a loud shout of derision—he looked so tiny in that vast space. But he heard nothing—feared nothing. Unflinchingly he faced those thousands, turning only once for a last look of love towards Mercia; and, with a little nod of assurance to her of his unwavering courage, he passed on, and the doors closed behind him, leaving Mercia alone once more.

CHAPTER XXI

MERCIA SAVES MARCUS

MERCIA sank upon her knees, with her face pressed against the iron doors. She was quietly sobbing, but her grief was not for herself. Silently she prayed to Him to give her strength to endure to the end. There were none with her to solace or comfort her; those who, a few moments ago, had filled the cell, praying and singing, were now lying dead in the arena, and their souls were with Him in paradise.

So the noble-hearted girl fought out her bitter fight alone; but in all her anguish, Marcus was not forgotten. She prayed that her death might bring him life, that her example might uplift him, that her undaunted faith might inspire him to belief.

Presently, the door leading to the corridor was unbarred. Two officers entered, ushering in Marcus, who started on finding Mercia alone. Dismissing the guards, he closed the door, gazing with infinite tenderness at the white figure kneeling at the gates. Mercia, lost in thought, had not heard him enter.

For a time Marcus could not speak; his heart felt like bursting with grief for this beautiful girl. Here, in this loathsome dungeon, she could still preserve her courage, and could still, he had no doubt, pray for forgiveness for her persecutors. Between her and a

MERCIA SAVES MARCUS

hideous death lay only a few fleeting moments, and such shield as his love could raise. Hungrily he stretched out his arms over her, proudly willing to give all he possessed in the world to shelter that frail girl in his strong arms and comfort and save her. Thrice he essayed to speak, but could not. What he would say choked him. At last, he murmured softly—

"Mercia!"

At that moment his name was mingled with her prayers, and it seemed as though his spirit had called her. She knew nothing of his coming thither, had not deemed it possible that she should ever see him again. Softly, a second time, he called—

"Mercia!"

Then, slowly, she rose, as one awakening from a dream, and looked around her. When she saw that he was indeed by her side, her heart gave a mighty bound that robbed her of her power to speak for a moment. When she recovered, she asked, in faltering accents—

"What would you with me?"

With a tender gaze and in earnest tones, he replied—

"I come to save thee."

"To save me? From what?"

"From death." And Marcus looked with horror towards the entrance to the arena.

"How canst thou save me?"

He hesitated; he could not yet summon the courage to tell her that her life depended upon her apostasy. At length he said, evading her direct question—

"I have knelt to Nero for thy pardon."

"And did he grant it?" Mercia asked the question,

THE SIGN OF THE CROSS

but she had no hope of pardon; she felt that she was doomed.

"He will grant it upon one condition." He paused, and Mercia inquired—

"What is that?"

"That—that——" He could not bring himself to ask her to abjure her faith. Mercia waited, and then softly asked—

"Well?"

There was nothing left for Marcus but to tell her the truth. Her precious life must be saved, no matter what the cost; and he said—

"That thou dost renounce this false worship——"

"It is not false! It is true and everlasting!" was Mercia's calm reply, and Marcus felt that her clear conviction was absolutely untouched by his assertions. Still he fought for her life.

"Everlasting? Nothing is everlasting! There is no after-life; the end is here. Men come and go; they drink their little cup of woe or happiness, and then sleep—the sleep that knows no awakening."

"Art thou so sure of that? Ask thyself, are there no inward monitors that silently teach thee there is a life to come?"

He hesitated to reply directly to this question, and evasively exclaimed—

"All men have wishes for a life to come, if it could better this."

"It will better this, if this life be well-lived. Hast thou lived well?"

A thousand shameful memories of his past life swept

across the mind of Marcus, and his eyes fell before her questioning gaze. Had he lived well? He could scarcely bear to think of the existence he had passed. In halting accents, he murmured—

"No. Thou hast taught me that. I never knew the shame of sin until I knew thy purity. Ah! whence comes thy wondrous grace?"

"If I have any grace, it comes from Him who died on Calvary's Cross that grace might come to all."

"Thou dost believe this?"

"I do believe it?"

"But thou hast no proof."

"Yes," replied Mercia, placing her hand upon her heart, "the proof is here."

"Ah!" he argued, "thou dost believe so? All men, all nations have their gods. This one bows down to a thing of stone, and calls it his god; another to the sun, and calls it his god. A god of brass—a god of gold— a god of wood! Each tells himself *his* is the true God. All are mistaken?"

"All these are mistaken," was the quiet rejoinder.

"And thou? What is thy God? A fantasy—a vision—a superstition. Wilt thou die for such a thing?"

"I will die for my Master gladly."

He felt this was no exaggeration, no boast. She meant it, and would sacrifice herself for her faith. But he could not endure the thought, and fervently he pleaded with her—

"Mercia, hear me! Thou shalt not die! I cannot let thee go! I love thee so! I love thee so!"

THE SIGN OF THE CROSS

"Thou hast told me so before, and wouldst have slain thy soul and mine."

"I grant it—I did not know! I was blind! Now I see my love for thee is love indeed. Forgive me that I did so misjudge thee and myself. The brute is dead in me—the man is living. Thy purity, that I would have smirched, hath cleansed me. Live, Mercia, live, and be my wife!" And he sank upon his knees before this simple girl with all the reverence a man might feel for a saint in soul, an empress in worldly rank.

Mercia was deeply moved. The man she loved with her whole heart loved her, and with a reverence and devotion that were beyond question deep and sincere.

"Thy wife? Thy wife, in very truth?" she asked, with a little sob of joy.

"In very truth my wife, my honoured wife."

"Oh, Marcus, Marcus!" murmured Mercia. All was forgotten save her joy in his love. She had long since forgiven him.

"Thou wilt be my wife?" urged Marcus.

Then came the thought to Mercia of the price she would have to pay for her earthly happiness, and tremblingly she asked—

"And renounce my faith?"

"That must be," was the sad reply.

"That can never be," exclaimed Mercia, and the firmness of her tone struck into Marcus' very soul. But still he pleaded—

"It must be! Think, Mercia, think!"

"There is no need to think. We do not need to think to breathe while we have life; the heart beats, the blood flows through our veins without our thought. God hath made us so. So I, without thought, worship Him—I need no thought to make me true to Him. He hath made me so; I cannot be otherwise—would not be otherwise."

"If thou didst love me?"

"Hear me, Marcus. I know not how or whence it came, but love came for thee when first I saw thee."

"Mercia!" he exclaimed, springing towards her.

"Nay, stay where thou art, Marcus, and hear me. This love I speak of came—I knew not whence nor how, then; now, I know it came from Him who gave me life. I received it joyfully because He gave it. Think you He gave it to tempt me to betray Him? Nay, Marcus, He gave it to me to uphold and strengthen me. The world has passed away from me, and as on the threshold of the other life all worldly thoughts are left behind, and all wordly things, I have no shame in telling thee that I love thee . . . next to Him."

"And thou wilt live?" he burst forth passionately.

"I will be true to Him."

"Thou wilt live?"

"I will not deny Him who died for me."

"Mercia, if thy God exists, He made us both, the one for the other. Hearken! I am rich beyond riches—I have power, skill, strength; with these, the world would be my slave, my vassal. Nero is hated, loathed—is tottering on his throne. I have friends in plenty who would help me—the throne of Cæsar might be mine, and thou shalt share it with me, if thou wilt but live. The crown of an Empress shall deck that lovely head, if thou wilt but live—only consent to live!"

"My crown is not of earth, Marcus; it awaits me there." She pointed heavenward. His arguments had moved her deeply, but had not shaken her resolve. She was filled with a divine strength that nothing could weaken, much less destroy. Life with him, as his wife, would excel all other earthly bribes; but not even for that would she betray her Master.

"Mercia, in pity!—by thy love for me, and by my love for thee, live! Live for me and for my love, I pray thee! Do not leave me!" And the strong, fierce man sobbed aloud in his agony.

With infinite love and tenderness in her tones, Mercia cried—

"I love thee, Marcus, but I must leave thee—it is His will that I do—to go to Him."

But he exclaimed passionately—

"I cannot part from thee and live, Mercia! I have, to save thy precious life, argued and spoken against thy faith, thy God; but, to speak truth to thee, I have been sorely troubled since first I saw thee. Strange yearnings of the spirit come in the lonely watches of the night; I battle with them, but they will not yield. I tremble with strange fears, strange thoughts, strange hopes. If thy faith be true, what is this world?—a little tarrying-place, a tiny bridge between two vast eternities, that from which we have travelled—that towards which we go. Oh, but to know! How can I know, Mercia? Teach me how to know! And teach me how to keep thee ever by my side."

MERCIA SAVES MARCUS

Her sweet face was uplifted, the pure soul shining through it, lighting it with a heavenly glow, as she answered—

"Look to the Cross, and pray, 'Help thou my unbelief!'"

"But to keep thee by my side?" he pleaded in broken accents.

"Give up all that thou hast, and follow me," replied Mercia in the words of her divine Master.

"Follow thee? Yea, but whither?" was the earnest question.

"To the better land—there, where He waits for us, with outstretched arms, ready to pardon, eager to welcome."

And Marcus, remembering his wasted life, his misspent youth, wonderingly, fearfully, anxiously asked—

"Would He welcome even me?"

"Yea, even thee, Marcus," was the answer of Faith.

Now there sounded on their ears another call from the trumpets. The brazen doors slid back, the guards entered, followed this time by Tigellinus. Nero had deputed him to personally receive the answer that was to decide Mercia's fate. Would she live or die? The Empress, seated in the Imperial box, watching the horrible sports, was tremblingly anxious to learn the girl's resolve. How would she decide? Would she abjure her faith and live for Marcus—or remain steadfast and die? Die to leave Marcus free!

Sternly, impassively, Tigellinus advanced towards Mercia, who stood calmly awaiting his question. In harsh accents it came, addressed to Marcus—

THE SIGN OF THE CROSS

"Prefect, the hour is come. Cæsar would know this maid's decision. Doth she renounce Christus and live, or cling to Him and die?" After a moment's pause, he added, "Answer."

Turning towards her, Marcus, with piteous entreaty in his voice, murmured—

"Mercia!"

"Answer."

Now, in clear, steady tones, quiet but deeply moving, at least to one hearer in the gloomy prison, Mercia answered—

"I cling to Him, and die."

Then she turned to the man she loved so truly; at thought of him she trembled a little, and her voice was all quivering with her held-back tears, as she softly sighed—

"Farewell, Marcus!"

Marcus, for a moment, answered not. A fierce battle was raging in his soul. What was he to do? Let her fare forth to her death alone? Abandon that brave, true heart in its last brief struggle? No! And yet, what was left him? He turned and looked upon her, and, with the swiftness of the lightning's flash, the light of conviction illumined his soul. Her belief, her faith, enwrapped him as with a garment. Doubt died, hope sprang to his heart! A rush of peace encompassed the whole of his being. He had decided!

"Farewell? No, not 'Farewell!' Death cannot part us. I, too, am ready! My lingering doubts are dead—the light hath come!"

MERCIA SAVES MARCUS

Then, taking Mercia's dear hand in his, he turned to Tigellinus, saying—

"Return to Cæsar; tell him Christus hath triumphed. Marcus, too, is a Christian!" Bending upon Mercia a gaze of pure, ineffable, holy love, and drawing her closer to him, he cried, "Come, my bride!"

"My bridegroom!" answered Mercia, returning his gaze with one as rapt and unworldly.

He, still clasping her willing hand, continued—

"Thus, hand in hand, we go to our bridal! There is no death for us, for Christus hath triumphed over death! Our love will give us victory over the grave. Come thou, my Mercia, my bride indeed—come to the Light beyond!"

His face shone with the same glorious radiance that had transfigured the features of Mercia. And thus, hand in hand, those two went calmly forth to the sacrificial altar, where they were made one indeed—united in bonds never to be broken; never, through all the vast mystery of eternity—bonds forged in the heart, riveted by sorrow, sanctified by faith, blessed by belief, and glorified by His presence who had promised to them, even as He had promised to the penitent thief, dying on the cross beside Him—

"Verily, I say unto thee, to-morrow shalt thou be with Me in Paradise."

THE END.

www.ingramcontent.com/pod-product-compliance
Lightning Source LLC
Chambersburg PA
CBHW022111230426
43672CB00008B/1344